GUIDE TO DRESSAGE

LOUISE MILLS WILDE

FOREWORD BY HILDA GURNEY

Breakthrough
PUBLICATIONS
MILLWOOD, NEW YORK 10546

To my
long-suffering family who
patiently tolerate all this
horsing around

Guide to Dressage copyright © 1982
by A.S. Barnes & Company, Inc.

Revised Edition 1987 by Breakthrough Publications, Inc., Millwood, NY 10546

Library of Congress Cataloging in Publication Data

Wilde, Louise Mills.
  Guide to Dressage, Revised.

  Bibliography: p.
  1. Dressage. I. Title.
SF309.5.W48   798.2′3   81-3621
ISBN 0-914327-05-4   AACR2

Printed in the United States of America.

Contents

Part II FIRST AND SECOND LEVELS

Acknowledgments

Excerpts from *The Complete Training of Horse and Rider* by Alois Podhajsky (Doubleday and Company, 1967). Reprinted by permission of Doubleday and Company, Inc. British rights by permission of George G. Harrap and Company, Ltd.

Excerpts from *Horsemanship* by Waldemar Seunig, translated from the German by Leonard Mins (Doubleday and Company, Inc., 1956). Reprinted by permission of Doubleday and Company, Inc.

Excerpts from *Notes on Dressage and Combined Training* (1972), *Supplement to Rules on Dressage and Combined Training* (1975), and the *Rulebook* (1978) published by the American Horse Shows Association, Inc. Reprinted by permission of the American Horse Shows Association, Inc.

Excerpts from *Training the Young Horse and Pony (The British Horse Society, 1961)*. Reprinted by permission of the Pony Club of Great Britain.

Excerpts from *Equitation* by Jean Froissard, copyright © 1967, 1977 by Arco Publishing Company, Inc. Reprinted by permission of Arco Publishing Company, Inc.

Excerpts from *Training Hunters, Jumpers, and Hacks* by Lieutenant Colonel Harry D. Chamberlin (Hurst and Blackett, Ltd., 1938). Reprinted by permission of Arco Publishing Company, Inc.

Foreword

The opinions of knowledgeable horsemen have been compiled in *Guide to Dressage*. The reader is given the advantage of understanding the various theories of dressage schooling by comparing the thoughts of experts. Mrs. Wilde, an active dressage competitor, has carefully chosen quotes from many of the world's most famous horsemen as they relate to competitive dressage. Various methods of schooling for and riding the American Horse Shows Association dressage tests are carefully covered.

This book, written by an American horsewoman for American dressage enthusiasts, is easily read and will greatly enhance the horseman's library.

Hilda Gurney

Bronze Medal, Olympic Games, 1976; Gold Medal, Pan American Games, 1975 and 1979; Silver Medal, Pan American Games, 1983.

Introduction

This is a different sort of dressage book. It is not a "how to" book in the usual sense of the word, although some readers will probably want to use it in that way. *Guide to Dressage* is primarily meant to be a guide for the person who is taking dressage lessons and needs a book to go along with the instruction. Consequently it is, in part, a theory book that will help a pupil to understand why an instructor gives certain directions and advice. It also defines all the terms and expressions of dressage clearly and graphically so that a student will know what the instructor is talking about. In addition, I have tried to give a "feel" for what the beginner is really up against, and what it will be like to carry out the elementary dressage training program.

Guide to Dressage does these things partly by gathering together from the standard dressage texts the definitions, theories, and training techniques of experts on each phase of dressage, beginning with seat and aids and proceeding in an orderly way through the training of horse and rider for the American Horse Shows Association dressage tests. Why should a rider not go directly to the original sources? Because the classics are often impossible for the beginner to understand. This is partly because they were written by experts who found everything easy and who really were writing for other experts, and partly because each text is organized in its own way and, of course, does not relate to the AHSA tests. Therefore, I have gathered the clearest commentaries on each subject, arranged them in a logical order, and, when necessary, explained them and pointed out the similarities and differences of the various theories. More experienced riders will probably want to obtain the books that fit best with their training techniques and read more broadly in them.

Bringing quotations together in this way has many advantages. Besides helping the beginning student, it also makes it possible for any dressage rider or trainer to find the various views and suggestions of the experts for dealing with any problem he may be experiencing. A person can simply skim or skip the elementary subjects if he wishes and read about his concerns of the moment.

For those not actively attempting to ride dressage, but interested in observing it or understanding what its principles are, there will also be much of interest. I have augmented the quotations whenever necessary with descriptions and illustrations showing the objectives of dressage, so that almost anyone can recognize them "in the flesh" and understand what he sees at a show, clinic, or training session. I have tried not to use any technical term or phrase without a truly adequate explanation.

For anyone wanting an orderly overview of the whole dressage process without too much technical detail, I suggest looking over the chapter titles and then skimming the paragraph headings and italicized topics. In this way the reader can survey the training methods and objectives of dressage without getting bogged down in the details, and, of course, he can go deeper and read more about any aspect of dressage that particularly puzzles or interests him.

The illustrations do not attempt to show perfection. Pictures of correctly executed dressage exercises can be found in many other places. Most of the illustrations are careful renderings of photographs of average horses and riders taken at local shows and clinics. Margaret Mittelstadt did this work very competently. I also explain how to analyze the drawings for what they reveal about a horse's performance. The good and bad features in each picture are pointed out to help the reader learn to judge the quality of a performance for himself.

I hope readers will like the plan I have followed in writing this book, and I would enjoy corresponding with them. If an especially useful quotation has not been included, I would like to know what it is. If a reader finds an error or knows a better way of detecting some quality in a horse, let me know. I only ask that the section in question be read several times, very carefully, and every effort be made to understand what I am trying to say.

I wish to thank my friend and teacher, Hilda Gurney, for her help. Hilda is a widely known and very busy instructor, judge, and international competitor, but she still found time to read and generously comment on each chapter as it was written. She examined the working photographs and made many useful criticisms and helpful suggestions.

I am also grateful to my daughter, Carol Wuenschell, for preparing the diagrams. There is no substitute for having an illustrator who is knowledgeable about your subject and immediately at hand for discussions and consultations. The illustrations should make abundantly clear anything that the text does not.

1981
Long Beach, California   L.M.W.

part

1 Training Level

1 What Is Dressage?

The interest in dressage in the United States is increasing rapidly, and the many newcomers have a common problem—trying to understand what dressage is and what use they can make of it. Usually they have a background in some other form of horse competition—equitation, hunters, Arabians, gaited horses, pleasure, endurance, and so on, and they wonder whether dressage training will help them and their horses in their usual activities, whether they would like to do dressage in addition, or whether they should abandon their past pursuits and concentrate on dressage. They wonder what is involved in learning, how much instruction they will need, and how difficult dressage is. These questions can only be answered gradually as the full realization of the nature of dressage unfolds, and its bearing on their original horse objectives becomes apparent.

The primary—but not the only—purpose of this book is to guide those who are interested in what I shall call *competition dressage*; that is, preparing themselves and their horses to perform the American Horse Shows Association (AHSA) dressage tests at dressage shows. Except for the most talented riders, this requires an instructor. Occasionally there is a person who can attend clinics or watch shows and then go home and, with the help of an observer on the ground and, perhaps, a book, duplicate what he has seen. But such talent is rare. The vast majority of us require instructors, and this book is meant to supplement the instructor's practical training with explanations and theory quoted from the authoritative writings of experts. *Guide to Dressage* should help a student to understand why the instructor gives the advice and directions he does.

If you do not have a teacher, or merely wish to experiment by yourself to see what dressage can do for you and your horse, then you will read books, watch any shows or clinics available in your area, and select and try whatever techniques or exercises seem likely to solve your problems or make your riding more fun. You will probably be pleased with the results; but you cannot expect to accomplish everything you see depicted in this book. I once trained two English pleasure horses by attempting to follow dressage books because at the time, there was no dressage teacher in my area. I had lots of fun doing what I thought was dressage. But I know now that a dressage purist would have called it bad dressage, and that my horses would not have been viewed favorably by a dressage judge. Even so, they benefited to some extent. So I do not wish to discourage riders and horse-lovers who will continue to experiment with their own brand of noncompetitive dressage. If these riders read further, however, although they will find many techniques and suggestions they can use, I hope they will soon begin to see the differences between what they can do by themselves and what they might achieve with instruction.

People say all sorts of things about dressage, and their conflicting statements do not help the beginner in his efforts to understand it. Some people say that dressage is good for all horses and that you are doing basic dressage if you make any use at all of dressage exercises and methods. But dressage exercises can be done well, or badly; they can be done in a way that a dressage judge would approve, or in a way that would appeal to judges of other types of horses. Some people say that all good training is dressage. By this they seem to mean that every good training method (that is, effective and humane) is derived from dressage whether the trainer knows it or not. I certainly would not go so far. I am sure there are many good trainers who get high-quality results in a humane way and do not owe anything to dressage. It is also possible to find trainers who have heard of dressage and who have adopted some of its exercises with absolutely no understanding of its spirit and purpose. For example, someone might exhibit a horse with an incorrect sort of half-pass or pirouette, perhaps even obtained by brutal methods, and say he is doing dressage. Of course he is not. All this is very confusing, especially to newcomers who are thrilled at the prospect of taking up dressage and are in a hurry to start learning from the first teacher they can find.

The word "dressage" is pronounced drě' säzh (*zh* pronounced like the *s* in "pleasure"). According to my French dictionary the first syllable accent is correct, but most Americans seem to place the accent on the second syllable. Dressage, of course, is a French word and literally means "training." But here in America we need to further define the word in a useful way that distinguishes it from other types of training. To begin to get an appreciation of what dressage is, let us read some definitions from the various classical sources that will be referred to throughout this guide. The authors will not be introduced here, instead we will meet them later as they are quoted individually on various subjects. None of these definitions is very satisfactory for our purposes, but they will help us to clarify our own ideas.

> . . . *dressage is the art of improving one's horse beyond the stage of plain usefulness, of making him more amenable, easier to control, pleasanter to ride, more graceful in his bearing and better to look upon.* (Henry Wynmalen, Dressage, *p. 20.*)

> *In English it has come to . . . denote the schooling of the riding horse in the middle and advanced stages of school work only, and in the school paces, which do not include the extended gallop.* (Nöel Jackson, Effective Horsemanship, *p. 21.*)

> *The object of Dressage is, by systematic work, to make the horse calm, light and obedient, so that he may be pleasant in his movements and comfortable for the rider.* (De la Guérinière, *quoted by Jackson in* Effective Horsemanship, *p. 20.*)

> *The object of the classical art of riding is to train a horse not only to be brilliant in the movements and exercises of the High School, but also to be quiet, supple, and obedient, and by his smooth movements to make riding a true pleasure.* (Alois Podhajsky, Complete Training of Horse and Rider, *p. 29.*)

. . . the training is based on methodical work which concentrates on gymnastic development, and which achieves the highest proficiency in completely natural abilities, without being forced or stooping to the use of tricks. Then the horses will suffer no harm; on the contrary, they will be able to fulfil their work and tasks for many more years than they would have done without proper training. (R. L. Wätjen, Dressage Riding, *p. 2.)*

The purpose of schooling a horse is to be able to get about on him and to go wherever one wants with a minimum of exertion and effort for the rider and with a maximum of ease and therefore preservation for the horse. The schooling which the horse gets for this purpose is called 'dressage.' . . . It comprises the gymnastic training of the horse to maximum efficiency and education to obedience. (Wilhelm Müseler, Riding Logic, *p. 57.)*

Dressage . . . means the gradual harmonious development of the horse's physical and mental condition with the aim to achieve the improvement of its natural gaits under the rider and a perfect understanding with its rider. . . . regularity of the rhythms of walk, trot and canter. . . . the engagement of the hind quarters with an active back action. . . . By virtue of a lively impulsion . . . free from the paralyzing effects of resistance, the horse obeys willingly and without hesitation. . . . The horse should remain straight on straight lines. . . . At changes of direction, the horse should adjust the bend of his body to the curvature of the line he follows. . . . The horse [in all his work] remaining "on the bit" . . . does not need the visible aids of the rider. (These requirements are compiled from the 1978 AHSA Rulebook, *pp. 149–160.)*

I urge the reader to study these quotations carefully, asking himself: Is this what I would expect of any well-trained horse? Is there any difference between the horse that is being described here and a well-schooled horse of whatever type or types I am used to? In other words, how is the dressage horse going to be different? To really understand what dressage is, we must know how we expect it to differ from that which is familiar to us.

As I read these definitions, it strikes me that we expect most of these things of every well-schooled horse. And this is not surprising, for these definitions are of European origin and, in Europe, dressage is about the only form of systematic and comprehensive training that exists. The many types of horse competition that we take for granted here do not exist in Europe. Only in America are there Western horses—including stock horses, trail horses, and pleasure horses—park and gaited horses, hunters and jumpers, English pleasure horses, Tennessee walkers, and three kinds of equitation. In Europe, riding horses shown in horse shows include principally dressage horses and jumpers. Therefore it is only natural that many of the traits expected of any schooled horse should be mentioned in these definitions of dressage, such as obedience, lightness, understanding with the rider, invisible aids, pleasant to ride, graceful in bearing, comfortable, smooth, improved gaits, physical and mental development.

In America, however, we have many specialties. Most of the traits mentioned in the quoted definitions are sought in all horses, but some are not. Gaited horses are supposed to be fiery, not calm. Western horses are not taught the same sort of contact with the bit, or the same sort of rein control, as are English horses. Park horses are *above* the bit, not *on* the bit. Pleasure, equitation, and trail horses could hardly be called "brilliant" or be said to display "lively impulsion." If you do not want dressage traits, then dressage is the wrong sort of training for your horse. And even if you do, dressage is not the only road to obedience, lightness, or invisible aids. If you are having trouble obtaining obedience; if you realize that your aids are painfully obvious; if your horse's gaits are rough, or he pulls, or is spooky, you need not necessarily turn to dressage. Dressage trainers will have their solutions to these problems, but so will other good trainers and instructors who may know nothing of dressage. And if the temperament or conformation of the horse is at fault, dressage exercises cannot necessarily be counted on to bring about a cure.

You must also realize that there is nothing magical about dressage. Whether you are training a horse by dressage methods or not, you will still have to be a diligent, sensible, and fairly strong rider to get the results you hope to achieve. If you have been a weak, permissive, overly kind rider, you will have to become firmer and more demanding. If you have been a rough-and-ready, cowboy-type rider, you will have to learn new patience and restraint.

Dressage training alone will not automatically prepare a young horse for all sorts of competition. A few years ago I sold a five-year-old that had not worked out for me as a dressage horse. His new owner immediately showed him in an English pleasure class, and was disappointed with the results. The fact was that the animal did not know how to work in a group situation, or how to suit his speed to the group. He had always been worked alone. And I had never taught him a slow, "pleasure-horse canter" because this is not desired in dressage. I hope that he has since been taught his new job.

Go to a dressage show if you can. The correctly trained horses are very calm and seem to perform effortlessly. The rider appears to be doing nothing. Yet the horse is working hard, and the rider may be out of breath and exhausted after a five- or six-minute ride. The beginning horses will have a lower head carriage than you may expect, while the higher-level horses move with a controlled energy and distinctive head carriage not seen in any other type of horse. (See Figures 1 and 2.)

Read the definitions and objectives again and look for the points unique to dressage. Some of the distinguishing features you will be able to pick out yourself. Other terms sound rather ordinary but have special dressage meanings. Those that will be discussed because they help us to understand the main features of dressage are:

1. Straightness and suppleness.
2. Gymnastic training or schoolwork.
3. Improvement of the natural gaits—free and regular paces.
4. Impulsion and being "on the bit."
5. High School.

Straightness and *suppleness,* so far as I know, are not stressed in any training except dressage. They are closely related. Suppleness is rather broad in its meaning and will be treated more fully later. Straightness means that the hind feet always follow in the path of the forefeet (except when doing lateral work). It is easy to think that your horse is straight when he is not. To mention just one example, many horses habitually canter with their haunches slightly farther away from the fence than their shoulders. (See Figure 46.) Stand where you can watch horses cantering directly away from you, and you will see what I mean.

On turns there are other problems. In order to be "straight" while traveling on a curve, the horse must be laterally supple, or

Figure 1.   Suitable head carriage for a lower-level horse. Neck is low, face in front of the vertical.

Figure 2.   Collected horse—Third Level. Good position of horse and rider. A longer stirrup might seem desirable, but this is a tall rider and he must keep his spurs within reach of his horse's sides.

flexible; that is, he must be able to bend his body slightly to conform to the arc of the turn or circle. If the horse is not supple and the body remains uncurved, the hindquarters may fall in (follow a shorter path than the forehand) or fall out (follow a longer one), or the shoulders may fall in (the horse cuts the corner). (See Figure 3.) We have all ridden horses that had to be steered around corners with the outside rein and the horse looking outward because otherwise the horse, stiff and trying to make life easy for himself, would cut the corner or, indeed, the whole end of the ring. Feeling whether the hind feet are following directly behind the forefeet is usually one of the first things a dressage pupil learns. Once you have felt the difference between turns done by a supple horse and turns by a stiff horse you will never forget.

Dressage is a system of training that utilizes *gymnastic exercises.* These exercises are sometimes called *schoolwork* because, I suppose, the indoor riding hall where they used to be practiced was called a "school." The exercises were invented to strengthen the horse, make him supple, straight, and light, and develop his gaits; in short, to eliminate all resistances and make an athlete of him. These exercises have been performed for hundreds of years and are called classical dressage. They are called for in dressage tests to measure the progress and correctness of the horse's training.

It is hard to say whether the exercises are now a means or an end. They are still a *means* to achieving the ultimate ends of perfect suppleness, impulsion, collection, and so on, but they are also an *end* in themselves for they are fun to do, attractive to watch, and they enable one to compete successfully and win one's share of ribbons. Whether the exercise is shoulder-in at trot, a small circle at canter, an extended walk, or a rein back, there is an element of beauty and achievement in it when done well and also a gymnastic purpose—to develop the inside hind leg, improve collection, put on muscle, supple the back. Dressage is unique, however, in that the exercises performed at shows are not *just* ends in themselves and are not subject to changes of fashion. They were invented to develop and improve the horse—to be good for him—and to achieve these aims they are always the same, although there may be some variation in emphasis from trainer to trainer.

If the gymnastic exercises are to achieve their purpose of developing the horse, it is necessary to get the horse going freely forward in a relaxed manner and accepting the bit. This, at least, is what is expected at Training Level. At First Level we would go a little further and say that the horse should be on the bit with some degree of impulsion. Then the good results can come—the suppleness, straightness, collection, lightness, lateral movements, and eventually High School if that is desired. It is not just *doing* school exercises that is important, but *how* they are done. They must be done so that they develop the horse. The horse must be straight, and going forward with pure gaits, regular rhythm, and correct contact with the bit. It is comparatively easy to ride a simple dressage test with reasonable accuracy; but accuracy is only one requirement, and not the most important one, for a good performance.

The *improvement of the natural gaits* (or paces), which requires *freedom* and *regularity*, is never forgotten as the trainer carries out the gymnastic exercises. The aim is a complete range of each natural pace (walk, trot, canter) from a collected form through a medium form to an extended form with freedom and regularity throughout. The three forms of each gait formerly were called "collected," "ordinary," and "extended," but the Fédération Equestre Internationale (FEI) in 1973 changed their terminology and eliminated the terms "ordinary walk," "ordinary trot," and "ordinary canter." This was good, because there is nothing "ordinary" about any proper dressage gait. They all have to be taught to the horse.

The paces (or gaits) must be "free," that is, not cramped or stiff. The horse should move energetically with long strides; shoulders, stifles, and hocks should flex and extend fully and easily. I dislike equating freedom of movement with speed, but it does give an idea of what is meant. The AHSA stated in *Notes on Dressage* (1972), page 2, that a trained horse should be able to go approximately 117 yards per minute (four miles per hour) at the walk, 235 yards per minute (eight miles per hour) at the trot, and 352 yards per minute (12 miles per hour) at the canter. Compare these speeds with the speed expected of a pleasure horse and the difference will be apparent.

The paces must also be "regular." That is, the rhythm of the hoof beats must be correct and unchanging. A regular walk has four equally spaced beats; a regular trot has two; and a regular canter has three beats (never four) followed by a brief period of suspension. Besides being correct, the rhythm should not change appreciably through the three forms of each gait. In other words, the horse should take the same number of steps per minute whether performing at collected trot, medium trot, or extended trot. The averge horse will not do this unless trained. Instead he will quicken as well as lengthen his strides when pushed to extend and will take more steps per minute. Conversely, before learning the collected trot and canter expected of an advanced dressage horse, he will shorten *and slow down* his steps if he is "collected." The steps may indeed get shorter, but they should not get slower. The horse should be able to maintain this unchanging, regular rhythm through turns, circles, lateral work, and even flying changes.

Impulsion and being *on the bit* are possibly the most important and most characteristic aspects of dressage, but they are also very difficult to comprehend until you have seen and felt them. Consequently I will say only a little about them now and take them up more fully in *Part II*, which will be devoted to the requirements of First Level and Second Level. Impulsion is something that underlies all correct dressage work. The best analogy I can think of is the "breath support" that underlies the vocal production of a trained singer. Without breath support he could not control attacks, releases, and volume of tone precisely, or project both the loudest and the softest sounds so that, without a microphone, they can be heard by every listener in a large opera house.

When the horse has impulsion he goes forward with more energy than is necessary for the gait and speed required, and he performs each figure with precision. He lifts his feet completely off the ground and brings each hind foot well forward under him at each step, usually stepping into the hoofprint of the corresponding forefoot when trotting. If the rein is eased a little, the energy comes out forward in longer steps. If it is not eased, the energy goes into higher steps and longer suspension at trot and canter. Brilliance and precision are added to the horse's gaits by impulsion just as they are added to the singer's voice by proper breath support.

In addition, if the head and neck are in the correct position for the level of training, and the contact with the bit is steady without the jaw being stiff, then the horse is "on the bit." This also can be expressed by saying that the bow is bent—a little. The "bow" is the top line of the horse from nose to hocks. Gradually the bow will be bent more as training progresses. The poll will flex, the neck rise and arch, the croup go down, the joints of the hind legs bend more, and the hocks stay more under the body. This tension forms a reserve of controlled energy underlying the horse's steps. This is dressage collection. (See Figure 2.) It starts with being on the bit with impulsion. The novice can only hope to get the merest glimpse of what impulsion and being on the bit mean and their importance to dressage. In the beginning, at Training Level, the rider works for freedom and regularity and acceptance of the bit.

The last characteristic of dressage is *High School* (Haut École in French). At just what point in training High School may be said to begin is not very definite. I think most people would say that the only High School movements included in dressage tests are pirouette, piaffer, passage, and repeated changes of lead at the canter. On the other hand, at least one writer would include many simpler exercises in the term High School if they are done in

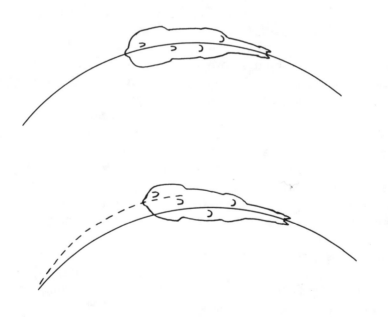

Figure 3. One horse is bent correctly. Both body and neck are curved and the hind feet are following the forefeet. The other horse has bent only his neck. His body is straight and his hindquarters are falling out.

perfect collection. (Wynmalen, *Equitation*, page 121.) The "airs above the ground" are High School but are scarcely practiced anywhere except at the Spanish Riding School in Vienna. Then there is circus high school, which has two chief differences from classical dressage. One is that it includes unnatural movements—that is, movements invented by man such as the Spanish walk, waltz steps, gallop on three legs, and the like. The other difference is that in the modern circus the classical movements and other high school movements are taught without the foundation of complete gymnastic development, which should come first so that they can be performed easily, gracefully, and with fluid transitions. In other words, the horse is trained as quickly as possible to give a flashy performance of advanced movements for the lay public.

To sum up, like any good training, dressage training is systematic and the aids are unobtrusive and consistent. The horse develops confidence in his trainer and becomes attentive and obedient. He learns to do his job dependably and efficiently. In addition his joints are suppled, appropriate muscles are developed, and he becomes more athletic. He becomes more relaxed, rhythmic, and light, and eventually develops great impulsion and collection. In true dressage the horse is treated kindly, though firmly, throughout his training, and the trainer seeks his cooperation rather than depending on force or coercion.

Dressage is sometimes criticized as destroying a horse's initiative for outdoor work. When working in the arena, every move is dictated to the horse and his position and bearing are exactly prescribed. He is expected to concentrate closely on the rider's aids. A cross-country horse, on the contrary, is usually expected to have the capacity to take care of himself rather than depend on his rider for detailed instructions about everything he does. Hence outdoor trail rides and cross-country work in which the horse has some independence should be interspersed with ring work, if desired; thus the horse will be able, on the one hand, to proceed efficiently when left to himself, and, on the other hand, to listen and be obedient whenever his rider takes over. Many multipurpose horses seem to have been taught and shown in other specialties before their owners undertook dressage. So if you start a young horse in dressage, you will also have to teach him other things if your goal is a multipurpose animal.

Beginners often expect that dressage will be easy—that is, not strenuous—and there are phrases in the definitions which were quoted above, like "easier to control," "comfortable for the rider," and "minimum of exertion and effort for the rider," which tend to support this common misconception. Actually anyone who takes up dressage must expect to work hard. There is a saying that, in the beginning, the rider sweats and the horse does not. Later on the rider and the horse both sweat. Only much later does the horse alone sweat. This maxim is not true in all cases—depending on the temperament of the horse and the physical condition of the rider—but it is very true in most cases, and the rider must, accordingly, be prepared for strenuous exercise.

Is dressage easy and enjoyable for the horse? It certainly requires hard work in the ring, but the result of the gymnastic development should be increasing ease for the horse as training progresses. Some horses seem very content working at dressage exercises; others become bored if their work does not include outdoor excursions or jumping. The trained horse may get about with "maximum ease" outdoors, as Müseler says, but only if he is not asked to proceed at a school gait. Dressage gaits require more energy per mile than more natural gaits. Dressage gaits have brilliance at the expense of ease.

2 Getting Started

People often wonder whether they are good enough riders to undertake dressage. Since lessons from competent dressage instructors are apt to be quite expensive and may involve traveling a considerable distance, I feel that it is desirable to achieve a basic competence first. This may involve taking equitation lessons from a local equitation teacher if necessary.

It is hard to determine whether a rider is sufficiently prepared or not. The important thing is to be able to sit still and keep a steady contact with the reins while giving aids. Many people do not realize how much they move their bodies and how unsteady their hands and legs are. They lean forward when they want to go faster and lean backward when they slow down; they kick with their heels, and their arms unintentionally react by jerking; they lose their balance slightly and save themselves from being left behind by hanging onto the reins. They think they have a steady contact with the horse's mouth, but frequently the reins sag for a moment or two, showing that the contact has been broken. Some do not hold the reins firmly. Consequently the reins are always slipping through the fingers, causing the rider to readjust them constantly. Other people do not sit straight; one hip may be higher than the other, or one shoulder ahead of the other.

A good equitation teacher will correct these and other faults until the rider is relaxed, yet can control his movements and not give unintentional signals to the horse with legs, reins, or weight. The rider will be taught to follow the horse's mouth at the walk and canter, and to keep the hands still while posting. He will learn how to control a well-trained horse by merely squeezing with the legs, not kicking.

If you take equitation lessons to prepare for dressage, or if you are already an accomplished equitation rider, you will have a few changes to make later depending on the type of equitation you have learned. If you ride hunt seat, you will need to ride with a longer stirrup for dressage and sit more vertically. If you ride saddle seat, you will have to change to a snaffle bridle and hold your hands lower because the dressage horse has a lower head carriage than a park horse. You will also have to acquire a different saddle. The forward seat saddle is used by some riders for lower level dressage (see Figure 4), but the park saddle is never so used because it places the rider too far to the rear. What if you are a Western rider? Since the reins must be held in two hands for dressage, you will have to change to a snaffle bridle and handle the reins in the English fashion. The position of body and legs in the stock seat is almost identical with the dressage seat, but, of course, you will need an English saddle. These changes should not prove unduly difficult. If you are not sure whether your proficiency is adequate to proceed to dressage, a considerate dressage instructor might be willing to give you a lesson and then tell you whether you need further equitation lessons before continuing with him.

One more question remains: can you school a horse? In southern California, where I live, nearly every aspiring dressage rider schools his own horse. Many have previously schooled other types of horses and know how to go about it, but some have not. So the instructor has to teach the rider how to do something new and how to teach his horse as well. It is surprising how well it works. Almost any skillful rider seems to manage, provided he is determined, patient, hard working, and thoughtful, and provided he has confidence in his instructor. I do not believe you can work well with an instructor if you have mental reservations about his methods. You have to do as he says 100 percent, especially if you are a beginner. If you object to some of his instructions, you had better ask questions or state your objections; and if you cannot reach an agreement, look for another instructor.

Figure 4.   This rider is using an extreme forward seat saddle, which is highly undesirable. The stirrup bar is so far in front of the lowest point of the seat that it is impossible to ride with longer stirrups. The rider has, however, modified her hunt seat by sitting vertically. The rein is sagging, indicating a loss of contact.

Some instructors are only interested in horses sufficiently talented to give promise of doing well in competition. These instructors feel that their reputations depend on this. Other instructors take a broader view and are willing to help a pupil improve any reasonable horse with dressage. Do not feel that you need lessons from a famous expert. Many persons showing at, say, Third Level, are themselves capable of offering excellent instruction to beginners, and the cost is less.

How do you select a competent instructor? I think it is important that he has trained and shown successfully at the levels he teaches. It is also necessary that you find his directions and explanations understandable. I suppose the ultimate test of a good instructor is whether his pupils and their horses perform well. Do the horses move as they should? It is not necessary that they win ribbons, but after they are reasonably experienced they should get scores of 50 percent or better. Finally, does the instructor always talk and act in a way that reflects the true spirit of dressage?

How often will you need lessons? Some beginners are able to progress with a lesson once a month. Others are not. If a monthly clinic is all that is available, try to ride both days if it is a two-day clinic. The second lesson will help to fix in your mind the feel of the movements and the techniques to be used. Also, make a day of it and watch the other students' lessons as well as taking your own. You will see other horses doing just what yours does, and can watch horse and rider to see the effects of the techniques the teacher uses to overcome problems. A dressage rider must learn to see, feel, aid, and teach.

A lesson every two weeks is adequate for most riders. You will ride your horse about eight times between lessons on such a schedule. Usually you and your horse will do your best the day after a lesson when it comes to remembering and repeating something that you got right for a few minutes—or seconds—the previous day. Then your memory will begin to fade. But other things have to be practiced to improve. Sometimes you have to learn a certain combination of aids, and you simply must try many times before it becomes well coordinated and automatic. Transitions are another thing that must be practiced many times in order to improve. Occasionally you may reach "a plateau" and find that you cannot seem to master something and make progress. More frequent lessons for a while may solve your problem.

The other question that concerns beginners is the selection of a suitable horse. A free-going horse of good conformation of almost any breed is usually satisfactory for the lower levels. Besides the favored breeds, Thoroughbreds, Hanoverians, and Trakehners, I have seen successful dressage horses that were Morgans, Anglo-Arabs, Appaloosas, Arabs and half-Arabs, Quarterhorses (of Thoroughbred type), even a Standardbred, a Lipizzaner, a Welsh pony, and a few horses of unknown ancestry. A horse that "moves like a Saddlebred," however, or one that is "a natural for a park horse," should be avoided. Also avoid down-hill horses, short thick necks, thick throats that cannot flex, too finely attached heads (danger of becoming overbent), hind legs out behind, straight shoulders, short upright pasterns, short choppy gaits, and, of course, any suggestion of irregularity of gait. Disposition is extremely important. The horse must be able to perform calmly in a strange place in a snaffle bridle and without a martingale.

How about the age of the horse? I have seen horses as old as 12 or 14 being started in dressage. The chief advantage of an older horse is that his disposition and behavior, especially at shows, is known, and if he is carefully selected you can be sure you are investing your time and effort in a horse that will be a dependable performer. Older horses present different problems than young horses, and the problems may or may not be more difficult to solve. The older horse is usually stiffer and will have to change some of his habits. The trainer must be patient and skillful to accomplish this. I personally would not want to start with an older horse that was in any way "difficult." Of course, if I owned an older horse that I did not want to sell, I might decide to see what dressage would do for his problems, whatever they might be.

The young horse has the advantage of being more malleable and giving more years of service. If carefully handled, he should develop no bad habits. But anyone who has schooled a young horse knows the time required to turn a "green" animal into a settled performer and the disappointments that may occur. Also, you can't push a young horse very fast. The whole idea of dressage is to develop the horse, not exploit him. As a rough rule I would say that a horse should not be shown at Training Level until he is at least three years old, or at First Level until he is four.

There are three attitudes a person might have toward his horse. The first is: "This is *my* horse. I love him and will never sell him." In this case, unless the horse is hopelessly unsuitable, go ahead and dressage him. You should be able to get "passing" scores and work up from level to level if you work hard and have good instruction. It is perfectly respectable in dressage to show and advance if you get scores in the range of 50 to 60 percent, even if your horse is never a winner. The second attitude is: "I will acquire a suitable horse, pay as much as I can afford, and train and advance as far as our abilities permit." If you do not have much to spend, let several instructors know that you are looking for a horse, and then be patient. Dressage riders who have to give up the sport are often more than usually concerned to sell their mounts to suitable owners who will continue dressage training and you might get a bargain. The third attitude is reflected in a desire to excel and win. If this is your attitude, you could buy a proven winner (which will be expensive) or you could start with a young horse considered by someone who is an expert to have a suitable temperament and to be a really excellent mover. If things do not work out, you will sell and try again until you succeed.

If you choose the proven performer, do not underestimate the cost or the amount of training you will require in order to show the horse effectively. If you decide to school an outstanding youngster, do not be in a hurry to advance. Dressage training is the "gradual harmonious development" of the horse. With all the interruptions that normally occur—vacations, bad weather, cast shoes, injuries, and illnesses—allow at least one year per level. If you hurry in the beginning, you will pay the price in the end by ruining the horse or running into insuperable difficulties that will make it necessary to go back and repeat part or all of the training you thought you had finished.

3 The AHSA Training Level Tests

The lowest test level provided by the American Horse Shows Association is called Training Level. (Prior to 1974 it was called Preliminary Level.) At the present time there are four Training Level tests. Test 1 is the easiest, and new requirements are then added test by test so that they gradually become harder. All the AHSA tests are revised from time to time, which gives riders a welcome change from the old routines. In the 1983 revision, extensive changes were made in an effort to improve the tests as a training sequence. The 1987 revision is minor. This *Guide* will follow the 1987 requirements closely.

As stated by the AHSA, the *purpose* of the Training Level tests is:

To introduce the rider and horse to the basic principles of dressage competition. Training Level requires "Obedience" to the aids of the rider without fight or evasion when ridden on light contact. One is searching for free, rhythmic, forward movement, relaxed and obedient, stretching into the bit in a calm, receptive manner.

The *general requirements for the horse* are, in summary, Regular and free gaits, impulsion, and submission. The *rider* is supposed to demonstrate a good position and seat, and correct and effective use of aids.

The following *paces* (gaits) and *figures* are required in the tests: Working walk, free walk on a long rein, working trot rising and sitting, working canter, canter departs from trot on the correct lead, large circle at trot and canter (65 feet in diameter), change of rein on the diagonal, down the center line, halt, and stand still. Test 4 also contains a halt in the body of the test. When new tests or revisions are issued, you will have to compare them with the old tests to see whether there are any changes that will affect your training program.

In order to cover all these subjects in an orderly way, I will start by discussing *seat and aids* since logically this should be the rider's first concern. After his own seat and aids are reasonably adequate, the rider is ready to begin to develop the *basic requirements in the horse*. Therefore an explanation of the meaning of the requirements for the horse will follow. Once the rider has some idea of his training objectives he will want to know the *methods* by which the objectives are attained. This will be the third subject taken up. Finally, we will come to the actual *performance of the tests* by which horse and rider are introduced to the principles of dressage competition: the memorizing of tests, the correct way to execute movements and figures, and the principles on which the tests are judged.

The Dressage Seat

This book is going to consist largely of quotations from standard works. The quotations will be accompanied by explanations to help the reader understand what the writers meant, and to give him methods for determining whether or not the objectives are being achieved.

We will start with a description of the French dressage seat quoted from Noel Jackson in *Effective Horsemanship*. (See Figure 5.) Jackson is an Englishman who, after many years of riding, hunting, and polo all over the world (he was in the diplomatic service), had an opportunity to attend the Portuguese cavalry school at Mafra, Portugal. In his book he sets forth the system he learned there. The Portuguese school is in close touch with the French, and what he learned was essentially the French concept of dressage.

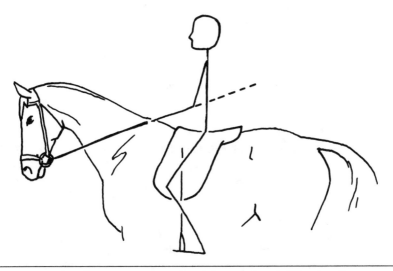

Figure 5. This illustration is reproduced from Jackson's *Effective Horseman-ship*, page 34. Jackson calls this the normal position for walk,
sitting trot, and collected canter. Dotted line emphasizes straight line
from elbow to mouth.

*I propose to discuss a modern seat that I have found suitable—with
different lengths of stirrups—for Dressage, cross-country riding,
jumping, and polo. It is the seat evolved by Colonel Danloux, who
was Ecuyer en Chef at Saumur from 1929 to 1933. After much study
and trial it was then adopted officially as the seat for the French army, and remains the French national seat to this day. . . . To
achieve this seat you will need to cultivate:*

Flexibility, *by the relaxation of all your muscles and joints.*

Balance, *which might be defined as adapting your centre of gravity
to that of your horse. It will help you to do this if you sit forward
and deep into the lowest point of the seat of the saddle, rather than
on top of or on the back of it.*

Adherence, *by which is meant maintaining contact with the saddle
and the horse with as large an area of your thighs and legs as is consistent with keeping your knees flexible. You will more easily do
this if, instead of gripping strongly with your thighs and knees, you
relax and stretch the muscles of your thighs—initially by riding
without stirrups—so that your seat and legs can descend deeply into
the saddle, and you can get your calves and the inside of your legs
below the calves close to it, and to the horse's sides. Gripping*

strongly with your thighs, **above** *the broadest part of the horse's body . . . has the effect of squeezing you upwards and* **out** *of the saddle. . . . If you keep your legs below the calves close into the horse's sides,* **below** *the broadest part of the horse's body, it will tend to draw you* **down** *into the saddle, and give you a stronger seat. . . .*

. . . .

. . . For Dressage, riding on the Flat, and for polo, you should rely mainly on **balance,** *and cultivate* **flexibility** *rather than a strong seat. For jumping and cross-country riding, however, you should* **adhere** *more strongly to the saddle and your horse with your legs, while maintaining the flexibility of your knees, body, and arms.*

. . . .

. . . You should keep your body erect but relaxed, with your head up, and you should look horizontally and in the direction you are going. Your neck and shoulders should be relaxed and your upper arms should hang slightly forward of the vertical, your forearms being in line with the horse's mouth. Keep your elbows and wrists supple and ready to flex to allow your hands, through the reins, to remain at one with the movements of the horse's mouth. Your wrists and hands, with your thumbs on top, should ordinarily be in the same line as your forearm, holding the reins above and just in front of the horse's withers, with your hands sufficiently separated to be out of each other's way, and with the reins, when the horse is going straight forward, roughly parallel to the horse's neck.

. . . .

. . . The pivotal point between you and your saddle should be your calves rather than your knees. In this position your leg below the knee will be more or less behind the vertical, according to the length of stirrups you adopt. Your stirrup leathers should be vertical, although they can with advantage be twisted slightly round your shin bones. Your heels, without the ankles being in any way stiff, should fall naturally below the level of the balls of your feet; and if the soles of your feet are turned outwards—again without stiffness—the insides and front of your thighs will lie more closely to the saddle, and your calves and legs below the calves will be more into the horse's sides.

I should next perhaps compare the Danloux seat with the one you may already know. To start with, you should sit slightly further forward in the saddle than is usual. . . . The reasons for this are that the horse can most easily carry weight on either side of the back part of his withers, where his spine and rib cage are strongest. This *takes the rider's weight off the horse's loin muscles and enables him all the more easily to use them. It is also the place that is subject to the least vertical movement in the horse's paces, and consequently the most comfortable place for the rider to sit. Another difference is in the position of the rider's lower leg. . . . I was taught . . . to grip the saddle with my thighs and knees and to keep my lower legs slightly away from the horse's sides. . . . Maintaining contact with the leg below the knee would, I was assured, either deaden the horse's sides, or upset a sensitive horse. I now know that this is not necessarily so. It depends on how it is done and how the horse has been trained.*

The objection to gripping with the thighs is that it tends to squeeze the rider out of the saddle, when he should be trying to relax down into it; while an additional objection to gripping with the knees is that it causes the rider to stiffen them so that one of the three shock absorbers—ankle joint, knee joint, and hip joint— . . . is reduced in its effectiveness. . . . This is the difference between the Danloux seat and Caprilli's. [The forward seat used in jumping was invented by Captain Federico Caprilli, an Italian army officer, about the year 1900. The current American hunt seat is one form of it.] Those who follow Caprilli keep their knees into the saddle and pivot on them. . . . For Dressage the rider's adherence need not be very strong; but his lower leg should remain in light contact with the horse's sides: and alive, ready to apply his aids smoothly and discreetly without the jerks that seem to be inseperable from making and breaking contact. At later stages in Dressage this will assume increasing importance, for really smooth and discreet aids are not possible without light contact. Provided the aids are kept alive, this contact need not deaden the horse's sides. Indeed, the horse grows to have confidence in it, and to develop more sensitivity than with constant making and breaking of contact. The same is true, of course, of the bit; without smooth contact between the horse's mouth and the rider's hands, in which the horse can have confidence, a still head carriage and accurate obedience are virtually impossible to achieve. (Jackson, pp. 33–37.)

The next description of the dressage seat is that of the late Colonel Alois Podhajsky, formerly commandant of the Spanish Riding School in Vienna. (See Figure 6.) Colonel Podhajsky was head of the school during World War II and his heroism in saving the school formed the basis of Walt Disney's 1963 motion picture, *The Miracle of the White Stallions*. Colonel Podhajsky was also an

Figure 6.   The seat described by Colonel Podhajsky. The rider depicted is
Franz Rochawansky of the Spanish Riding School of Vienna. The
horse is performing the piaffe, which is a trot on the spot. Note that
a vertical line would pass through the rider's shoulder, hip, and heel.

international competitor and an Olympic contender, winning the
bronze medal in dressage in 1936. His book, *The Complete Training of Horse and Rider,* is very useful, giving many detailed explanations of exercises and methods.

> *While the horse is standing still, the trainer explains the correct
> position to the rider. This begins with the foundation, namely the
> seat. This should be pushed well forward into the centre of the sad-
> dle. Both seat bones should rest firmly in the saddle. . . . The seat
> should be open and not be pinched together in order to allow the
> rider to sit as deep as possible in the saddle. . . .*
> *Both hips, which decide the position of the upper part of the
> body, must be vertical to the saddle. . . . If the hip comes behind*

this vertical line, the rider will sit as if he were in a chair, the back would be rounded, the knees would come off the saddle, and the legs would slide too much forward. This seat would be as much a fault as sitting on the fork, *which comes about when the hip comes in front of the vertical line with the consequence that legs and knees would be taken too far back. The effect of this seat is even more harmful than the "chair" seat because the rider sits more on the thigh than on his backside. The upper body would become unsteady and the rider would easily lose his balance, besides which any pushing aid of the weight would be impossible.*

. . . .

The rider's back *must be upright with the small of the back braced. The spine must not be hollow and the back must remain supple and flexible. This is necessary to enable the rider to follow all movements of his horse as if he were part of his own body. The back must remain firm and upright to allow the rider to use the small of the back as an aid; otherwise he would not be able to prevent the horse from pulling him out of the saddle when lying on the rein.*

. . . .

The shoulders *must be so taken back that the chest is arched without tenseness. . . .*

The head *should be carried with a firm but not stiff neck. The chin should be slightly drawn back. It should not be pushed forward and the head should not look down. . . .*

The thigh *should turn inwards from the hip and lie smoothly and firmly on the saddle without being clamped to it, . . .*

If the knees *are raised and too far forward they will provoke the "chair" seat. If they come too far back, the leg will be nearly vertical to the ground and throw the rider onto his fork. The knees must lie flat on the saddle and must never move from it. A gap should never be seen between the knee and the saddle.*

The lower legs *should form a wide angle with the thighs and lie close to the horse's body, hanging down by their own weight without tension. They should be on the girth. The foot, parallel to the horse's side, is the prolongation of the leg turned inwards throughout its whole length. The heel should be the lowest point of the foot.*

A vertical line *drawn from the shoulders of the rider to the ground should touch his heel and a vertical line from the knee should touch his toes.*

. . . .

The rider must now learn to maintain the correct seat in all paces. . . . If the rider finds difficulty in sitting, he may hold onto the sad-

dle, that is, pull himself into the saddle. He should not balance on the top of the saddle, but grip the horse with his knees.

. . . .

When the rider holds onto the saddle, his outside hand will hold the pommel and his inside hand the cantel. If the position of the hands were reversed . . . his outside shoulder would fall back and would not be at a right angle to the horse's spine. (Podhajsky, pp. 211–215.)

Finally, here is a description by a modern German dressage expert, Richard Wätjen. (See Figure 7.) Wätjen was a prominent trainer, teacher, and competitor who spent ten years at the Spanish Riding School early in his career. His book, *Dressage Riding*, describes the correct performance of the classical dressage movements, but does not attempt to tell how they are taught.

The rider should hold himself upright and in a natural position, with his back braced, and sitting well down in the middle of the saddle at its lowest point, which is in fact the centre of gravity. The rider's knees must be drawn back so far that the inside of the thighs lies flat against the saddle. He should hold his feet naturally in the stirrups with the heels well down and his feet almost parallel to the ground. The lower part of the legs should hang down loosely, the inside part in light contact with the horse's body, so that the leg aid can be applied quietly and calmly, the leg gently touching the side of the horse. . . . Stirrups that are too long cause restless legs, and this leads to an unsteady seat. Stirrups that are too short prevent the rider from sitting gracefully down in the saddle and he appears to be sitting on a chair. To a certain extent the length of the stirrup depends on the horse's conformation and its progress in training.

The upper arm should almost form a right angle to the forearm. The rider should hold his hands about four inches away from his body, so that when the wrists are slightly turned inwards, the little fingers should be opposite each other; the hands vertical, and fairly close together. The rider should hold his shoulders square, letting them drop naturally. The upper arms should rest gently against the rider's body, so that they form a support for his hands, enabling them to exercise a calm and continual influence. The rider's back should be straight, but not rigid and stiff, so that the simultaneous leg and rein aids are transferred through the rider's back directly to the back of his mount. The combination of a straight back and supple hip joints enables the rider to adapt himself to the horse's movements. He should sit quietly but firmly, independent of the movements of his horse. Hands, with pliable wrists, must remain as calm and steady as possible. Otherwise the pace and the following of movement will suffer, with the mouth becoming insensitive and not, as so many think, active. The same applies to the legs. Constant tapping is useless, even detrimental, since the steadiness of the seat suffers. The horse also grows accustomed to this continuous tapping and becomes indifferent to normal aids. Furthermore every aid should be applied with the upper part of the body held steady. (Wätjen, pp. 9–10.)

There are differences among the seats described by Jackson, Podhajsky, and Wätjen—the knee grip and the position of the arm and hand, for instance—but in most ways they are similar. The braced back may be ignored for the time being. It will be discussed in *Part II.*

The special points of the dressage seat are as follows:

1. *Long stirrups.* When the legs are stretched down as straight and far as possible, the stirrup will not strike the ankle bone, but one or two inches below it. (See Figure 8.) When the feet are in the stirrups and the heels a little down, the central axis of the rider's

Figure 7.   Richard Wätjen is depicted at the halt. This is the seat he describes. Most pictures of Wätjen show his leg behind the girth and his reins very long. Reproduced from page 10 of *Dressage Riding*.

thigh, when extended, will pass a little *below* the point of the horse's shoulder. In the so-called "chair seat," on the other hand, this imaginary line will pass *above* the point of the shoulder. (See Figure 9.)

2. The *weight is on the seat bones*, not on the thighs. This will occur if the buttocks are not pinched together, the thighs are relaxed, and the body is vertical. You can check this by putting the fingers of one hand under the seat bone on the same side and then

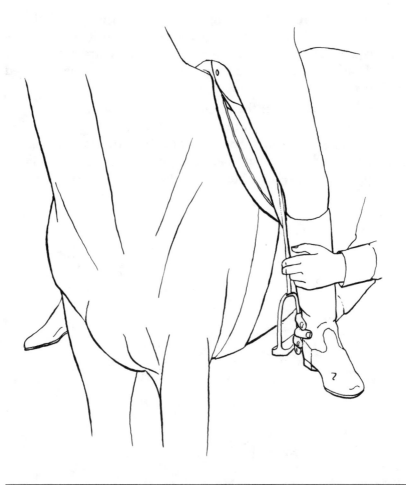

Figure 8.   Method of approximating correct length of stirrup for dressage. Rider sits squarely in saddle and stretches both legs straight down, letting toes hang. Assistant's middle finger is on protruding ankle bone. Left hand holds stirrup close to foot. When adjusting stirrups for hunt seat, stirrup will bump ankle bone.

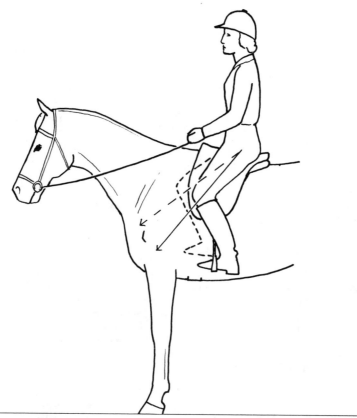

Figure 9.   Dressage seat with prolongation of line of thigh passing below the point of the shoulder.

experimenting by alternately tensing and relaxing the thighs, alternately pinching the buttocks together and relaxing them, and by tilting the body forward and back. You will soon find how to get maximum pressure on your fingers: it should feel as though the bone is going right down through your hand. You will probably find that you are accustomed to gripping with your thighs and inclining your body slightly forward. (See Figure 10.) You will have to "think tall" and consciously relax many times before you can form a new habit. You will also probably find that your seat does not press down on the saddle (or does not even touch it all the time) at sitting trot and canter. "Sitting down in the saddle" can be achieved only by relaxing the upper part of the legs, sitting vertically, and being supple, especially in the hip joints.

Figure 10. This rider has a nice long stirrup and good leg, foot, and hand position. Her body, however, is not vertical and her weight is not on her
seatbones. The horse is depicted at the moment of suspension and is
tracking up. The right hind foot is going to land on the spot just vacated
by the right forefoot. Another way of confirming that the horse is
tracking up is to note that as the feet move forward and back, they
almost touch under the horse's body.

Practice the dressage seat at a slow enough sitting trot to be
comfortable. You will not be riding at a slow trot after you start
schooling your horse, but you can do it at this stage to get the idea
of how flexibility and relaxation of the thighs make it possible for
the seat to follow the movements of the saddle and rest steadily
upon it. The ankles also will have to be flexible to keep you from
losing the stirrups. It will feel as though your toes are going gently
up and down when the horse trots.

With a young horse, the dressage seat is not used immediately.
Trainers do a lot of posting trot in the early stages because it is not
comfortable to do sitting trot until the horse has made a certain
amount of progress. Even when riders do sit down at canter, and
later at trot, a "light seat," which is more like hunt seat, is used for
a while. The body is tilted just enough forward so that the weight
is on the thighs rather than on the seat. From the horse's point of
view, this means that the front part of the saddle will be weighted

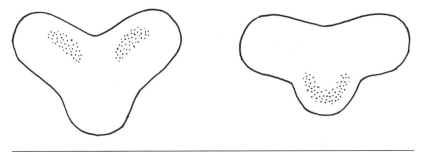

Figure 11. The part of the saddle pad that is soiled by the forward seat, *left,* and by the dressage seat. Dirt is concentrated most heavily in the areas shown.

rather than the seat. You can tell what part of the saddle you are weighting by observing the dirty area on a soft saddle pad. Use a thin, clean pad and examine it after use. (See Figure 11.)

3. The horse is influenced by the *calf of the leg,* and it is usually described as being "on the girth." Actually the top of the boot (the fat part of the calf) is on the girth and the lower part of the calf is behind the girth. The way to check this is by having someone look at you from the side. The girth should be visible above the toe and instep and then pass under the top of the boot. (See Figure 10.) The seat bones must rest on the lowest point of the saddle. Then, if you are sitting on a dressage saddle, the back of your heel, your seat bones, hip bones, shoulder, and ear can be in one straight vertical line. (Compare Figures 5, 6, and 7.) This is the classical dressage position.

My dressage saddle measures only 5¾ inches from the lowest point of the seat to the center of the stirrup bar. You cannot sit this way on some forward seat saddles because the seat is further back. I have measured saddles that are 7¼ inches or more from the lowest point of the seat to the center of the stirrup bar. (See Figure 12.) So if you use such a saddle, do not expect to have the classical dressage look. Sometimes extra stuffing in the back of the saddle will correct this problem.

Whatever type of saddle you use, you should sit in the lowest part of the seat, use a long stirrup, and have your foot far enough back so that the girth can be seen above the toe. You will probably have to hold your foot back and your calf against the horse's side at first, but in time this becomes a habit. Use a thin saddle pad so

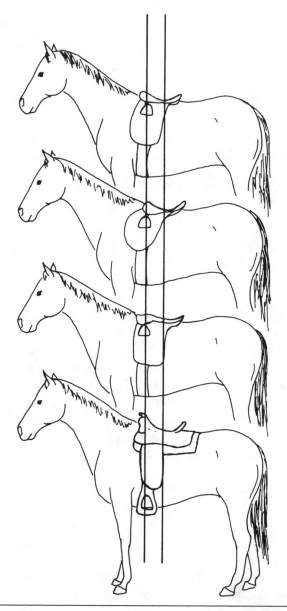

Figure 12. This composite drawing shows the relative positions of stirrup
leather and deepest part of seat of four saddles. One line goes
through the stirrup bar. The other line marks the lowest point of the
seat of the dressage saddle (a Fulmer saddle—English). The distance
to the lowest point of the other saddles is seen to be considerably
greater. The classical dressage seat is possible only in the dressage
saddle.

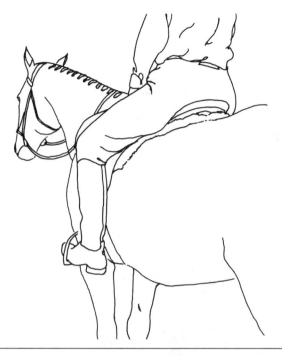

Figure 13.   One thin pad should be used for dressage to make good leg contact possible. If extra padding is needed it should be under the seat only.

your calf can touch the horse, and make sure there is no roll at the back of the flap that gets under your leg and holds it out away from the horse's side. (See Figure 13.) If your horse's back is sensitive and needs more cushioning than a single pad, a wool blanket (as shown in Figure 74) will not keep your calf away from his side. If you cannot keep your knee against the saddle when the calf is against the horse, the correct position of the calf is the more important goal.

4. The *hand and arm position* is not unusual, but it should be stressed that the important thing is the straight line from elbow to bit. Most instructors seem to like the wrist and hand to be a straight prolongation of the forearm. The actual height of the hand varies, depending on how high or how low the horse carries his head and how long the rider's arms are. In the beginning it is low, sometimes level with the top of the withers, or the hands may be still lower—on each side of the withers. (Compare Figures 1, 2, and 14.)

Figure 14. Riding with a "light seat" on a young horse. The whip is being carried correctly. The horse's neck is low, poll not flexed, accepting the bit. The rider's hands should be a little lower so as to make a straight line from elbow to bit. Left hind toe kicking up dust shows that there is not yet much impulsion.

5. The *foot* is most elegant if the toe points straight ahead rather than turning out. This is supposed to be achieved by turning the leg at the hip. If you stand up with both legs perfectly straight and raise one foot a fraction of an inch off the floor you can turn the toe outward, straight ahead, or inward by rotating the thigh bone in the hip socket. The ankle and knee remain entirely immobile. Try it with each leg while standing and then try it on horseback. Just how successful you are will depend on your conformation and that of the horse. Whether the knee is against the saddle or not also depends on the size and conformation of horse and rider.

Aids

In dressage the inner side of the calf, not the back of the calf, is supposed to act on the side of the horse. To check this, note where the dirt collects on your boot. Ideally there should be no dirt on the strip of leather that goes up the back. If dirt extends to this strip, you are using your legs by turning your toes out and bending your knee to press the calf against the horse's side. The correct way is to close your legs more like a tongs, bringing your toes closer together without increasing the bend of the knee. Of course, this results in a pretty mild aid. It is the ideal for a well-schooled horse. During schooling, there will be many times when you will turn your toes out in order to use your legs or heels vigorously.

The legs can be used in several different ways. They can exert a steady grip like a vise. This squeeze can be maintained and increased until the horse responds. They can be used to give little, quick, bouncy squeezes by pressing the toes together without the calf ever losing contact in between. Tapping with the legs means that the contact of the boot and the horse's side is broken, and the leg then makes a new contact, more or less emphatic. When one leg alone is used it can press steadily or can be moved back where it touches without pressing, or it can give short little presses in the position on the girth or in a position farther back. A very well-schooled horse may respond to one or both toes being merely pressed down in the stirrup. This raises the heels and moves the lower calf up and back against the horse's side. The legs almost always remain in contact but do not press, squeeze, or tap unless it is desired to give an aid.

Initial work is done with a snaffle bit only. The double bridle is not even permitted until Fourth Level. The snaffle rein enters the hand between the ring finger and the little finger and leaves between index finger and thumb.

The whip is held in the inside hand and must cross the thigh just above the knee. (See Figure 14.) The little finger holds it up in this position. The dressage whip with its heavy mushroom butt is desirable because it is very nicely balanced. When you wish to use it, you move the hand to the side—without disturbing the contact of the bit with the horse's mouth—and then twist the wrist, still without disturbing the contact any more than can be helped, so that the whip taps the horse just behind the calf of the leg. The whip should be about 36 inches long. Do not use a crop.

Whenever the horse and rider "change the rein," the whip should be passed to the new inside hand. Here is one way to change the whip: Take the left rein into the right hand, thus freeing the left hand. Then reach across the horse's neck with the left hand and take hold of the whip with the thumb toward the butt end. Flip the tip forward, up over the horse's ears, and down to its new position. Take the left rein into the left hand again. The horse must not be afraid of the whip and may have to get used to its being passed from one side to the other. Some trainers carry a whip in each hand to avoid shifting one whip back and forth.

The reins are almost always kept "stretched," that is, lightly taut. The contact is given up momentarily when the horse flexes the jaw or when the rider desires to yield the rein. In both cases contact is gently resumed very quickly. The reins can be kept stretched only if the hand follows the horse's head at walk and canter, and remains still at trot even when the rider is posting. Reins must be shortened for posting trot but are usually the same length for working walk, sitting trot, and canter.

All rein aids commence with the bit already in contact. This is very important as tugs, vibrations, or the French half halt would be very severe if they started with the rein slack. In that case the horse's jaw would be painfully bumped instead of merely being pulled on. An observer can tell that the contact is not being maintained whenever one or both reins sag or flutter (float) instead of remaining straight. (Compare Figure 4 with Figure 14.) They should not sag even during canter departs.

Reins can be tightened by moving the whole arm back from the shoulder, or by bending the wrist so the thumbs point toward each other, or by tightening the fingers (bringing the fingernails into the palms). Obviously the last is the most subtle and would be effective only on a sensitive horse with a steady head.

The hands can steer by pulling on one rein until the horse bends his neck a trifle, or by moving both hands to the side to which the turn is being made so that the outer rein bears against the neck. If both hands move to the left, the right hand comes *to* the withers but does not cross over to the other side; the right rein touches the neck, the left rein is clear of the neck, the horse looks a trifle to the left and turns to the left. The horse must not look to the right as he might do if he were being neck-reined Western style.

Dressage aids need not necessarily be different from the aids you are accustomed to, provided your usual aids are invisible, or nearly so, and provided they will not cause confusion later when you have advanced to more complicated movements. About the only aid which should be visible is the moving back of the outside leg for canter departs and lateral work. Even Grand Prix riders can be observed moving the lower legs backward and forward when performing flying changes. The chief confusion that is likely to develop in more advanced riding is also connected with the canter depart.

Americans generally use the outside rein and outside leg for canter departs. At least in the early stages of training, they turn the horse's head to the outside with the outside rein and push the haunches away from the rail with the outside leg. When the horse is in this diagonal position they drive him on into canter. The dressage horse has to be straight at all times, so he must not be pushed into this diagonal position. Also, he must not look to the outside. In fact he must look a trifle to the inside on turns or circles, and the canter depart is required while trotting on a circle in Training Level tests. Later the horse has to change leads at the canter and immediately turn in the direction of the new lead. So it is important, in the Training Level tests and for later advanced work, to have the horse straight in canter departs and looking the way he is going. If your horse is in the habit of departing into the canter from a diagonal position you will have to eliminate this, as the best English and Western riders do.

Another thing. If your horse is accustomed to a double bridle, he probably raises his neck when the snaffle is used alone and brings his nose in only when the curb rein is tightened. You will have to ride with just the snaffle in dressage, and teach him to drop his nose and flex at the poll to the snaffle bit alone. I mention these things here because they are aid problems. They will be taken up again as appropriate.

Basic Systems of Aids

The aids include the legs, reins, weight, whip, and spurs. In addition, the voice is used in training although it cannot be used in a test at a show. The term "aids" also refers to the way they are used. For example, you can say, "The legs are an aid." You can also say, "The leg aid for shoulder-in is repeated, short pushes by the inside leg on the girth." Aids may be divided into *basic aids*, which are used to obtain each gait and increase its energy or speed and to steer around an arena, and *specific aids* for movements such as half-pass or flying change. In this section only basic aids will be examined. Specific aids will be treated in later sections when the various movements and figures are discussed.

Although, as I have said before, basic dressage aids need not necessarily be different from regular English aids, except for the points just noted, there exist several systems of dressage aids that you may find surprisingly different. Unfortunately it is hard to find them described in the standard works, but I will try to give you some idea of what a dressage instructor might expect of you.

A system may use the same aids for each gait. Most Americans are used to such a system. They squeeze with both legs (or knees) to increase the pace. But there is a quite different dressage system of this type (using the same aids for each gait) that is taught by Robert Hall, coach of the 1968 and 1972 British Olympic dressage teams.

In the Hall system the inside leg is always the driving leg. (The inside is the side toward the center of the ring.) This leg vibrates (gives quickly repeated, short presses) against the horse's side. Even when riding outdoors, one side has to be the "inside" and the other the "outside." The rider posts on the "outside" diagonal and drives with the "inside" leg. The whip is always in the inside hand so it can back up the inside (driving) leg if needed. Of course, the rider reverses the aids from time to time outdoors, just as he would reverse his direction periodically when riding in an arena. The horse is always restrained with the outside rein, not with both reins. This rein is vibrated when a decrease of speed or gait is desired. This is not a compulsion for the horse, it is a signal. The reins can actually be lengthened at the same time so the horse can extend his neck as he slows down. The outside leg behind the girth is used, if needed, to keep the hindquarters from flying out or to push them to the side. If the hindquarters are moving correctly the outside leg does nothing, remaining passive on the girth. The inside rein is used to give the direction when a turn is indicated. Of course both legs and both reins maintain contact at all times.

There always has to be some special signal for canter departs to indicate the lead desired. In the case of Robert Hall's system, the outside leg is moved back but not pressed against the horse. This indicates the lead. Right leg back, left lead; left leg back, right lead. The reins do nothing because the horse already has a slight position of head and neck to the inside, and the length of rein is not changed. The rider continues to sit upright. The inside leg is used if necessary to ask for the depart, vibrating against the horse's side in its usual place.

With a system such as Hall's, where the same driving aid is used for each gait (also the same restraining aid), only the strength of the aid and the degree of yielding of the rein indicate to the horse whether the rider wants a change within the gait (more speed or energy) or a change of gait (walk to trot).

If you do not use the same aids for each gait, you eliminate this problem, and several examples of such a system could be cited. One is described in *Give Your Horse a Chance* by Lieutenant-Colonel A. L. d'Endrödy, former member of the Royal Hungarian Olympic Equestrian Team. This remarkable book was written while the author was a prisoner of war during World War I. It is incredibly detailed, probably too detailed for the average reader.

Action of the driving leg in walk and trot

The horse, both in the walk and trot, performs identical movements with its hind legs. . . . The steps of both hind legs participate equally in promoting the horse's forward movement. When the aim is to accelerate its movements in these paces, it is necessary to speed up the movement of both hind legs equally. To achieve this effect, the driving signals have to be applied alternately to both sides. For instance, a short light pressure or knock of the rider's right leg for the desired movement of the horse's off-hind leg, and a touch of the left leg for the movement of near-hind leg, and again by the right leg for the off-hind leg, and so on.

The action of the driving leg in the canter and gallop

The method of giving drive-on signals in canter and gallop differs from that in walk and trot. The root of the difference lies in the fact that in these paces each of the horse's four legs has a certain function in thrusting the body forward, and they perform this function by different movements.

This distribution of functions of the legs provides several equally valid possibilities for the application of signals, each of which has its particular advantage. . . .

From my own point of view, the best method in the canter and gallop seems to be to give the signal on the inside in a touching-like manner, by which the forward-thrust of the inside hind leg is animated. . . .

Thus the drive-on signal (executed with the inside leg) should be applied in the canter at that moment when the hoof of the inside foreleg appears in front of the particular shoulder, and in the gallop when the hoof of the outside foreleg appears in front of the shoulder. (d'Endrödy, pp. 43-44.)

Another system using different aids for the various gaits is taught by Charles de Kunffy, well-known contemporary writer on dressage and former Hungarian International Equestrian Team member. The de Kunffy method calls for alternating leg aids at walk in rhythm with the horse's strides just like d'Endrödy. At trot, however, brief little squeezes with *both* legs in the trot rhythm are used; at the canter, alternating leg aids again. The squeezes at trot coincide with the moment when you would say "down" if you were saying "up, down, up, down," in time to your posting on the outside diagonal. The squeeze is caused by pressing the toes toward each other and then relaxing them. It may be very gentle (the legs "breathe with the horse") or quite emphatic. When the toes go in, the calves roll a little forward and the knees go out. When the toes return to their normal position, the calves roll a little back and the knees turn in.

The driving aid at canter is alternating, but not at equal intervals as at walk. The inner leg "nicks" as the leading shoulder of the horse comes back and releases as it goes forward. The outer leg pushes during the intervals between. The rider starts by making the inner leg nick inward in accordance with the movement of the shoulder and then adds the outer leg, letting it follow the movement of the horse's barrel (brush forward). Soon the rhythm can be established by feeling the movement of the horse. For the canter depart, the weight is momentarily on the outside seat bone and the outer leg is back.

Other aids could be described, especially for canter departs, but my purpose is not to confuse the reader—and there is danger that I may have already done so—but to give some idea of the various aids possible and offer the reader some help in following the instructions of his particular instructor. Although various claims are made for the different systems, it does seem as if the horse can work well with almost any system so long as the rider is consistent.

The alternating leg aids at walk are so commonly used, and horses seem to respond to them so well, that I would like to close this section by quoting a very good explanation of the theory and practice of this useful aid by Henry Wynmalen in his book, *Dressage:*

> . . . *a driving aid cannot influence the action of any given limb after such limb has already left the ground; whilst this consideration may*

*become largely theoretical in other gaits, with a much quicker suc-
cession of footfalls, it remains eminently practical in the case of the
more leisurely walk.*

*It follows that in the walk, to be fully effective, the action of the
rider's driving leg-aid must coincide with the moment in which the
hindleg to be activated touches down. In other words, to be fully effective, the rider's driving leg-aids are used alternately, coinciding
with the alternating footfalls of the horse's hind legs. There is in that
no difficulty, since the rider can feel these moments distinctly by the
peculiar swing of the horse's body; he has but to follow that swing,
from side to side, with each of his legs and, when a driving aid is to
be given, accentuate the inward swing of each leg slightly; his aid
will then synchronize with the corresponding footfall of the horse's
hindleg. (Wynmalen, pp. 183–84.)*

Perhaps Wynmalen has hit on the reason why this aid works so
well and is so widely used, while there is so much variation in the
aids for the other gaits. Wynmalen was a Dutchman who became a
naturalized English citizen. His dressage stems from the French
school. His books, although popular and containing clear explanations, also contain unfortunate mistakes. In particular, the pictures cannot be relied on to correctly illustrate dressage
movements. There is no doubt, however, that he had the true
dressage spirit of kind and humane training, which one is sure to
absorb from reading his two books, *Equitation* and *Dressage*.

Basic General Requirements for the Horse

The statement of these requirements is at the ends of the tests
where three special marks are awarded for them. (There is also a
special mark for the seat and aids of the rider.) Stated in full they
are:

Gaits (freedom and regularity).

Impulsion (desire to move forward, elasticity of the steps, relaxation of the back).

Submission (attention and confidence; harmony and lightness and
ease of movements; acceptance of the bit).

I will take up the last one first.

Not much needs to be said about *submission* and its corollaries: *attention* and *confidence*, and *harmony, lightness,* and *ease* of the movements. The words are pretty much self-explanatory. Submission is the opposite of resistance, irritation, and unwillingness. If the horse is attentive, he responds promptly to aids and is not easily distracted by extraneous sights and sounds. His ears are often directed backwards toward his rider. Beware of pricked ears. The horse turns his ears in the direction of his attention. If the horse has confidence in his rider, he will look calm and happy. Everything he does should look simple and natural, that is, "harmonious, light, and easy."

The horse must also *accept the bit.* That is, he must go willingly forward against a lightly stretched rein and must not in any way fight or avoid the contact of the bit on the bars of his mouth. He must not fight it by tossing or shaking his head, or avoid it by raising his head (Figure 15), poking his nose, opening his mouth, or tucking his chin into his chest (Figure 16). Of course, he must not go to the other extreme and pull, or lean on the bit and expect the rider to hold his head up for him. His head must be steady. He should have a wet mouth, and if he chews the bit and drips foam, so much the better.

With older horses that are just being started in dressage a hard mouth is a common problem, and the horse must be taught to loosen his jaw before he can have a good contact. Many older horses also have habits of fighting the bit, avoiding contact, or taking a stronger contact on one side of the mouth than on the other. Or they may have always been ridden in a standing martingale on which they are used to "leaning." These bad habits can be gradually minimized or overcome by intelligent training.

The rider, for his part, must provide a steady support; this means that he must be able to keep his hands still when trotting, and follow the horse's mouth when walking and cantering. Many riders, however, if they have conscientiously learned to maintain a "light" contact, actually have a contact that is *too* light—it is so light that it is not steady, and the reins look as though they are "floating" rather than "stretched." The correct dressage contact is a stretched rein. A stretched rein is straight at all times. It never sags or wavers. So even if your horse has a nice steady head carriage, you may have to shorten your reins a little and induce him to go forward with a slightly stronger contact than you and he are accustomed to before he can be said to accept the bit.

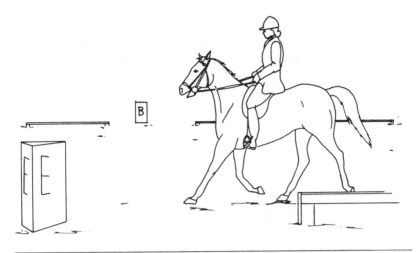

Figure 15.   Incorrect head carriage and contact. The horse is "above the bit" and appears to be pulling. He is not accepting the bit. His steps are stiff and short as shown by right fore and hind being well separated.

Figure 16.   This horse is "overbent," that is, the face is behind the vertical. The sagging rein shows that he is also "behind the bit."

If a horse is not submissive the trouble may be that his rider's aids are inconsistent and confusing, with the result that he does not know what to do. Or the aids may be clear enough, but the horse may be unable to do what is required. He may not have been trained long enough or gradually enough. Or some item of tack may be wrongly adjusted or dirty and causing pain. It is also possible that he has a nervous and fretful disposition and may never become confident and dependable. Dressage training can correct many faults when carried out intelligently and tactfully, but it cannot correct all faults.

The horse should also have regular and free gaits. *Regular gaits* are gaits performed with the correct sequence of footfalls in an unchanging rhythm. People often do not realize the number of irregularities that actually can occur in a horse's footfalls at each gait. Some quotations will help to clarify the point.

> *In the walk the horse moves his legs one after the other so that four hoof beats may be heard. . . . It is a bad fault if the horse moves forward with both legs of one side at the same time, when only two hoof beats will be heard. It is also a fault when the legs are not put forward in the same rhythm and the same length of stride, or the horse makes hasty steps. . . .*
>
> *In the trot the diagonal legs must be raised from the ground simultaneously and be replaced on the ground together, making two hoof beats. (Podhajsky, pp. 31–32.)*
>
> *One of the most common faults in the trot is the hurried steps of the forelegs in which they reach the ground before the diagonal hind leg, so that two separate hoof beats are heard instead of one. These horses carry a greater proportion of their weight and that of their rider on their shoulders. If the hind leg is put down before the diagonal foreleg and again two hoof beats are heard, it is known as a hasty hind leg. This fault will also occur when the horse does not bend his joints sufficiently and drags his hind legs along the ground. It is also a fault when the horse does not bring his hind legs sufficiently under the body and appears to make a longer stride with his forelegs, which accordingly have to be withdrawn to equal the stride of the hind legs. . . . Another fault is when one hind leg steps more under the body than the other, thus making the strides uneven.*
>
> . . . .
>
> *The canter consists of a series of bounds. In the correct canter three hoof beats should be heard. . . .*

. . . The canter is incorrect if four hoof beats can be heard, which happens when the hind leg is put down before the corresponding diagonal foreleg. This fault appears when the horse loses impulsion by incorrect collection and does not canter with sufficient elevation. Some people are of the opinion that a four-beat canter is a collected canter, but this is incorrect; in this case the horse does not execute correct bounds of canter but "hobbles" along. . . ; only in the racing gallop should there be four hoof beats. (Podhajsky, pp. 34–35.)

A common fault with weak horses is the disunited canter, in which the horse canters with the left leg leading in front and the right leg leading behind, or vice versa. The rider will be able to recognize the fault by an uncomfortable feeling through the horse's back. (Podhajsky, p. 36.)

A horse with any of these problems should not be selected for dressage because it would virtually disqualify him. Actually such problems are rather rare in horses moving naturally; they usually creep in when a horse is pushed or collected beyond his current ability. For all practical purposes, it is the *regularity of the rhythm* that should concern the rider when working with a green horse. (See page 11.) In other words, the footfalls are most likely correct but should occur in a steady and unchanging rhythm. The rhythm should not change when the horse goes through a corner, performs a circle, or comes down the center of the arena. At first, horses tend to slow down their rhythm on circles or at any time when they must leave the track and tend to increase it again on the straight. Regularity comes with training. Perfect regularity cannot be expected at Training Level.

Free gaits means that there is nothing stiff, tense, or cramped about the horse's movements, and that he takes long, low, elastic strides. Lifting the feet high off the ground or taking short steps is undesirable, and so is dragging the feet instead of lifting them. On this subject a quotation from Waldemar Seunig is helpful. Colonel Seunig was a military dressage rider, trainer, and teacher who was influenced by Vienna and Saumur. He was still teaching in his eighties, long after retirement. Seunig died in 1976. His book, *Horsemanship,* translated from the German, is unusually clear, even if a little more thorough than many readers would wish.

When the horse is shown in free action, the hind hoofs should tread two or more hoof-widths in front of the foreleg hoofprints at a walk. This forward engagement of the hind legs accords with their job of acting as lever and support in the direction of the centre of gravity, which is shifted forward in free, unconstrained action. . . .

In the trot the natural thrust is more sudden that it is at a walk, and it hurls the body forward, so that the length of the stride is increased by the distance covered in the suspension phase. Without external inducement the hind hoofs will just about reach the tracks of the front hoofs even when the horse's mechanism is perfect. But if increased thrust and natural swing are added, which should be produced by a touch of the whip . . . remounts that have the right conformation for trotting will repeat the picture of the hind legs' exceeding the front hoofprints by a considerable distance that we described above in our discussion of the walk.

It is best to observe the gallop of remounts at the end of their run. The more freely and smoothly the successive jumps sweep over the ground and the more ground they cover, . . . the better the gallop. (Seunig, pp. 37–38.)

The usual American terminology for the overstepping at walk and trot which Seunig describes is that the horse "overtracks" at walk and extended trot. At a natural, free trot we would say that he "tracks up" if the hind hoofs "reach the tracks of the front hoofs." Or put in other words, the horse takes long steps or engages the haunches. If the horse is stiff or tense and therefore not moving freely, he is not likely to do this. (See Figure 15 and Figure 17.)

At this point it may be well to carefully define the term tempo. *Tempo* used to mean speed—that is, miles per hour, or yards per minute. It is so defined and used by Podhajsky whose definitions used to be considered standard. Now, however, the AHSA has seen fit to define it as steps (not yards) per minute. *Steps per minute* has usually been called *rhythm,* and often still is. So now, if the tempo (or rhythm) is fast, this means the horse is taking many steps per minute. If the tempo (or rhythm) slows, he is taking fewer steps per minute. A freely moving horse will advance with a good tempo, that is, with long steps in a slow rhythm. A tense horse will take short steps, and if urged to increase his speed, he will increase his tempo too. That is, he will take more quick, short steps per minute in order to go faster. A good tempo for the trot is about 155 steps per minute or 13 steps in 5 seconds.

Three qualities in the horse are lumped together under *impulsion;* desire to move forward, elasticity, and relaxation of the back. The first, *desire to move forward,* is obviously an aspect of impulsion. (Impulsion will be discussed more fully in Part II. See pages 114ff.) Desire to move forward means just what it says. Is the horse always ready to go faster, in a good tempo, of course? Is he always ready, even eager, to accelerate from walk to trot to canter? Or does he appear reluctant, with a tendency to slow down of his own accord? Here we can quote Vladimir Littauer in *Schooling Your Horse*. Littauer uses the term "impulse forward" to cover desire to move forward and impulsion:

> *Any movement, even a lazy, "disconnected" one, is the result of a certain amount of impulse forward but, speaking more precisely, the term "impulse forward" means more than just a movement forward, slow or fast, at a walk or gallop. Impulse forward means the alertness with which the horse starts a gait or increases the speed or keeps the pace; the term also refers to the reserve of energy with which the horse travels. Thus a slow gait may have good impulse (collected gaits, for instance), while a fast gait may lack it (for example, a refusal on an easy fence, approached at a fast gallop).*
>
> *Some horses naturally possess a great deal of impulse while others have very little. In the first instance the trainer's problem is to keep this instinctive impulse down, while in the second case the trainer may have to animate his pupil. (Littauer, p.17.)*

When Littauer includes the "reserve of energy" with which a horse moves, and when he mentions collection, he is talking about a more advanced stage of impulsion. The "alertness" with which a horse moves forward is a good description of what is desired at Training Level.

Incidentally, Littauer is not an advocate of dressage training except for horses intended for dressage competition; but he has an excellent background in dressage, having been educated in the pre-World War I Russian cavalry. His book is not a dressage text—in fact, quite the contrary—but in many places he draws distinctions between what is and what is not dressage, which are clearer than anything that I have found elsewhere. Littauer adds:

> *Many of the Thoroughbreds with which I have come in contact belonged to the first category and hence my work often consisted in teaching the riders how to moderate their horses' natural impulse forward sufficiently to make them tractable. (Littauer, p. 17.)*

This is very important. The horse should give the impression of always moving forward willingly but yet not be excited or pulling or nervous, just alert and moving freely.

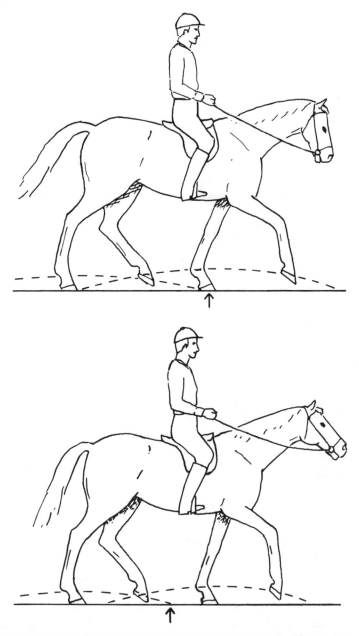

Figure 17.   In these drawings of a trotting horse, the dotted lines show the tra-
jectories of the right fore and left hind feet respectively. The arrow
marks the spot where the hind foot will be grounded. The top picture
shows a free-moving, relaxed horse that is tracking up. The lower
horse is lazy or stiff and is not tracking up.

The next quality mentioned is *elasticity*. Elasticity is partly an innate quality of the horse and partly the result of training. If the animal is not tense or overly restrained, his natural elasticity will be apparent. It is to be hoped that your horse has a naturally springy step and that his feet appear to tread the ground lightly, almost bouncing off the ground. If he is lazy and tends to drag his toes, touches with the whip will increase his impulsion and cause him to pick his feet up a little more. This will improve his elasticity. If a judge comments that the horse appears stiff, or that his feet stick to the ground, or that he looks cramped or lacks suspension, you may conclude that he is deficient in elasticity. When the joints of the hind leg bend more at each stride of working trot, elasticity increases.

Relaxation of the back will be discussed in Part II in the chapter on the working trot. But I do want to discuss *relaxation* in general at this point, because it is very important at Training Level. This requirement comes last, but it is the cornerstone on which the other requirements depend. Unless the horse is relaxed, his rhythm will not be regular, his paces will not be free, and his contact with the bit will not be steady. The horse must be calm to be relaxed. Littauer explains this relationship as follows:

> One should never forget that an extended position of the neck and calmness of the horse are closely connected. Effective, ordinary gaits, the extended neck, balancing movements of the neck and head, and calmness, form in nature an inseparable quartet—they must remain together in schooling. The moment the horse gets upset [i.e., ceases to be relaxed] his neck goes up, the balancing gestures cease and his steps become short and high. (Littauer, pp. 13–14.)

In the following paragraphs Seunig uses the term "unconstraint" almost (though not quite) as a synonym for relaxation, and what he says about unconstraint is pertinent here:

> Unconstraint *is the psychological and physical state of the horse in which it flexes and relaxes its muscles elastically only as much as is required for uniform locomotion . . . thus avoiding all unnecessary expenditure of energy.*
> *. . . unconstraint alone . . . is, one might say, a purely passive matter in which the horse's legs swing back and forth expressionlessly.*

> *A horse that is psychologically and bodily cramped will find it hard to flex and relax its muscles elastically and in a relaxed state.*
>
> *On the contrary, it will flex and relax them convulsively (tighten up) in order to resist the unpleasant, painful constraint of the load, thus losing the freedom of its gait and its natural ability to balance itself. Or the constraint of an inner tightness (fear, excitement) will be manifested in the same way and will become perceptible to the rider.*
>
> ·
>
> *A third type of constraint that arises neither from feelings of pain nor from those of fear is the muscle tension, the so-called "muscle tone" that is habitual in many highbred horses, which they must be allowed to work off on the lunge, or, even better, in freedom before they are mounted until the tension in the horse's muscles is dissolved so that the tightness in its joints disappears. (Seunig, p. 114.)*

Seunig has mentioned four factors which inhibit relaxation: pain, fear, excitement, and muscle tone. Another, which I have even noticed affecting myself, is cold. When I am out for a walk with the dog on a chilly evening, the cold makes me tense. Then I walk along without swinging my arms and take short, stiff steps. If I make a point of relaxing in spite of the temperature, my arms start to swing again, and I resume my normal longer steps. The same thing can happen with a horse.

How do you teach an excited, tense horse to relax? Let me lead up to it in a way that may seem a little roundabout. First, I wish to refer to two old definitions of the working trot found in AHSA publications. These definitions, although they have been superseded, are useful here. The working trot, which is called for at Training Level was defined as follows in the 1972 *Notes on Dressage and Combined Training:*

> *This is a pace in which the untrained horse can best carry his rider and himself without any special strain, and is most responsive to his rider's aids.* (Notes, p. 3.)

The 1975 AHSA *Supplement to Rules on Dressage and Combined Training* said, in part:

> *This is a gait in which an individual horse presents itself in the best balance and is most easily influenced and worked.* (Rules, p. 3.)

These definitions were not very helpful, but they did refer to the horse carrying his rider in the *best way* and in the *best balance*. Actually the trainer must teach the horse how he can *best* carry his rider in the *best* balance. The horse may not discover it for himself. When the trainer has taught this, he has achieved relaxation! Jackson explains:

> *When ridden for the first time the horse will have difficulty for a month or two in adapting himself to the change of balance caused by the weight of a rider on his back. Also, the general slackness of his muscles—and particularly of those muscles used for carrying weight—will accentuate these difficulties; so that he will be, at first, unable fully to use his loins or shoulders to carry himself and his rider freely forward, or easily to use his neck to balance himself. As a result he will hollow his back and move in short irregular strides. An early requirement, then, is to help him find his new balance with a rider on his back; to help him to discover how fully to use his neck; how to arch and swing his back: to help him, in brief, to find the attitude in which he can best carry a rider. (Jackson, p. 78.)*

Even an older horse that has been ridden for years may not carry his rider in the *best* way and frequently needs to be taught.

The problem that is seen most often at Training Level is a tense horse with a high neck taking short, quick steps. (See Figure 15.) If only the horse would lower his neck, he would almost automatically *relax* with a resulting arching and swinging of the back and lengthening of the strides. It is important to understand the relationship between relaxation, the position of the neck, and the activity of the back and legs. It is because of these relationships that relaxation is so important. It is pretty complicated, however, and you cannot expect to understand it all at once.

These relationships are referred to again and again by various writers, but the best description I have found is given by Noël Jackson. First he presents a diagram (see Figure 18) that shows the location of five groups of muscles. They are numbered from one to five, and he describes them as follows:

Group 1. In the Dorsal [Top] Part Of The Neck
A group of muscles—notably the trapezius, splenius, *and* spinalis—*which lift the head and neck. . . . They are arranged in*

pairs on either side of the ligamentum nuchae *a powerful and elastic ligament running from the horse's poll over the top of his withers. This ligament is prolonged in less elastic form as the* ligamentum nucho-dorsale *along the top of the spines of the horse's backbone to his sacrum. When stretched over the withers as a fulcrum by the horse lowering his head, it tensions the horse's spine and enables him to arch his back. . . .*

Group 2. In The Ventral Part [Under Side] Of The Neck

A complex of muscles—mainly the mastoido-humeralis—*that flex the head or neck either downward or laterally, or advance the shoulder.*

Group 3. Between The Shoulder Blades

A group of muscles that regulates the position of the spinal column and ribs of the thorax between the shoulder blades, for the horse's shoulders and forelegs are not attached to the rest of his skeleton by joints, but only by muscles and ligaments.

Group 4. Along The Back

A group of muscles—mainly the longissimus dorsi *. . . —which lie along and on either side of the spines of the vertebrae. They are extensors, or those that in contracting straighten or extend a flexed joint, in that they extend the pelvis and hind limbs backwards to push the horse forward.*

Group 5. On Either Side Of The Abdomen

. . . pairs of straight abdominal muscles, which run from the cartilages of the 5th and 9th ribs to the pubis (part of the pelvis). . . . These . . . are used . . . to bring the pelvis forward after extension of the hind legs. They are thus flexors (or those that in contracting cause a joint to flex) of the back in that they draw the pelvis forward . . . and arch the horse's back in the process.

The Relationship Between The Groups Of Muscles Illustrated

The muscles of Group 1 that raise the head and neck are in opposition to Group 2 that pull them down. The muscles of the back, Group 4, as extensors have the opposite effect of those of Group 5, which are flexors. Those of Group 1 are also opposed to those of Groups 3 and 5, because when the horse's head is brought up and his cervical ligament goes slack, the vertebrae at the base of the neck go forward and down between the shoulder blades, the muscles of Group 3 are stretched, the area of attachment to the base of the neck of the muscles of Group 4, in going forward and down, reduces the extent to which this group can be stretched backwards, and thus restricts the extent to which Group 5 can be contracted. In effect this means the extent to which the horse can engage his hind quarters under him. Conversely, when the muscles of Group 1 and the cervical ligament are stretched forward, the contraction of the muscles of Groups 2 and 3 raises the base of the neck, facilitates the extension of those of Group 4 and the contraction of those of Group 5, with consequent engagement of the horse's hind quarters and arching of his back. The first step, then, in training our horse should be to encourage him to stretch his neck forward and down in an extended attitude. . . .

Were we to allow the horse to raise his head and poke his nose by contracting the muscles in . . . Group 1, the muscles of Groups 3 and 2 would be stretched, the base of his neck lowered, his back hollowed, and the engagement of his hind quarters inhibited.

. . . .

. . . The first step . . . is to persuade the horse to lower his head to help him to stretch his cervical ligament. As he progresses . . . he will adapt his muscles to this attitude, even with a rider on his back, his hind legs will come more and more under him, to support more of his weight, and he will himself raise his whole forehand as a direct result of this. (Jackson, pp. 83–84.)

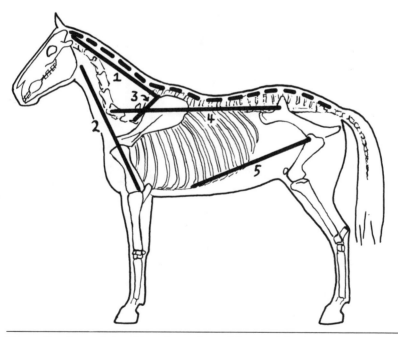

Figure 18.   Interrelationships of muscles and bones of the horse. Adapted from Jackson's *Effective Horsemanship*, page 82.

Raising the forehand will come much later in training and will be fully explained at that time.

This long quotation from Jackson is very important if you wish to fully understand what is happening. It will be necessary, of course, to carefully reread it from time to time. The key to comprehending it is to keep in mind that if two groups of muscles are opposed, one must relax when the other contracts and vice versa. In fact as one group contracts (shortens) the other group first relaxes (lengthens) and then, if the first group continues to contract, the second group must actually stretch.

To round out the discussion, one more short quotation is needed. Jackson mentioned stretching the cervical ligament. Here he gives an additional reason for doing so.

> *In the horse the muscles of the back and the cervical ligament have the very important function of tensioning his spine so that the muscles controlling his limbs have a firm attachment from which to work his forehand and hind quarters. The horse can make only very little effort while his spinal column is slack; and to produce strong muscular effort he must first tension it. (Jackson, p. 81.)*

4 Training Methods

The aspects of training which will be discussed in connection with Training Level are 1. relaxation and lengthening of the stride, obtained by lowering the neck; 2. free forward movement; 3. acceptance of the bit; and 4. the canter depart on the correct lead. The last of these, although not set forth as a specific Training Level objective, must, of course, be mastered. If you start a young horse you may have to handle this yourself during the breaking-in period before you approach a dressage instructor for lessons. And if you are going to use an older horse, you will want to modify the usual canter aids to make them compatible with dressage requirements.

The first three objectives are specifically required at Training Level and are also preliminary to putting the horse "on the bit." Techniques for *actually* putting the horse on the bit, which is one of the most important objectives in dressage, will be left for First Level. This is not because there is anything wrong with a Training Level horse being on the bit, but merely because you need not wait to show at this level until your horse is on the bit. The purpose of Training Level is "to introduce the rider and horse to the basic principles of dressage competition," so you should start getting used to competition—especially if you or your horse has not showed much before—as soon as you can perform Test 1 reasonably well and show some dressage potential.

Relaxation, a good contact with the bit, and free forward movement are closely related in practice. First I will quote from one of Lieutenant Colonel Harry D. Chamberlin's books, *Training Hunters, Jumpers, and Hacks.* Chamberlin was a United States cavalry officer. He was influenced by the French and Italian cavalry schools but developed his own method of systematic schooling which is set forth in his book. He says:

> . . . *all the objectives are interdependent and hinge one upon the other. They are the guiding lights always to be kept in sight; if one is missed it will be rare indeed that the next is found.* Only a comfortable head carriage will induce calmness. There will not be a comfortable head carriage, relaxation, or suppleness unless the bit is correctly accepted. *(Chamberlin, p. 61.)*

Although fully recognizing this interdependence, we will consider the objectives and how they are attained one at a time.

Relaxation and Neck Position

If the horse trots in a relaxed manner with a slow rhythm and long steps, this is good; but if he rushes forward tensely with his head in the air, relaxation will have to be deliberately cultivated. The three—relaxation, low neck, and long steps in a slow rhythm—are closely related, and we can lower the neck to bring about the other two. Some horses raise their heads as soon as a contact is taken with the bit; others always carry their heads too high, and rush instead of lengthening whenever urged to move forward. For these horses, instructors will usually prescribe special techniques for lowering the neck. Other horses that are normally relaxed will start to rush if they are excited, say, by the unfamiliar surroundings at a show. When excited they become tense and raise their heads. (See Figure 19.) Repeated visits to shows, together with sensible diet, of course, will gradually overcome this problem in most cases. But the neck-lowering techniques are useful here too, for they can be used at a show to remind an animal to relax and to get him calm sooner than would otherwise be possible.

I would like to quote Podhajsky first. He offers no specific remedy for too high a neck although he warns of the danger:

> . . . *it is of great advantage when breaking in young horses to allow them to seek the contact with a lowered head and, from contact ob-*

tained in this manner, to proceed gradually to a correct position. This is still more important for horses with weak backs or weak hindquarters and the rider must not make the mistake of trying to raise the head and neck prematurely, for this would later make correct work more difficult. A horse that raises his head and neck more than his conformation or degree of training warrants will increase his speed and try to evade the pushing aids of his rider when he tries to bring the hind legs further under the body. (Podhajsky, pp. 92–94.)

If the horse does not bring his hind legs further forward under his body, he does not lengthen his stride and will not "track up." Instead he hurries, and this is what Podhajsky wishes to avoid by encouraging a lower head and neck.

Chamberlin offers a specific remedy for too high a head carriage:

> *Where, because of poor conformation, high spirits, or rebellion against the bit, the colt raises his head too high when increased tension is taken, the rider's hands also move upward so as to maintain the straight line from the elbow to the bit. Instead of releasing the tension it should be mildly increased and the colt's head held in its*

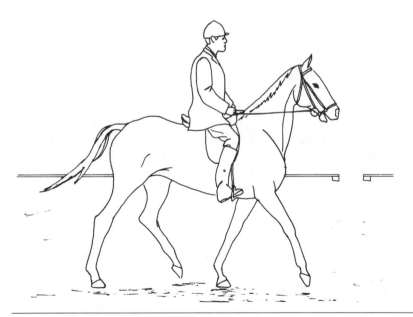

Figure 19. This horse has not been taught to lower his neck. He is tense and his head is up. As a result, he is taking short steps.

high position until, through discomfort, he seeks to lower it. Tact is required to seize the first, and the exact, instant when the colt endeavours to lower his head. Thereupon the fingers and elbows must yield, and the hands follow the mouth's downward movement. Soon the youngster realizes that raising his head only places him in difficulty, and that comfort exists when the head and neck are correctly placed. (Chamberlin, p. 87.)

A technique called "combing the reins" is described by Jean Froissard, a French writer. The following is taken partly from his book, *Equitation*, and partly from an article by him in the magazine, *Dressage*.

> *First teach it to the horse at the walk, if necessary, halt, but eventually it must be practiced at the trot. . . .*
>
> *. . . take both reins in the right hand, separated by your index finger, just as close as possible to the base of the neck, carry this hand to your chest, letting the reins glide through your fingers while maintaining a light tension. While your right hand is approaching your chest, your left gets ready to act the same way. Thus, by the time the right has finished its course, the left has taken over and maintains the contact, the hands acting alternately.*
>
> *. . . At the merest hint of the neck's stretching, yield to let it be, but never lose your contact with the mouth and keep remembering that none of this can be effective unless leg action keeps the hind legs engaged.*
>
> *Simple indeed, if we do not lose sight of a few points that are essential to success. It isn't enough for the legs to act . . . they must do so in cadence with the gait. If they don't, they sow confusion in the mind of the horse. Rein tension, though optional, must suit the horse. Some require little, others more; but keep the contact at all times. Your greatest difficulty is knowing how to yield in time when he starts into the extension; be constantly on the alert to allow and accompany the first small hint. . . . (Equitation, p. 50, and Dressage, Volume 6, p. 105.)*

This is almost exactly like a procedure I was once taught called "massaging the reins" or "milking the reins." The only difference was that the "massaging" took place from a point as near the horse's poll as you could reach and was in a direction parallel to the cheek pieces of the bridle until your hand was as high as you could reach. As in Froissard's "combing," it was also necessary to keep the horse going forward and to yield the moment the horse started down.* The objective of this work is to get the horse to *keep* his neck constantly in a low, stretched position at walk, trot, and canter.

Still another technique is found in *Training the Young Horse and Pony,* a useful little book put out for the use of the Pony Club by the British Horse Society. It applies equally to horses and ponies, although the word "pony" is used throughout. First it warns against use of a standing martingale to correct too high a head carriage. Since this is a warning with which dressage trainers would surely all agree, it is well to include it here:

> *Any restriction or force used will result in shortened paces and, more than likely, incorrect head-carriage. For instance, should the rider use a martingale in order to hold the pony's head down, having it so fitted that the pony can 'lean' against it, the pony will be using the wrong muscles in his neck and will miss it the moment it is removed. Consequently he will throw up his head, feeling for the strap which is not there, all of which will have aggravated a fault which will take long to correct.*
>
> *If a young pony is inclined to throw his head up into a dangerous position, it is advisable to use a standing martingale, properly fitted so that it only comes into action when the pony has thrown his head up beyond the point of control. Fitted in this way, it acts only as a safeguard for the rider and in no way hinders the pony's training.* (Training the Young Pony, *pp. 56–57.*)

This is the procedure that is recommended for lowering the head:

> *We must now study how to get the pony's head in the correct position. If the pony carries his head too high he must be 'asked' to bring it down. Nothing is gained by the use of force, because the moment the force is relaxed the head will once more take the false, high position. . . .*
>
> *. . . [Instead] . . . the rider sets about 'asking' the pony to lower his head (if it is too high) and relax his jaw.*
>
> *He proceeds at the trot . . . and takes a light but firm contact with the left rein (soft side). This contact must be kept throughout the lesson, no matter in what direction he is going. Now, by a slight tightening and relaxing of the fingers on the right rein (stiff side) the*

---

*I have heard the warning that after using the massaging technique to lower the neck, it is difficult or impossible later to raise the neck with the reins for advanced work. Apparently Froissard does not have this problem. (Froissard, pp. 65–66.)

> *rider 'asks' for a relaxation of the pony's jaw and a consequent lowering of the head. . . . The motion is like 'squeezing-water-out-of-a-sponge' and must not in any way be backwards. At the same time as the rider 'asks' with his right hand, he also uses his legs, the right leg giving a stronger aid than the left. If this is repeated every time the pony gets his head too high, he will soon learn to lower it and relax his jaw. . . . (Training the Young Pony, pp. 58–61.)*

The Pony Club manual recommends that the rein which is "kept" (in this case the left rein) should be the rein on the pony's "soft" side, and that the rein which is used to "ask" should be the rein on the pony's "stiff" side. The problem of the soft and stiff sides will be taken up in Part II, Chapter 9. If your instructor uses this method and distinguishes at this stage between soft and stiff, he will make this application clear, but it is not necessary when using this method. "Asking" can be done on large circles, always "keeping" the *outside* rein and always "asking" with the *inside* rein.

The name I have heard for this technique in America is "asking down." A contact should be taken with both reins before starting to "ask." The warning that the motion is "not in any way backwards" may be a bit misleading. The motion of the "asking" rein, of course, is backward and forward. What is meant is that the *arm* is not moved backward toward the rider's body more and more as the procedure is continued. Instead it stays in the same place so that each time after taking one or two inches, the rein gives the same amount. It requires great concentration on the part of the rider because the asking must continue until the horse *begins* to lower his head, at which moment it must stop and the rider's hands must follow the head down. But it must start again as soon as the horse *begins* to raise his head. If the trainer waits until the head is high again and then asks, the horse will learn to bob his head up and down rather than to keep it down.

This asking down is useful for older horses in the habit of carrying their heads too high and taking short, choppy steps. In this case, however, the mere tightening and relaxing of the fingers may not be enough; instead it may be necessary to bend and straighten the wrist in order to shorten the rein about two inches each time, giving firm tugs on the horse's mouth. Also, it might take six months of work to get the horse to *keep* his neck down consistently. With a young horse it should not take so long. Once the neck stays down when the horse is simply trotting on a large circle or trotting around the ring, it is still apt to pop up and require "asking down" every time the horse is asked to do anything, as for instance a turn, circle, shoulder-in, or halt.

Another method of lowering the neck is described by Jackson:

> With the horse the first essential step then is to persuade him to stretch the muscles in the dorsal part of his neck (Group 1) by lowering his head. [See Figure 18.] But how are you to do this? You will find walking and trotting the horse uphill helpful, because as he settles down he will lower his head and learn both to arch and swing his back. But perhaps the most effective exercises on level going are to turn the horse from side to side on the opening reins and to work him on circles; and the reason for this is as follows. The muscles in Group 1 are, as I have already shown, arranged in pairs on either side of the . . . [neck]. The horse holds his head up by contracting the muscles of both pairs at once. But if you bend his neck by turning him from side to side, and by riding him on a circle with his neck bent in the direction of the movement, you can stretch at least the muscles of one pair; and if you stretch first the muscles of one pair and then those of the other, the horse will soon begin to relax the muscles of both pairs and so to lower his head. The first practical exercise then is, first at the walk for some days and then at the short trot, to turn your horse from side to side in impulsion on the opening reins. The next step is to work him on circles . . . making sure, in both exercises, that you maintain impulsion and keep him flexed to the circumference of the circle and balanced laterally between his shoulders. It is for this lateral balancing that the leg that curves the horse's body is of particular value. (Jackson, p. 85.)

Curving the horse's body and balancing him laterally between his shoulders will have to be left for discussion at a later point, but the method may be of use even without these refinements. "In impulsion" means here that the horse is trotting briskly forward, while the "opening rein" means that the rein which turns the horse is carried well away from the neck toward the inside of the circle, and pulls backward as little as possible. Jackson sums up:

> By working your horse from side to side and on circles on the opening rein, well balanced laterally, you will very soon teach him to lower his head progressively as you move it from side to side, relaxing first the muscles of one pair and then of the other. . . .

> *Very soon he will lower his head on a simple resistance on first*
> *one rein and then the other, produced by closing your hand with a*
> *squeezing effect on the rein adjusted in contact with the horse's*
> *mouth. (Jackson, p. 86.)*

Another method is explained by Müseler. It is called "showing the horse the way to the ground," and it is done at a brisk trot on a circle.

> *At first the rider exerts a very slight pressure upon the outer jaw so*
> *that he can immediately 'give'. . . . This slight pressure must only*
> *last a second and has no other purpose than to draw the horse's*
> *attention to the outer rein: the important thing is the 'giving.'*
> *(Müseler, p. 82.)*

Another name for this procedure is "feeling forward" with the reins. In anywhere from a few minutes to half an hour, according to Müseler, the horse will begin to "give" and stretch his neck forward and take a feel on the bit. The process requires that the rider continually drive the horse forward onto the bit a little faster than the horse wants to go. Müseler says that it should be done on circles in both directions. The inner rein keeps the horse flexed to the circle and the outer rein only does the feeling forward. (See pages 82–83 in Müseler's book.)

We should not leave the subject of head carriage without saying something about the opposite problem, because it is possible, of course, for a horse to carry his head too low. The Pony Club manual says:

> *In the case of too low a head-carriage, the rider must use his legs to*
> *push the pony's head up, by making the hind legs more active. . . .*
> *(Training the Young Pony, p. 61.)*

A glance at Figure 20, reproduced here from the manual, will show that in the first position the neck is too low and the horse's face is behind the vertical. In the second position, the horse is taking longer steps (though still not tracking up) and has raised his head so that his face is in front of the vertical. The raising of the head is *caused* by the lengthening of the steps.

It is interesting to analyze the drawings a little more. The longer steps in the second position are shown by the hind feet being further apart (and, of course, also the front feet). The longer steps are

Figure 20. The rider must "push the pony's head up." Adapted from *Training the Young Horse and Pony,* **page 61. "A" and "C" should be lengthened and "B" shortened. When tracking up, "B" nearly disappears at the moment of suspension.**

also shown by the shorter distance between the forefoot and hind foot, which are close together under the horse's body. For these effects to show best, a photograph should be taken at the moment of suspension when all four feet are off the ground. If you are comparing the strides of horses in two photographs it is important that they be taken at the same point in the stride, preferably during suspension. These two drawings are at approximately the same point in the stride though not during suspension. The manual goes on to warn:

> *The rider must never attempt to pull the head up with his hands, as the result would be a false head-carriage, with the top of the neck bent in a concave position, which is very damaging to the training. Carrying the head up in this position has the effect of hollowing the pony's back and thus making it impossible for him to use his back correctly or to bring his hind legs under him. (*Training the Young Pony, *p. 61.)*

Other methods of raising the horse's head, however, can be used if the trainer has sufficient skill:

> *If the [neck] . . . is excessively rounded and the head tucked into the breast, the hands are carried far forward to a position over the poll. From here, one of two corrections may be administered; first, a sharp upward twist on one or both taut reins (euphemistically called a 'half halt') which causes the colt to raise and extend his head; or, second, with the hands fixed and set over the poll, strong resistance is set up and the bit worked back and forth through the mouth (vibrating effect) until, through annoyance and discomfort, he lifts and extends his head into a correct position. In either case he is rewarded upon assuming a correct attitude by prompt re-establishment of the light, normal contact. The 'half-halt' and 'vibrations' are always executed on taut reins. (Chamberlin, p. 87.)*

The half-halt described here is the French half-halt and is quite different from the usual half-halt, which is from the German school.

When a very green horse walks with his face vertical or a little behind the vertical, this may be only a passing phase that the rider need not worry about. Littauer has a picture of a colt walking in this way. (See Figure 21.)

Moving Freely Forward

Checking your horse's gaits against the speeds given on page 10 above will give a general idea of whether the horse is moving freely forward or not. The trot and canter speeds should be especially noted at this stage as it may take time before the horse learns to walk freely forward. A trot of 100 yards in 30 seconds and a canter that is distinctly faster than the trot should be the goals. Do not try to slow and "collect" the canter of the young horse as a pleasure horse trainer would do. An older horse, accustomed to cantering slowly, must be pushed along into what would probably be called a hand gallop.

Figure 21.   This drawing was made from one of Littauer's photographs. The rider is using the "forward seat" because Littauer's
book is mainly about "forward riding." Littauer says that this horse's
head is too low because he is very green and that the situation will
correct itself as the animal gains strength.

Many horses move forward freely without special training. If
yours is one of these, and, provided he does not "rush," you are
lucky to have a good mover. But if a horse is reluctant to go forward, and the problem is not poor health or lack of condition, it
may be that the rider is too gentle and kind. Vigorous measures
may need to be taken. Here is Littauer's suggestion:

> *While some horses are too eager to go ahead there are others
> which, being lazy by nature, prefer to dillydally, and particularly so
> when they feel even the lightest pressure of the bit in the mouth.
> With the second type the impulse forward must be developed
> through schooling. Here is one way of teaching it.*
> *. . . instead of using your legs hard give a voice command to trot
> . . . and support it with the closing in of your calves; if there is no
> response give a sharp whip as punishment. From the whip the horse
> will probably jump forward, but if you are quick enough with your
> hands to prevent a disorganized canter you will have an energetic
> trot departure, and you may pat your horse; you have to tell him
> immediately that that was what you wanted of him. Don't trot for
> long; bring your colt down to a walk, wait until complete calmness
> is reestablished and then repeat the lesson. Many colts will really*

"shoot" forward from just a squeeze with the calves after five minutes of this lesson. You may like to repeat it for a couple of minutes at the end of the hour, always being careful not to upset the horse. You will have to practice this lesson for several days; one lesson never establishes a habit. A similar lesson may be necessary for colts which have a tendency to slow down at gaits, or are reluctant to increase their speed. There is nothing as annoying as the necessity of continuously using legs forcefully. It is desirable for the horse to have a calm impulse forward, either natural or developed. (Littauer, p. 55.)

Seunig has this to say on the subject:

There are skulking, deceitful horses that are unwilling to reach forward with their stiffened hind legs. . . .

If an experienced rider desires to reinforce his leg control by using the spur, expecting it to exert a "forward-driving" action, he will be disappointed to find that such a tight, deceitful horse resists even more. The stimulus of the spur causes its muscles to become even more convulsed.

In such cases a stroke of the riding crop and riding forward without using the rein as a "fifth foot" will compel the horse to balance itself on its own four legs and will make it, willy-nilly, reach forward honestly with its stiffened hind legs. . . .

The situation is quite different with horses that drag their hindquarters and seem to be stuck to the ground. Such horses avoid even the effort of growing stiff. They could hardly be called tensed; they merely creep around lazily and seem to be begging to be awakened from their sleep. Fairly light touches of the spur on alternate sides, just behind the girth and in time with the gait, make such horses prick up their ears. This results in lively, fresh advancing, and in a few minutes can convert a sluggard into a riding horse with springy, energetic strides. (Seunig, pp. 129–30.)

If a horse is sluggish, the instructor is the person to evaluate the situation and either help the rider overcome the problem and induce the horse to move freely forward or recommend another horse.

Podhajsky distinguishes between lazy horses, weak horses, and those that rush:

. . . in all cases riding forward must be the main concern. This should not be misunderstood: riding forward does not mean *rushing off with hurried, unlevel steps, but gaining ground to the front with ever lengthening strides in an even and regular tempo.*

Lazy horses must be stimulated by legs and whip in order to create this forward urge, but the rider must distinguish between laziness and weakness. With the latter, shorter periods of work should be allowed in order not to discourage the horse by demanding too much. It cannot be repeated too often that one of the greatest faults a rider can commit is to demand more from his horse than is justified by his physical and mental condition.

A horse whose steps are naturally hasty should not be dealt with in the same way as a lazy one. Pushing him forward would destroy his paces completely. The rider should try to calm him down and help him to find his balance, and only then, by carefully applied pushing aids, should he try to obtain longer strides. (Podhajsky, p. 95.)

Contact

When starting a young horse, teaching acceptance of the bit is critically important, for without this basic requirement nothing else can possibly go right. The first steps when a horse is first ridden are described by Chamberlin as follows:

For mechanical reasons at the walk and free gallop the head and neck are carried somewhat lower than at the trot or collected canter. At every stride during the walk and gallop the head oscillates backward and forward. This oscillation assists the horse's movements just as the swinging of his arms assists a man in walking, running, or jumping. At the walk there is, in addition, a slight oscillation of the head from side to side. At the trot, on the contrary, the head and neck are not only held higher than when walking or galloping, but are fixed in position without material movement of any sort. These facts must be known, continuously bourne in mind and utilized in the development of good and educated hands, without which the trainer never can perfect his horse's education. Thus, when the reins are stretched and a horse at the trot is accepting the bit, the hands should remain practically immovable because, as just stated, the horse's head and neck do not oscillate. If the rider is posting, shoulders and elbows compensate for the body's movements permitting the hands to remain quietly in one place relative to the horse's neck. On the contrary, the hands, through the suppleness and elasticity of finger, wrist, elbow, and shoulder joints, should accompany the forward and backward movements of the head and neck at both the walk and the gallop in order to carefully maintain soft, continuous contact of unvarying intensity. It is understood of course that this contact with the mouth continues to be of light and unvarying intensity only so long as the horse goes calmly at the gait and rate desired by the rider. The tension will vary to correct disobedience, to change rate, gait, direction, or to halt. (Chamberlin, p. 55.)

He says further:

As promptly as possible after the trainer discards the longe, contact with the mouth is established. The reins are held, one in each hand, with the hands widely separated (a foot or more). . . . Little by little the reins are stretched lightly taut. This must be a gradual and gentle process, for the bars of the mouth and tongue of the unbroken colt are exceedingly tender, and the trainer's immediate objective is to teach the horse confidence in the bit's soft support. With a keen, free-going type—termed a 'hand' horse—this contact is readily instituted. With the opposite sort which is sluggish or lazy—a 'leg' horse—the rider will have to search continually for his mouth and energetically drive him, by use of the legs and spurs, into the habit of seeking his bit. (Chamberlin, p. 75.)

And again:

[The rider's] . . . constant endeavour should be to gain the confidence of his mount through the softness and elasticity of his hands. In other words, with the neck thrust out horizontally—and oftentimes lower—the colt at first is encouraged and later required to accept a steady, gentle support from the rider's hands, having sure knowledge at all times that no painful, unintentional or angry jerks will come to his mouth. This so-called 'normal support' varies from a few ounces' to three or more pounds' tension, and is progressively stronger as the horse's speed becomes greater. Under good training the horse soon learns to seek willingly this support without flexing his neck in the middle or near the shoulders. Neither does he poke his nose skyward, a fault called 'star-gazing,' which is assumed in an effort to escape the bit by a horse that never has been taught to accept properly its support. The amount of support given also is largely dependent upon the natural balance of the horse. A high-withered, well balanced horse wants only a light feel on his mouth; a low-withered, high-crouped horse generally needs strong support, particularly at speed. (Chamberlin, p. 54.)

If the rider has "good hands," that is, if he can maintain a soft, continuous contact at walk, trot, and canter without any unintentional jerks, there should be no trouble getting the horse to accept the bit. If the horse tends to stop or slow down the moment a contact is taken, then the rider must keep him going with the legs until he understands that he is to continue to move forward in spite of the contact. Littauer adds this refinement:

> The contact between the rider's hands and the horse's mouth is not established by the hand being moved to the rear. Just the reverse should take place; that is, the horse, moving forward with sufficient impulse stretches his neck and, due to the rider keeping a correct length of reins, the horse's mouth feels the rider's hands. Instead of the rider's hands pulling back on the mouth, it is the mouth which gently pulls the rider's hands forward. (Littauer, pp. 17–18.)

> But in response to what does the colt reach for the bit? In response to the rider's urging legs. In short, the process is as follows: the rider, while keeping reins of correct length, with no more than one or two inches of slack, urges the horse forward and the latter, increasing the energy of his movement, stretches the neck and head forward; the slack disappears and contact is established. (Littauer, p. 50.)

Making the horse stretch to the bit cannot be done with all horses. It depends, I think, on how the horse is carrying his head before the rider attempts to make contact. If he is trotting with his neck extended he may be unable to extend it even another inch so as to make the contact himself. (See Figure 22.) If his neck is *not* extended, then the rider's legs *can* "push his mouth forward toward the bit." Littauer's warning is really more appropriate later, when the horse is being put on the bit. I include it here because in one form or another it is found in many places. My own experience with several horses has been that there is no trouble in obtaining acceptance of the bit from a young horse if the reins are simply taken up until there is a light contact which is then maintained by the rider's "good hands."

Correct Lead at the Canter

It is desirable to teach a young horse to canter on the required lead without resorting to the usual positioning of the horse with

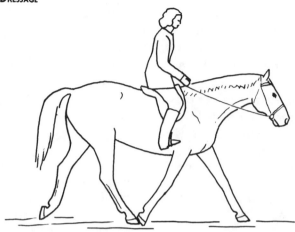

Figure 22. A horse that carries his head like this cannot make contact with the bit by stretching his neck even more. Note that he is relaxed and tracking up. Drawing is adapted from a photograph in Littauer's book.

the head to the rail and the haunches to the inside. If the youngster has been longed at the canter, he will know the voice command and will be accustomed to taking the correct lead when on a circle. Podhajsky depends mainly on this background and on having the horse bent slightly on a circle or when rounding a corner:

> *When work at the walk and trot has been established, but not before,* work at the canter *may begin. To start with the rider will ask the horse to strike off from a trot, which will be easier for him, and he must make use of the corners or the large circle which will put the horse in the right position to select the correct leg (commonly called "lead"). The corner into the short side of the school is the best place to make the first attempt because if it does not succeed, it can immediately be tried again at the next corner.*
>
> *In this stage of training, the horse must be pushed forward at the trot with both legs until, helped by the turn in the corner, he breaks into a canter; touching the horse on the inside shoulder with the whip and the use of the voice will reinforce the leg aids. The voice is especially recommended for it will be available when the whip is no longer used. When the canter has been started on the large circle, the rider will then "go large," that is, use the wide perimeter of the arena, as cantering on a circle would be too tiring for the young horse. The canter must be brought to an end before the horse drops back into a trot on his own account from fatigue.*

If the horse strikes off on the wrong leg (or lead) the rider should allow him to continue for a few strides before bringing him back to a trot and trying another strike-off. On no account must he bring the horse to an immediate halt, which would result in confusion and fear. . . .

If the horse when asked for a canter instead dashes off into a fast trot, he must not be allowed to strike off from this pace; he must be slowed down and calmed before being asked again. (Podhajsky, pp. 94–95.)

Somewhat later in training Podhajsky expects more of the horse and uses more complicated aids:

Up to this point the canter has been employed more or less to exercise the horse, but now correct work in the canter must begin. The rider will no longer be content to push the horse forward until he breaks into a canter, but will now demand a correct strike-off. This exercise offers further opportunity for the physical training of the horse.

The outside leg placed passively behind the girth gives the signal for the canter and prevents the horse from carrying his hindquarters to the outside, while the inside leg, pushing forward on the girth, makes the horse strike off. At the same time the rider must sit a little more firmly on his inside seat bone. With the transition to the canter the rider must be careful not to allow his inside leg to slide forward as so often happens, thus diminishing the value of the aid in this pace. The inside rein must place the horse in the right position and, with the support of the inside leg, prevent the hindquarters from falling in, which would cause a crooked strikeoff, a serious fault not to be allowed even with a young horse. (Podhajsky, p. 115.)

Notice Colonel Podhajsky's emphasis on keeping the horse straight. The inside rein "places the horse in the right position," that is, bends the head or neck very slightly to the inside. This feel on the inside rein is often enough to keep the haunches straight, that is, on the track behind the forehand.

What is the rider to do if he uses this method and gets the wrong lead? I feel that if you have no one to help you at this stage, the most important thing is to get the correct lead consistently and have your horse cantering on willingly. So it is better to resort to the more common method of positioning the horse—especially if you are already familiar with the method—and straighten the horse later. Chamberlin gives two versions of this method, one of which is almost sure to work:

> *There are two elementary ways of teaching the gallop departs.*
>
> *First method: Being at the normal trot, a very slightly increased tension is taken on the outside rein (right, if circling to the left) just prior to taking the gallop. A fraction of a second later the right leg is used strongly just a little in rear of the girth to force the croup inward (to the left). The moment the croup moves over, the left leg comes to the assistance of the right and their combined energetic action urges the horse into the gallop. The right rein's effect is to impede the right shoulder and free the left. Thus with his croup pushed to the left and the left shoulder advanced and freed, the horse is set in a natural position to take the left lead. The rider carries his body slightly to the left front as his legs act.*
>
> *The usual error in the application of these lateral aids (right leg and right rein) lies in applying too much tension to the right rein. This pulls the head and neck too far to the right and causes the horse to 'pop his left shoulder out to the left' to conserve his balance. He thus weights, rather than lightens, it, and so frees the outside shoulder. As a consequence the false gallop (with the off fore leading) is more easily taken. Only the slightest displacement of the head toward the outside of the circle is necessary. When taking the gallop the trainer either should sit firm in his saddle, or post on the outside diagonal and apply his aids just as his seat comes into the saddle.*
>
> *Second method: The rider, posting at the normal trot on the outside diagonal, takes the same action with his legs as in the first method. In this case, however, he carries both his hands and his trunk to the left and forward just as he sinks into the saddle. This action throws the near (inside) fore leg further forward and overbalances the colt in that direction. The rider's legs give impulsion and hasten the movements of the hind feet so that the horse strikes into the canter. The left rein goes slack and the right has the bearing effect. (Chamberlin, p. 85.)*

Chamberlin does not mean a faster pace than the canter by the word "gallop." He simply uses the word "gallop" instead of "canter," as do many other writers. Perhaps this is because both French and German have only the one word: gallop. By the "bearing effect" of the right rein, Chamberlin means that it acts as a neck rein.

Trying to apply several aids one after the other, or trying to apply them at a certain point in the horse's stride, may be difficult for a novice trainer and make him tense and jerky. So if you have this difficulty try doing it all at once, if that seems easier, and do not worry about trying to do it at exactly the right moment. If it works, fine. Just do it when you feel you are ready. Once your horse is reliable about getting the correct lead, you can analyze what you are doing and then try to minimize whatever makes him crooked.

In the case of an older horse, you may find that he is so accustomed to leading with the inside leg that he does so no matter what; then it is easy to adopt the aids you want to use. If you emphasize outside leg placed passively behind the girth (so as not to push the haunches to the inside), inside leg used firmly on the girth, and reins doing nothing except maintaining an even contact while you sit up straight and do not lean forward or to the inside, all will be well. If he does not automatically take the inside lead and requires to be positioned with head to rail and haunches away from the rail, you will have to continue this for a while, if necessary, until you are sure of always getting the desired lead. Then combine with the positioning the aids you want to use, such as weight on the inside seatbone and maintenance of contact with the inside rein. Sit straight, and do not lean in any direction. After some days, when you feel that the horse is well aware of the aids you are using, gradually begin to diminish the undesirable positioning by making less use of the outside leg. Be sure throughout that you get the desired lead at least nine times out of ten. Do not advance to the next stage unless your mount is nearly or quite perfect in this respect, or you will only end up in confusion. Canter only from the trot at this stage. Canter from walk is not required until Second Level.

As a summary I would like to quote Chamberlin on what he considers the objectives of the breaking-in period:

(1) *a good disposition (calmness);*
(2) *a hardy physical condition;*
(3) *prompt response to the action of the legs;*
(4) *acceptance of the bit with extended head and neck* (which means to put the colt on his forehand);
(5) *obedience to the simple rein effects at walk, trot, and canter.* (Chamberlin, p. 78.)

5 Showing at Training Level

Once your horse accepts the bit, carries his head in a reasonable position, and moves steadily and briskly at the three gaits, you ought to start showing at Training Level. You will be anxious to discover how your horse acts at shows, what judges think of him, and to get over your own nervousness. In some areas, however, even Training Level horses are on the bit with impulsion and probably are being schooled in Second Level exercises at home, so you may feel that you must wait until you have made considerably more progress before appearing in public. In this case, perhaps there will be schooling shows where you can get the necessary early experience.

At any rate, sooner or later you will feel that the time has come to show and you will begin to prepare for this important event. This will mean checking over or acquiring suitable clothing and tack, joining any necessary organizations, learning the tests, and practicing for the show. Finally comes the show itself, often quite a scary business, followed by thoughtful recollection of your rides and study of your score sheets. It is along these lines that this chapter will be organized. First a few pointers about tack and clothing and general turnout. Then the learning and practicing of the tests, and finally the performance of the test and the show itself.

Tack and Turnout of Horse

The AHSA requirements, which can be found in the *Rulebook*, are not very restrictive. The bridle must have a "plain" snaffle bit and some kind of noseband. A picture showing the permitted "plain" snaffles is included. The most commonly used bits have a fairly thick mouthpiece and one joint. Twisted and wire bits are prohibited. A rein wide enough so that it does not slip through the fingers is recommended. It may be braided or laced. All types of English bridles are seen—plain, raised, round-sewn, and lined event.

The dropped noseband is not favored by *all* dressage riders, but it is very commonly used, and in many places it is almost the infallible indication of a dressage horse. Unfortunately it is hard to get the right size, and consequently it is frequently not fitted correctly. I always have had to have mine altered before they would fit at all. Usually both the noseband and the chin strap must be shortened, and it is important that the chin strap should be free to take the best angle. A spike ring is no good. A ring with a leather circle sewn in around it is all right because you can cut out part of the circle so the chin strap is loose. The cheek pieces must be shortened to raise the noseband about two inches above the horse's nostril. If the side ring of the noseband is a little above the bit ring and the noseband is short enough so that the two rings do not interfere, it should be about right. Figure 39 should make this clear. It is equally correct to show with a cavesson noseband, flash noseband, or crossed noseband. When the noseband is buckled, the horse should be able to take a lump of sugar off your palm, but not an apple. The purpose of the noseband is to keep the horse's mouth almost closed and prevent tongue and mouth problems from ever getting started.

The saddle, of course, must be an English saddle. This does not mean that you have to buy a dressage saddle. Any English saddle on which you can sit correctly will do. There is a type of heavy stirrup with a thick white rubber pad called a "German dressage stirrup" or a "Fillis stirrup" that is popular but is not necessary. Because of their weight these stirrups bounce around less than other stirrups and are easier to retrieve when lost. Never use offset stirrups.

Boots, bandages, martingales, and any sort of auxiliary reins are prohibited. The rider may carry one whip up to 48 inches long, except in qualifying and championship classes.

In general it seems that horses may be turned out either like hunters or according to their breed, for example, Arabs and Morgans with full natural mane and tail. In my area the manes of Thoroughbreds are braided, but tails are not. Instead, tails are natural or shaved, and the end may be squared off a little below hock level. These matters vary according to the taste of the rider and local custom, there being nothing compulsory. Of course, horses should always be clean and neatly trimmed. There are no regulations as to toe length or shoe weight, but these are never exaggerated. Shoes with pads are allowed. One European custom that is occasionally seen is the checkerboard pattern on the croup. I understand this is done by wetting the hair with sugar water and then combing it in different directions with a two-inch comb.

Clothing and Turnout of Rider

Black hunt boots, coat, and derby hat or hunt cap are standard, with white breeches, stock tie, and pin. The top hat was popular recently, even at the lower levels, but is not now recommended. One sometimes sees coats and hats of some dark color other than black. This is quite acceptable. Gloves are optional. If worn they are usually white. Spurs are optional. All clothing should be clean and well fitting. Hair should be neat, and hair nets are required for longhaired riders. Hair must not cover the entry number if it is worn on the back. Some judges dislike dangly earrings. If in doubt about anything, observe at a show and see what the local customs are.

Organizations

One other matter which is best taken care of early is joining any necessary organizations. In my area you must belong to the local dressage society or pay an extra fee to enter its shows. Also you must join the AHSA or pay an extra fee to ride in AHSA approved shows at First Level or higher, but not at Training Level. Members of a local dressage organization can join AHSA as "individual affiliated members" and will receive the *Rulebook* but will not have all privileges. For certain awards you must also hold other memberships and register your horse with AHSA or the United States Dressage Federation (USDF). Since rules vary from time to time and place to place, be sure to read the show announcement very carefully before sending in your entry. If you receive the AHSA *Rulebook* it is a wise idea to read the entire section on the Dressage Division.

Having taken care of these preliminaries, you will next want to memorize and practice the tests you intend to ride. It would be a good idea to allow a month for this part of your preparation.

Learning the Tests

Do take the trouble to memorize the tests, and try riding them from memory, even if you feel at first that someone is going to have to call the tests for you at the show. Study the tests on the ground, not on the horse's back, and concentrate on learning patterns, not on learning letters. I find it helpful to draw diagrams of the test as shown in Figure 23. Then rehearse the test in some way that is helpful to you. Draw an arena and push a paper clip around it. Or run your tongue around the roof of your mouth. My favorite way of learning the pattern is to do the test on foot on a broad sidewalk, using the lines in the pavement to mark the ends of the arena. The small arena is two squares, the large arena is three. Since I do not know of any sidewalks where there is absolute privacy in the daytime, I use this method when I take the dog for a walk late at night. I walk, trot, and gallop—on the correct lead, of course.

The entrance and exit are so standard that they do not have to be specially memorized. The entrance is the same for the first three levels: Enter at the trot, halt at "X" and salute, proceed toward "C" at the trot. The first thing to learn about a particular test is which way to turn as you approach "C." The exit is also the same for all tests: Down the center, halt and salute at "X," and leave the arena at a free walk on a long rein. When leaving the arena you may turn either left or right at "C" and should then walk around on the track and exit at "A." Be sure to exit only at "A." You will be penalized 2 points for any other exit. I have seen riders do a little circle at "A" before leaving. This is reminiscent of hunter and jumper classes and is not desirable.

Now for the body of the test. First see whether there is a general pattern to the test. Often it helps to divide the test into sections and start by memorizing their order. For example, Test 1 has five sections: trot, canter, walk, trot, canter. The other Training Level tests do not lend themselves to this sort of analysis but the First and Second Level tests do. There are always two canter sections, however, so next note whether they are symmetrical, that is, whether the figures are the same but done in opposite directions. The canter sections are generally symmetrical, and the trot sections may also be. Test 1 is symmetrical in both trot and canter, but Test 2 is symmetrical only in canter.

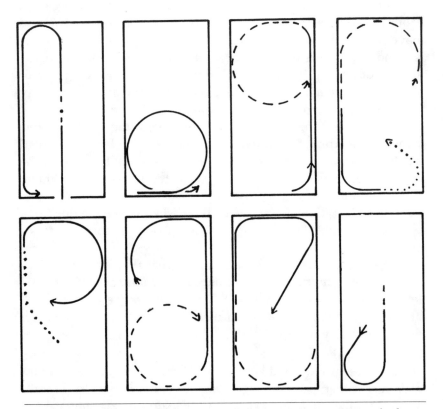

Figure 23. I make a set of sketches like this for every test so I can refresh my memory at a glance. The solid line represents trot; the long dashes, canter; the dots, walk. This is Test 2.

With this general outline in mind, you can now analyze and memorize the patterns. Taking Test 2 as an example, I would learn the patterns as follows: Turn left, down the long side, big circle at the end, up the long side, canter in the corner, big circle at once, trot in middle of long side, walk at end, change across diagonal on long rein, trot at corner, large circle at once, down the long side, canter in corner, big circle at once, trot at middle of long side, change rein on diagonal, up the center, and salute at "X." Finally, after all this is learned, note exactly where the transitions occur and where you do sitting trot.

Notice that in Tests 1 and 2 you depart into canter "between M and C." This is easier than Tests 3 and 4 where the transition is "at M." In the first two tests it is probably best to think of departing as you go around the corner. Test 1 also gives you some leeway in the canter-trot transition which is "between E and H."

The amount of sitting trot required at Training Level has varied from time to time. Fortunately most of Training Level Tests 1 and 2 is now done rising which is very much less taxing for both horse and rider. Later when the horse's back swings and "invites you to sit down," sitting trot is easier. Tests 3 and 4 have more sitting trot, but even so the trot sections are not very long.

There are reasons for some of the short bits of trot that may seem to make the tests more confusing. In the first place, all canter transitions are into and out of the trot at this early stage of training. Walk-canter transitions come much later. So there has to be some trot after walk and before canter, and also after canter and before walk. In addition, of course, there has to be some trot and a change of direction between the right and left canter sections. Usually the transitions are into and out of sitting trot because it is easier to do a smooth transition and use your legs accurately if you are sitting. The entrances and exits also have a logic of their own. At the lower levels entrances are always in trot with the halt and salute at "X." The exits are also always in trot, with the halt and salute at "X."

Practicing the Test

Once you have memorized the test so that you can recite it and also do it without hesitation with your tongue or paper clip, you come to the problem of finding a place to practice it on horseback. Very few of us have standard arenas to work in, so we have to improvise something. The most obvious solution, which requires only a large enough area and an assortment of jumps, is to lay out the arena using jump standards, poles, cavaletti, barrels, pieces of brick wall, and so on. This takes a lot of time, a strong back, and the ability to pace off distances. You could probably do it once or twice before a show, however, if there were no other possibility.

A solution that I have found very satisfactory is a portable arena made of rope and stakes. The small arena requires 400 feet of rope and 13 stakes. By driving the stakes into the ground at the locations of the letters and the corners, and then attaching the rope permanently to the stakes, I eliminated all future measuring and pacing. To keep the thing from getting hopelessly tangled when not in use, I keep it in a large bucket. To put the portable arena away I proceed as follows: Pull the "A" stake at one end of the rope and place it in the bucket. Carry the bucket to the corner, coil the slack rope and put it into the bottom of the bucket, pull and place the corner stake in the bucket next to the "A" stake. Carry the bucket to "K," coil the next section of rope and put it in the bucket, pull the "K" stake and put it next to the corner stake, and so on. When I have gotten around to "A" again (the thirteenth stake) I have a circle of stakes around the inside of the bucket with all the rope neatly coiled in the center. The arena can be put up again by going around in the opposite direction, stretching out the rope and driving each stake in turn.

I have one other suggestion for a practice area which you can use when you do not wish to go to the trouble of setting up a portable arena. The ring that I have to work in is about 85 feet wide and 200 feet long and it is oval. This is a common sort of ring and it is fine for a young horse; but once you start making real turns, it will not do. So by laying down four poles, I mark off an area across the middle of the arena that is exactly 20 meters wide (65 feet). I place the poles so that they do not block the track around the rail. This is very useful indeed. When I reach one of my poles I can leave the track, make a proper turn, and go across the arena where I make another turn onto the track again. It guides me in making large circles (65 feet in diameter) and small circles (33 feet in diameter). It is useful for turning down the center and stopping at "X." If I want to mark any point I use a handful of shavings. It is not useful for changing the rein on the diagonal, as the angle is wrong, but it is good for departing into the canter at a prescribed place and for many other maneuvers. (See Figure 24.)

Whatever you use for a practice arena, let us hope it has low sides and is level and has good footing. When you leave the rail and try your new area with its low sides, a strange thing will happen. The horse will feel like a different animal. The purposefulness will have gone out of him. He just will not see any reason for doing these strange maneuvers out there in the middle of nowhere. In fact, until he is on the bit and going with impulsion, it may be rather discouraging. The circles will not be as round or as even as when you had a fence for a guideline. You may also find when you first try it, that a 65-foot circle is an enormous thing. It is hard to find the correct curvature, and sometimes the circle tends to get smaller and smaller. However, everyone else is having the same trouble. The arena at the show will have a bit of a track worn around it (if you are not one of the first competitors) and eventually you will be on the bit with impulsion and the problem will diminish.

When you are practicing, try to think ahead. For example, while you are doing a circle, think what comes next. Do not concentrate on the circle until suddenly you come to the end of it and instantly have to remember what happens next. If your mind does go blank

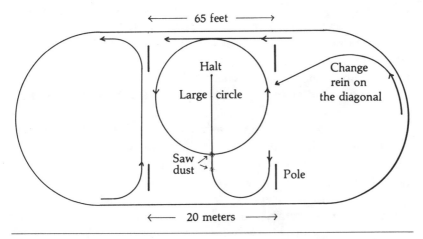

Figure 24. This drawing shows how four poles can be laid down in a large ring to mark off part of a dressage arena of the correct width across the middle. The other lines suggest figures that can be ridden.

during a test, just continue whatever you are doing along the track and hope the pattern will come back to you. In many cases you will remember in a second or two, and the judge may think you made a slightly delayed transition. If, on the other hand, you forget completely, the bell will ring and you should trot up close enough to the judge to hear him easily. He will tell you what to do. Remember, you have only lost two points and the judge probably feels sorry for you rather than being annoyed. He certainly will not hold it against you for the rest of the test.

These are just my suggestions about learning the tests. You may have other ideas. I do hope that you will not do what one person did. She tried to memorize the test in the arena on horseback, holding the test in her teeth and frequently stopping to look at it. Some people warn against practicing too much and routining the horse. The danger is that the horse might learn the test, or parts of it, and anticipate movements, doing them ahead of the places where they are prescribed. I thought this unlikely until I acquired my present horse, an Arab-Paint cross. He did it at his first show!

The Day of the Show

It is important to bear in mind that the purpose of the Training Level is to "introduce the rider and horse to the basic principles of dressage competition." You have a lot of bugs to get out of a complicated procedure. Having gotten your horse washed and braided, packed up and into the trailer, you finally arrive at the show. Be sure to allow plenty of time after you arrive so as not to be hurried. You get your bearings on the grounds, find a program and your number, and discover whether the show is on time and which arena you are riding in. You tack up and dress. You proceed to the warm-up area and take the required time to either warm up or calm down, depending on the horse's temperament. When the horse is in just the right frame of mind, really moving forward but not too fresh or too tired, you ride over to the arena where you take a few minutes' rest and review the test while the preceding rider completes his test. While the judge is dictating his final remarks to his secretary, you ride around the outside of the arena so your horse can get used to the surroundings. When the bell finally rings, you continue without haste toward the entrance, make exactly the sort of turn you had planned, and enter the arena.

You actually have 90 seconds to enter after the bell sounds, so do not hurry.

It will take you a while to become accustomed to all this, and it will take the horse a while to get used to it, too. You have to discover exactly what is the best sort of preparation for your horse before he enters the arena, how his behavior at a show differs from his behavior at home, and how best to cope with him at a show. It may take several shows before you feel even reasonably comfortable about all this.

Performing the Test

Now let us consider how the test is supposed to be performed, and how the judge views the Training Level horse. We have thoroughly discussed how the horse should trot, canter, perform a canter depart, contact the bit, and carry his head and neck. We have also discussed the rider's hands and seat. Now we will assume that you and your horse have mastered these points as well as can be expected at this stage of training, and that you have memorized the Training Level test.

Entrance

You are supposed to be straight when you enter and proceed straight down the center line. The halt should not be abrupt. Let the trot slow down, and let the horse walk a few steps before halting. At the halt he should be straight, square, and still, and maintain contact with the bit. He must not "stretch." The hind canons should be vertical. Shift the reins to the left hand, salute, smile at the judge, and as soon as he acknowledges your salute, shift the reins back into two hands and proceed. The horse is expected to walk a few steps and then trot. He should move straight ahead.

Now what is actually likely to happen? At this stage, before the horse is firmly on the bit, you will probably not be very straight. Horses like paths and rails, and if there is no guide of this sort, they tend to wander. But do not worry unduly. The important thing is to proceed at a good trot. Try to put your horse into the trot while you are still some distance from "A," and then, even before you enter the arena, aim for "C," actually look at the letter in question and ride toward it. It is surprising, but your horse will go more briskly and probably somewhat straighter if you are actually looking a long distance ahead.

Apply the aids for the halt soon enough so that you can reasonably expect your horse to halt at "X," but remember that a smooth halt, though it is a little before or after "X," is better than a jerky or dragged-out one right *at* "X." If you have to drop the contact so your horse will stand still, do so—though it is better if you can maintain a light contact with your left hand while saluting.

The horse will probably not stop straight or square. Again, this is not too serious. Not being straight means that his haunches shift to one side a little as he slows down and stops so that he is not quite parallel to the long side of the arena. Some horse always shift the same way. If the haunches shift, say, to the right, you may be able to hold them straight with a stronger pull on the right rein. Stopping square means that the four feet are at the four corners of a rectangle. To do this, the horse must take a half step with the last foreleg to bring it up to its mate, and also with the last hind leg. In time you will teach your horse to square up in this way, but you may not have done so as yet. It is not very important at Training Level. Besides, it is more important for you and your horse to get into the arena and become used to the whole procedure and able to think while performing before you worry about this refinement.

When you move forward after the salute, again the horse may not move dead straight ahead. Do not worry. When you have reached the stage where you can notice whether or not all these things are going correctly while performing a test, it will be time enough to try to do something about them.

Exit

Most of the same remarks apply to the exit. After the final salute, you will move forward at a walk. If it is a schooling show, or a show in an area where dressage is just getting started, the judge may signal to you to halt again when you are closer and take time to speak with you about your performance. When he is through, proceed to leave the arena correctly at the free walk. It used to be that the horse was being judged at this final walk until he left the arena at "A," but this is no longer the case. Judging now ends with the final halt and salute, but you must still be sure to leave the arena only at "A," or be penalized for an error.

"Free walk on a long rein" simply means that the horse walks with a minimum of contact. The reins should show more of a curve or sag from the hand to the bit than at working walk. Figure 25 shows "free walk on a loose rein" which is no longer in the tests. At either free walk, the horse should lower his neck and walk with longer steps than at the working walk. There should not be any flexion at the poll. Push him as fast as he will go without breaking into a trot or becoming irregular. He should overtrack—that is, the hind footprints should be some distance in front of the forefoot prints.

Body of the Test

A turn is a quarter of a circle. You are not supposed to be able to trot on a curve smaller than 10 meters in diameter at this stage, or canter on a curve smaller than about 15 meters in diameter; hence the turns at the end of the arena after the initial salute and before the final salute should blend into smooth 10-meter half circles. Many people wait until they are too close to "C" or "A" before starting to turn. A perfect half circle would start at a point between "H" and "M"—or even sooner if you could tell that your horse disliked the judge's umbrella, or the flowers, and was not going to get very close to them. Judges are tolerant about this, especially at Training Level.

Large circles (20 meters) are not easy to do. In the first place, riders often make them too small, and if the rider doesn't do this, the horse usually does. In the second place, if the circles are not too small they are usually irregular in shape. The rider tends to turn too abruptly, correct this by straightening, then turn too sharply again. Or he does the corners near "H" and "M" as though he were going around the arena on the track. This makes the "circle" more of an egg shape. The only solution is to practice in an enclosure of the correct size, mark the points where the circle touches the track with some sand or sawdust or scratches in the ground, and then try to get a feeling for the correct curvature. Remember that a circle started at "A" or "C" goes through "X" (in the small arena) and coincides with the track for a few feet on each side. Perhaps it will help to think of a circle as a direction: You give the horse a certain direction (curve) and if he stays at that direction, a circle results.

Figure 25.   Free walk on a loose rein. It would be better if the horse were stretching his nose a little more forward. He has, however, lowered his neck, and the rider has surrendered contact. The horse is over-tracking. This can be seen at the walk by measuring the distance between the hind feet and noting that it is greater than the distance between the right fore and left hind.

You really should spend five or ten minutes of each practice session working on a large circle. Don't just do a circle now and then, but work steadily on the circle, trotting and cantering without interruption. If you are working in an arena you can work at one end between "A" and "X," or in the middle between "B" and "E."

Finally, a word about transitions. Technically they should be performed when the rider's body passes the prescribed point. At Training Level, however, it is much more important for them to be smooth and for the horse to keep his head steady. So look ahead, note the correct spot, start your aids far enough in advance, and then don't worry if they do not happen exactly where you intend.

Principles of Judging

The judge scores each movement in a dressage test immediately upon its completion. The score can range from 0 to 10 with these meanings assigned to the numbers:

10 Excellent	5 Sufficient
9 Very Good	4 Insufficient
8 Good	3 Fairly Bad
7 Fairly Good	2 Bad
6 Satisfactory	1 Very Bad

0 Not performed or Fall of Horse or Rider

The total score is then expressed as a percentage of the total possible points. The meanings of these percentages is very easy to understand. A score of 50 percent would be obtained if the horse was scored 5 on every movement, or 4 on half of the movements and 6 on the other half, or any mixture of scores that averaged out at 5. A score of 55 percent would result if half the scores were 5s and the other half 6s, or any mixture that averaged 5½. And so on.

It might seem that 70 percent and 80 percent scores would be common since we have many "fairly good" and "good" horses, but such is not the case. Instead it works this way: The judge has a "standard" in mind of what is "passing" *at the level being judged,* and he first mentally classifies a movement as "passing," that is, up to standard, or as "not passing," that is, not up to standard. If it is not passing, it gets a 4 (Insufficient). If it is *just* passing, it gets a 5 (Sufficient). If it is somewhat better than just passing, it gets a 6 (Satisfactory). If it is super, it gets a 7 (Fairly Good). Scores of 3 are also fairly common when the performance is considerably below standard. And that about covers it: 3 to 7. Five degrees of discrimination. Possibly this is about as much as a judge is capable of when dealing with an average distribution of talent.

Other numbers are there for use when something really out of the ordinary occurs, but that is uncommon. Most scores actually are 4, 5, or 6, and percentages are usually in the high 40s, 50s and low 60s. A score of 50 percent or better denotes a respectable performance. Usually the winning score is in the 60s.

At Training Level the horse's general way of going is probably the thing that is most important. It enters into the judge's evaluation of each movement as well as being scored separately at the end of the test. In other words, relaxation, free forward movement, contact, and the qualities of the three paces are what count most. The rider's seat and use of aids, which also receive a score at the end of the test, probably do not enter into the score of each movement except insofar as they influence the performance of the movement by the horse. Most judges do not stress the "geometry" of the ride at this level—that is, the size of circles, location of transitions, accuracy of center lines, diagonals, and so on. I do not mean that a ride that is precise in all these respects will not win over a ride that is sloppy. What I mean is that an accurate ride on a horse with poor paces and tense, short strides will score lower than a smooth, sweeping, inaccurate ride by an elegantly moving horse. Of course, if the level of competition is high, the winner will have to display good paces *and* accuracy.

What is the moral of the story? Concentrate on developing the general qualities of your horse, and then spend a fair amount of time practicing the test before a show. Remember that without a freely moving, relaxed horse and proper contact, perfect geometry is worth very little.

Finally, you must not expect to do as well as you have done at home or at lessons. A well-known judge commented that on the average, a horse is 20 percent below potential when performing at a show. You tend to expect your horse to do the best of which he is capable on each movement. Naturally he is not going to do this when he does a series of movements one after another in a space of three or four minutes. In fact, you cannot expect him to even do his best on *most* movements when he is in unfamiliar surroundings and his rider is as nervous as he. So do not expect too much at first. Training Level is designed to be just that—training for horse and rider. If you and your horse do as well as you can reasonably expect, be satisfied, regardless of your score. Read the judge's comments thoroughly and discuss the score sheet with him after the class is over if you do not understand something. Then resolve to work hard and ride a better test the next time.

6 Longeing

Longeing is a training technique in which the trainer works the horse on foot. The horse is controlled by a long whip and a single line attached to a longeing cavesson, halter, or bridle. The trainer stands in one place and continuously pivots as the horse circles around him.

Probably most trainers—including dressage trainers—start their young horses on the longe line (longe rhymes with sponge). It enables the trainer to teach some obedience and discipline and the meaning of several verbal commands. The technique can also accustom the horse to the whip and to various items of gear including saddle and bridle. Once a horse has learned to longe he can be exercised and the freshness worn off before mounting, although sometimes it is necessary to turn a very fresh horse loose in a field or arena for a while before expecting him to work in a disciplined fashion on the longe. The understanding of verbal commands will make early mounted lessons easier. In addition, longeing is frequently useful in exercising a horse when you are unable to ride for any reason, or when the horse has a sore back or some other condition that prevents his being ridden. The technique is also used in teaching a horse to jump.

Besides these very practical advantages which apply to all horses, some dressage trainers do a good deal of quite sophisticated work on the longe in developing the trot and canter. So if you are breaking a young horse, it would be advisable to longe before starting mounted work. If you have an older horse who has been longed, it will be easy for you to learn the technique. If neither you nor your horse can longe, you will have to learn together. Your dressage instructor may expect you to know how and may wish to have you use longeing in the general development of your horse, or from time to time in working on various problems. It will be to your advantage if you and your horse know the basic procedure so you can quickly learn whatever techniques the instructor advises. Basic longeing is not difficult, but until you get the hang of it you may feel clumsy and awkward.

I would not advise you to go to the expense of buying a longeing cavesson, surcingle, and side reins, which can be quite expensive. Wait to see whether you need them. You *will* need a webbing longe line and a whip, however. The longe line is 25 or 30 feet long, with a snap and swivel at one end and a loop for a handhold at the other. For a long time I used a driving whip with a three-foot piece of bamboo as an extension of the handle and a yard or so of cord added to the lash. I now have a very nice, jointed longeing whip that is much lighter and more convenient than my makeshift version. Above all, do not try to longe with a short piece of rope for a line and a short whip that will not reach the horse. If you do you will be bound to work on too small a circle, and your horse will get very little benefit from longeing. If the whip is 15 feet long over all, your outstretched arms add 5 feet so you can reach a horse working on a 40-foot diameter circle.

You can start your longeing efforts by snapping the line into the side of the noseband of your halter. Many people longe on a halter. Wynmalen, in particular, recommended it. However, your only direct form of discipline is short jerks on the line and these may not be very effective when the line is attached to a halter. Of course skillful handling of line and whip and working in an enclosure may enable you to control and teach your horse with very little need for disciplinary jerks. Jerks are more severe if the line is attached to a longeing cavesson with its heavy metal noseband. If you do get a cavesson, it must be carefully fitted. There must be enough padding on the noseband and chin strap so that the jaw and nose are not bruised or rubbed raw, and the jowl strap must keep the cheek piece from slipping up onto the horse's eye.

Since directions for basic longeing are to be found in many places, I will not go into the elementary details of teaching the horse to circle the trainer. Try to get someone who knows how to help you if you and your horse are both new at it. Be sure you learn to handle the line and whip safely, keeping the line properly coiled or folded in your hand so you cannot be caught or tangled in it.

Trainers differ as to whether the longe line should ever be attached to the bit. If you do not have an experienced trainer helping you, I would suggest trying this only as a last resort if the horse is unruly on the halter and you have no cavesson available. The safest way to attach the line to the bit is to run it through the inside snaffle ring, up around behind the ears, and down to snap into the outside snaffle ring. Then the bit cannot be pulled through the horse's mouth, and the pressure is applied on both sides similarly to the way you might pull on both reins to stop a horse. Of course when you reverse directions, you must reverse the attachment of the line. To keep the bridle rein out of the way put it over the horse's neck, then twist the two sides together under the horse's throat, and pass the throatlash through *one* of them before buckling it. This keeps the rein from hanging down and pulling on one side of the bit. (See Figure 26.)

The object of longeing should be to have the horse go around steadily at the desired gait on a perfect circle, keeping a light tension on the line. The horse should not pull outward, but neither should the line sag very much. He should respond to verbal commands, urged on when necessary by the whip or restrained by light jerks on the line. Accomplishing this is not always easy.

Sometimes the horse will not go on as large a circle as you wish; he lets the line sag, and the circle gets smaller and smaller. The classic remedy is to point the whip at his shoulder or head, or flick him on the shoulder with the lash. If this does not help, remember that the faster he goes the harder it is to turn; and the larger he will of necessity have to make the circle. So try driving the horse on a little more energetically. It is also possible that a horse will decrease the circle to avoid tension on the line. If you let the line hang slack every time he cuts in, you will unintentionally encourage him to do exactly what you *do not* want. Instead you

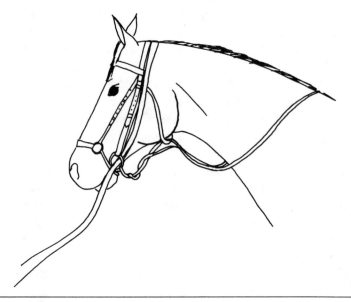

Figure 26.   The best way to attach longe line to snaffle bit, if it is necessary. It goes through the inside snaffle ring, up behind the ears, and down to snap into the outside snaffle ring. Note how the snaffle rein is kept out of the way.

should take in the slack and let him go in a smaller circle *with contact* on the line, until eventually you can get him to trot a little more energetically so he will again have to enlarge the circle.

If the horse cuts in abruptly, usually at the same spot each time around, you can try to prevent this by driving him on with the whip just *before* he reaches the spot. If this causes him to break into a canter, do not punish him. Let him canter, and wait until he drops back into a trot. Continue to urge him on at the proper spot until he gets tired enough to stay on the circle without cantering. Then praise him and let him rest.

If, on the other hand, the horse tries to rush off on a tangent, it will help to longe him in an enclosed area. If you have only the corner of a large enclosure to work in, try laying poles on the ground or setting up some jumps so they form the missing sides of a square.

When your horse is mounted he will be expected to always stop straight and stand still, so you should insist on straight stops when longeing. The horse should always come to a stop facing straight ahead on the circle, and not be allowed to turn and face the trainer. This also enables you to send him on again after short halts. If he does turn, walk to him and move him back into the correct position from which he moved. When he gets the idea and stops straight, be sure to speak approvingly.

There are many special longeing techniques, ways of adjusting side reins, ways of attaching the longe line to the bit, and so on. Some are ways of overcoming particular problems; others are just an individual trainer's way of handling whip or line. Here are a few quotations to give you an idea of some of the possibilities.

First, Seunig. He is referring to the whip when he uses the term "controls":

> If the controls are always exercised from the same initial position, differing merely in degree, from the bottom upwards and from the rear to the front as driving controls, and from top to bottom and along the lunge as controls returning the horse to the circle or enlarging the circle, the horse will very soon learn to distinguish between them and follow them correctly.

> . . . .

> If the horse tugs at the lunge at excessive speed and cannot be brought to a . . . halt . . . by repeated and increasing pulls inwards on the lunge and by the voice, the leading hand releases contact for an instant and then tugs rapidly and forcefully on the lunge. This control, called a saccade, may be repeated, if necessary, until the horse obeys. The trainer may also be compelled to employ these saccades in a milder form as a control to slow down the pace. (Seunig, p. 100.)

> There are horses that always pull on the lunge and try to turn out. The lunge trainer tries to make these horses contact their bits more easily by alternately raising his hand up to his shoulder and letting it down again. (Seunig, p. 99.)

Seunig has several pages of advice about longeing which the beginner may find helpful.

Podhajsky also has detailed instructions, as longeing is an important part of the training at the Spanish Riding School. Here is a small sample:

> If the horse leans to the outside the trainer should try to keep him on the circle by repeated short actions of the hand and not by a steady pull. . . .

> . . . if the horse begins to rush off he will be calmed down by . . .
> circular actions of the longe against the movement and by the use of
> the voice.
>
> . . . if the trainer always uses the same word and tone for chang-
> ing speed or halting, the horse will soon answer to the command.
>
> If the horse overbends, the trainer will again use a circular action
> of the longe but in this case it will be the same direction as the move-
> ment while pushing the horse forward with the whip. (Podhajsky,
> p. 81.)

Figure 27 shows more clearly what he means.

Now let us see what the various levels of accomplishment on the
longe can be. *Stage one* can be referred to as simple obedience. The
horse goes around in a circle. He recognizes and obeys the commands "Walk," "Trot," and "Whoa." He walks and trots steadily.

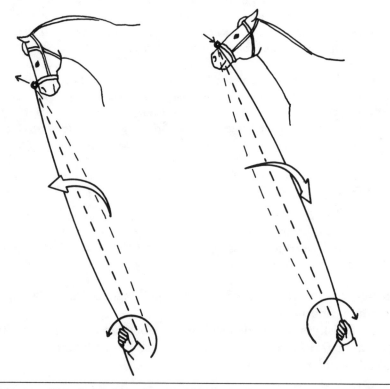

Figure 27.   This sketch shows how Colonel Podhajsky recommends using a circular action of the longe line *with* the motion to raise the head or
against the motion to slow the horse.

He learns to balance himself while moving on a circle and to follow a smooth arc. He does not pull or try to rush off. This much can be accomplished by almost anyone, with a little help, and should be accomplished before approaching a dressage instructor. There is no point in having a highly skilled instructor teach you elementary things.

Stage two—relaxation, suppleness (flexibility), free forward movement, and contact with the bit can be observed and improved. You can certainly observe them, and your instructor may help you use longeing to improve them. It depends on the problems of the horse and the preferences of the trainer whether he will want your horse worked on the longe or only under saddle.

At the risk of too much repetition, I will once again review the main objectives of training and show how they can be observed while longeing.

Rhythm and relaxation. Rhythm is the regularity and unchanging speed of the hoofbeats. If the horse is constantly varying his speed—darting forward, gradually slowing down, or going by fits and starts—he obviously does not have rhythm. Relaxation means that all tenseness and nervousness have been eliminated. Just working on a comfortably large circle promotes relaxation. The circle should not be less than 35 feet in diameter once the horse has learned to go around well, and a larger circle is desirable, especially at the canter. Carrying the head too high is a form of tenseness that causes a hollow, stiff back and is the very opposite of relaxation. The horse must be encouraged to lower his neck, if it is too high, until it is nearly horizontal (see Figures 28 and 29), and to take a comfortable feel on the bit (if you are using side reins). One way in which this is taught is by "asking down" with the longe line. A relaxed horse will take long, low, regular (rhythmical) strides. Since the strides are *long*, the rhythm will be *slow* relative to the speed at which the horse is traveling. Too fast a rhythm is called "hurrying," "rushing," or "running." When you are riding you can feel the rhythm. When you are longeing you can see it.

Lateral suppleness (flexibility) is also part of relaxation. If a horse is relaxed and does not have any basic stiffness in his muscles or joints, he will conform his spine from poll to tail to the curve on which he is traveling. Note whether the prints of the outside forefoot and the outside hind foot are exactly on the same circle. If the hindquarters are traveling on a slightly larger circle, the horse is not bent supply to the circle. We say the hindquarters are "flying out" or the hindquarters are "not tracking the forehand." (See Figure 30.) If this is the case, the circle should be enlarged to make it easier for the horse. Later it may be gradually decreased as suppleness improves.

Figure 28.　The colt is just being started on the longe. His head is high and the line is loose. He will have to learn to lower his head and take a contact.

Figure 29.　The mare is well trained on the longe. Her head is low and the line has good contact. She is trotting on a good-sized circle.

A free-going horse, who would like to dash away, will frequently look to the outside as he circles. His hindquarters will be apt to track the forehand, not because he is flexible, but because he is looking outward. With such a horse you can try making the inside rein a hole shorter than the outside rein. However, be satisfied to get him to look straight ahead at first. If you shorten the inside rein enough so that the horse looks to the inside, the hindquarters will probably fly out.

. *Free forward movement* is another basic requirement at Training Level—and in all dressage work. A pretty good index of it is the degree to which the horse "tracks up." When the fore and hind hoofs (on the same side) make only one print on the ground, the horse is said to be "tracking up." When trotting on a circle, the outer hind print must fall exactly *on* the outer fore print. The inner hind print may fall *on* the inner fore print or close *beside* it under

Correct—neck and body curved or bent to arc of circle.

Incorrect—neck and body straight, horse looking outward, hindquarters tracking but horse not supple.

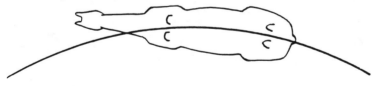

Incorrect—only neck curved. Body straight, quarters flying out, horse not bent.

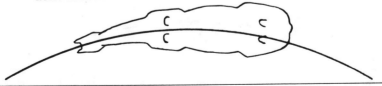

Figure 30. Lateral suppleness when longeing.

the center of the horse's belly. Neither hind print, however, should be *behind* the corresponding fore footprint. (See Figure 31.)

If they are behind, there is a lack of relaxation, a lack of free forward movement, a problem of conformation, or the circle is too small. If the horse starts out trotting in a tense manner, just getting him to relax and lower his neck may be enough to get him to track up. If he is relaxed and trotting with rhythm but does not track up, he should be driven forward more energetically by voice and whip until he lengthens his stride enough to track up. If you cannot get him to track up, he may be lazy, tense, have a long back, straight hocks, stiff hind legs, a little soreness or lameness somewhere, or there may be something wrong with the way the forelegs move. Only an experienced trainer would be able to pinpoint the cause of the problem and decide whether that particular horse ought or ought not to track up.

Outer hind not on same circle as outer fore, quarters not tracking forehand—also not tracking up.

Outer hind on same circle as outer fore, inner hind under center of belly—nearly tracking up.

Hindquarters tracking forehand—horse tracking up.

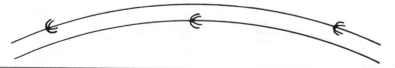

Figure 31.   Footprints of horse trotting on a circle. Forefoot print is rounder, hind foot print is narrower.

The final objective was *contact with the bit*. This, of course, requires the use of side reins. You can make a pair cheaply from an old pair of reins, or have them made, by following the suggestions in Figure 32. One end is looped around the girth below the saddle flap, and the snaps are attached to the snaffle bit. The fancy kind of side reins with elastic inserts are not necessary, and in fact some trainers do not like them.

With the side reins in place and adjusted to the proper length, which is quite long at this stage, the horse should reach for the bit and take a feel on it, carrying his head low and steady, and with the line of the face in front of the vertical. (See Figure 33.) He will be "on the forehand," but this is normal at this early stage. If the horse "over-bends" or "gets behind the bit" (avoids contact by rounding his neck and pulling his chin in toward his chest) the solution is to drive him on a little more energetically. In this way he will be induced to take longer steps and will have to extend his nose, for a horse cannot usually place his forefeet on the ground in front of a line that is an extension of the front line of his face. Figure 34 illustrates this point.

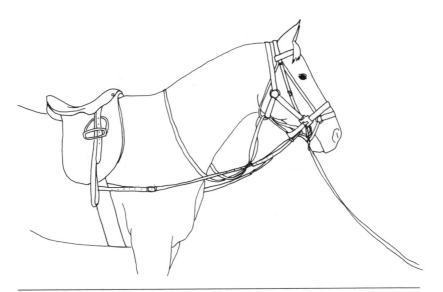

Figure 32. Simple longeing gear. Halter over bridle with longe line snapped to side of noseband, rein up out of the way, sidereins attached low on girth and of good length for early stages of longeing. Sidereins like these are easy to make. All that is required is an old pair of reins, two snaps, four buckles, and a leather punch.

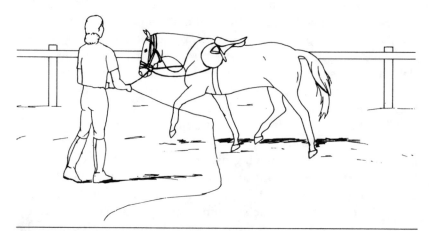

Figure 33.   Young horse taking a nice contact. The sidereins are of equal length
and the mare is bending her neck, so the outside rein is taut and the
inside rein is slack. Some trainers prefer to shorten the inside rein so
the horse can take an equal contact on both reins.

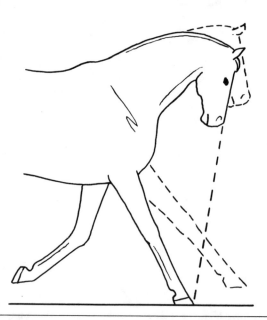

Figure 34.   The horse is unable to ground his forefoot in front of the point
marked by the line of his face. Thus, when he is overbent (face
behind the vertical) his stride is restricted. If the horse lengthens his
stride, he is compelled to raise and extend his head.

Of course, it is very easy to get the side reins the wrong length, and it is really best if this phase of training is under the supervision of an experienced trainer. One warning: When the reins are correct for trotting they are too short for walking, so the horse ought not be asked to walk once the reins are attached to the bit.

To sum up, if the horse is supple (not looking outward, and hind legs tracking forelegs), relaxed (neck low and no sign of tenseness), moving freely forward (tracking up), with a good rhythm (regular and slow) and taking a feel on the bit with the side reins the right length, then we could say that the horse is trotting correctly. If you could accomplish all this on the longe you would accomplish a good deal, although it would still be a long way to obtaining the same performance under saddle. Actually you probably could not accomplish this much by yourself. When a rider is following printed instructions and has no experienced person to guide him he never knows whether his horse is really relaxed, how lively is "lively enough," how long a stride is "long," how low the neck should be, or what rhythm is correct.

There is just no substitute for a teacher or trainer who has watched many horses, and can look at yours and tell you how much of anything is the right amount for your horse at the stage he is in. Also, an inexperienced person cannot take in the whole picture at once and see just which element is lacking or which is wrong. For instance, you might merely observe that your horse had stopped tracking up, and proceed to drive him faster with your whip. But if you could take in the whole picture it might be obvious that the problem was that the horse's head had come up and that until he lowered his head and relaxed, driving him on would only result in faster steps (hurrying or loss of rhythm) instead of longer steps.

If you are going to longe, however, you should certainly observe all that you can about your horse and his way of going. The problems encountered vary a good deal with the type of horse. For example, a high-spirited horse will probably exhibit free forward movement right from the start. The problem will be to obtain obedience, relaxation, and rhythm without losing the very valuable quality of liveliness. A lazy horse, on the other hand, will rather soon be relaxed and rhythmical, and the problem will be just the opposite—to develop a free-going trot without losing the relaxation and rhythm.

So far I have not said anything about the canter. This is more difficult than the trot, and I will confine myself to making a few suggestions. As soon as the trot is going well, you can try the canter. It is useful in livening up the trot, and the two gaits can be alternated, especially if the trot tends to be lazy. The canter should be attempted only from the trot, as taking the canter from the walk requires the ability to collect the walk, which you cannot do on the longe. The horse should be performing a lively trot (but not be rushing) and be taught to make a clean transition without first speeding up the trot, losing rhythm, and falling awkwardly into the canter. To obtain the correct lead, you must not be pulling on the longe *at the moment* of the transition. The longe must momentarily be loose. And the circle should be very large.

Here is Seunig's description:

> The trainer brings the horse somewhat inside the circle by pulling slightly on the lunge, yielding as soon as it has responded to this pull and at the same time applying a driving whip control. The horse's complying with this release by moving outwards creates the most favorable position for a gallop depart, and an unconstrained and supple trotting horse will involuntarily change into the gallop. Later on, the hand and whip controls will be reduced to mere symbols, the command, always given with the same intonation, sufficing. (Seunig, p. 103.)

If the horse pulls on the longe while cantering, but is not being disobedient, it means that he is not well enough balanced for a circle of the size being asked. Either enlarge the circle, or do more work at the trot to improve the balance.

When slowing from canter to trot (or trot to walk) the dressage trainer wants the horse to continue to go freely forward at the slower pace; hence he does not demand an immediate, abrupt transition. If necessary he repeats the command several times in a soothing tone and accepts a rather delayed response and a gradual transition, provided the horse goes forward at a good trot (or walk).

If it should happen that the horse is unruly and you cannot control him at the canter, or if he often gets the wrong lead, it is better not to attempt longeing at the canter without assistance. He will not be learning obedience, and you will only be making trouble for yourself if you get him confused about his leads. On the other hand, if the horse takes the canter promptly and canters quietly and steadily without pulling, and with the hind legs tracking the forelegs, you are doing about all that you can expect at this gait. Horses usually go better in one direction than the other. Be careful not to work mostly to the easy side at the canter (or the trot) just because it is easier.

Skillful longeing, like any other training, requires intense concentration. Once a good gait is attained, the competent trainer is constantly on the alert to notice the *beginning* of deterioration in any aspect of the work and to apply instantly the appropriate remedy. Only in this way does the horse really learn what is expected of him and develop improved gaits.

part **II** **First and Second Levels**

7 The Requirements of the Tests

The AHSA dressage tests are meant to be guides to training as well as competitive devices; therefore one should study them to see what new movements and figures are introduced at each level. Not only the levels, but the tests within each level are designed to show progression. There are four First Level and four Second Level tests, so in all, eight stages or steps in the training process are spelled out.

Not all trainers would agree with the order in which each movement and figure is presented. New tests always provoke heated discussions among riders and trainers, not only as to progression, but sometimes even as to whether certain exercises should be included in tests at all. These latter ones are usually exercises useful in training, but not deemed suitable by some people for a public presentation. We will try to ignore the arguments as much as possible and simply study the progression of requirements as they appear in the 1987 tests, examine various theories and methods of training, and finally consider how you should train in preparation for competition.

Before proceeding, it would probably be a good idea to distinguish between movements and figures and add a third category—transitions. Analyzing the tests in terms of these three categories will make it easier to plan and carry out a training program. First, it should be noted that a *movement* is a method of locomotion, such as working walk, trot with lengthened strides, or shoulder-in. A *figure* is a path along which a movement is performed, such as changing the rein on the diagonal or a 10-meter circle. Finally a *transition* is a change from one movement to another or to a halt, such as a change from working walk to free walk, from trot to canter, or from shoulder-in to lengthened trot. Difficulty increases as more difficult movements are introduced and as they are performed on more difficult paths. The difficulty of a transition depends on the place where it is performed as well as on the gait change.

The AHSA First Level Tests

The *purpose* of the First Level tests is stated to be:

> To determine that the correct foundation is being laid for the training of the riding horse, that the horse moves freely forward in a relaxed manner and with rhythm, its spine always parallel to the track of the prescribed movement; that it accepts the bit . . . shows . . . softening of the lower jaw, some flexion at the poll, lateral bending and quiet transitions.

The *general requirements for the horse* are listed in the collective marks at the end of the test. They are the same at First Level as they were for Training Level, but they are so important that I will repeat them here in full.

Gaits (freedom and regularity).

Impulsion (desire to move forward, elasticity of the steps, relaxation of the back).

Submission (attention and confidence; harmony, lightness and ease of movements; acceptance of the bit).

The *movements, figures,* and *transitions* can best be presented in a table. The Training Level requirements will be included to make the table complete and to show the entire training progression to this point. There is nothing official about this table or the classification of items in it. I have merely done what seems logical to me. In fact, there were a few things which it was hard to categorize. For instance, is "turn on the haunches" (in Second Level) a movement or a figure? It really seems to be both. Anyhow, I hope the table will be useful to you. When new tests come out, you can compare them with the 1987 tests and make any necessary changes in the table.

		First Level			
	Training Level	Test 1	Test 2	Test 3	Test 4
MOVEMENTS	(Working) walk (Working) trot, rising and sitting (Working) canter Free walk on a long rein	Working walk Working trot Working canter Lengthen stride in trot rising	—	Leg-yielding Lengthen stride in trot sitting Lengthen stride in canter	—
FIGURES	20-m circle at B, E, A, or C Change or rein on diagonal across half or full arena Down center A to C 20-m figure 8 in trot at X	15-m circle at B or E in trot and canter	10-m half circle and reverse in trot 3 loop serpentine with 20-m arcs in trot	10-m circle from center line in trot 10-m circle at B in canter	MBXG in trot
TRANSITIONS					
Gaits	H-W-T-C-T-W-H W-Free walk-W	T-H-T Working trot, lengthened trot and back	—	Change lead through trot Working canter, lengthened canter and back	—
Places	Canter departs: Between M and C or F and A At M or F going into short side On large circle at B Canter-Trot between E and H or E and K Canter-Trot at the letter	Canter depart: At M coming out of the short side	—	Leg-yield off center line in trot	Leg-yield off track in trot

Requirements for the Horse

As with Training Level, we will discuss the general objectives first, and then examine the exercises in detail. Most of the qualities desired in the horse at this level were also mentioned at Training Level. We will not discuss them again, but they are very basic. Moving freely forward, relaxation, regularity, and accepting the bit are just as important at First Level or Fourth Level—or, indeed, at Grand Prix—as they were in the beginning and should never be lost sight of. There are, however, some additional objectives to focus on.

The Training Level horse was supposed to accept the bit with a light contact. Now a little more advanced sort of contact with softening of the lower jaw and flexion at the poll is expected. These ideas, along with the stretching into the bit which was mentioned in Training Level, will be developed in the chapter on the working trot.

The First Level purpose also states that the spine should always be "parallel to the track of the prescribed movement." The conforming of the spine to the path being followed is called "flexibility" or "lateral suppleness," and we will go into this subject thoroughly. There are actually two kinds of suppleness. *Lateral suppleness*, also called *flexibility*, means that the spine can bend from side to side so that the horse can be curved when he goes around turns or circles. The other kind of suppleness is *longitudinal suppleness* and means bending the spine up or down, for example, raising the loin, bending the croup down, or arching the neck.* Lateral suppleness enables "the spine of the horse to be parallel to the track of the prescribed movement." This is so that the hind feet can follow the same path as the forefeet, thus making the horse "straight." (See page 7.) Odd as it may seem, the horse must be supple—able to bend—in order to be straight. When he is on a straight track his body and neck are indeed straight, but when he is on a circle, the hind feet only travel in the path of the forefeet if he is bent or flexed to the circle. Conforming the spine to the circle or turn also has the advantage that the horse can go around the arc with his body very nearly vertical to the ground;

---

*Seunig, whom I frequently quote, does not use this terminology. He uses the term "longitudinal suppleness" for what the AHSA call lateral suppleness. (Seunig, page 104.)

otherwise he must lean inward like a bicycle on a turn. (See Figures 35 and 36.) This quote from Seunig makes it clear:

> . . . *the closer the . . . axis of the horse comes to the circumference of the circle, in other words, the more perfect its . . . flexion,* * *other conditions . . . remaining the same, the less will be the action of centrifugal force and the less does its centre of gravity have to be shifted inward. The more defective its . . . flexion, on the other hand, the more will an untrained horse have to lean into the circle in order to resist centrifugal force. . . . (Seunig, p. 119 note.)*

Figure 35.   Horse not bent to the turn. Hence, he is leaning into the turn like a bicycle.

*I have omitted the word "longitudinal" where it is confusing.

Figure 36. Upper level horse doing an eight-meter circle. His spine is parallel to the track of the circle and his body is very nearly vertical.

Sometimes it is desirable to lean into the circle. A barrel racer, for instance, is supposed to lean inward. That is the way he can get around the fastest. In dressage, however, we are not in a hurry and want to go around without any alteration in speed or rhythm. So we learn to bend the whole horse. We are also careful not to let the neck bend more than the body, because there should be a *uniform* curve from poll to tail. The body can bend only a little bit while the neck is quite flexible and can easily bend a lot, which it is not supposed to do.

Bending the horse would be relatively simple if the horse were merely stiff and straight to begin with, but instead he is usually crooked, so he must be straightened and then bent. There is a great deal in the literature about crookedness and its causes and cures. We will discuss this presently.

Now getting on to the qualities mentioned in the collective marks, something more must be said about impulsion. Impulsion is an extremely important quality. Judges continually make comments about it, usually "Not enough impulsion," or "Impulsion lacking." It has been discussed in a preliminary way in Part I. (See pages 11, 48, and 66). Writers frequently mention the need for it but do not define it very adequately. Here are some typical references to it:

> . . . *a horse can only display his full beauty when able to move correctly with impulsion and suppleness. (Podhajsky, p. 99.)*

> *Impulsion is the horse's keenness in performing tasks. . . . It reflects the animal's striving to go forward and carry out with eagerness the action required of it. Impulsion enhances the quality of the entire motion. . . . (d'Endrödy, p. 237).*

> *Impulsion should not be confused with mere speed, for it is largely a matter of how the horse responds to his rider's impulsive aids at all paces, particularly by engaging his hind quarters well under him. (Jackson, p. 96.)*

How can the rider or observer know whether the horse is sufficiently responsive and eager? The expression "engaging the hind quarters" is the clue. For practical purposes, this usually means "tracking up." If your horse tracks up at the working trot, his impulsion will probably be adequate. Other similar expressions mean the same thing: "Engage the haunches well forward"; "engage the hocks under the mass"; or more simply, "engage the hind legs."

This is actually a very peculiar use of the word "engage" when you stop to think about it. To "engage" means "to bring into contact with" as "to engage gears" or "to engage the enemy." So, what is being "engaged"? It can only be the *hind feet* which contact the ground! The part of the hindquarters that is engaged is not the hocks or haunches but the feet, and they are engaged well forward; that is, they are well forward under the horse's belly when they touch the ground. For some obscure reason, "hind quarters," "hocks," and "haunches" are used interchangeably with "feet" even though it is obviously only the feet that can engage with anything.*

Anyway, if the horse is being very energetic and is eager to go forward, without being tense, he will take long steps with the hind legs and place the feet well forward under the body. This is the

---

*The word "engagement" is also used sometimes to refer to the bending of the joints of the hind legs. See pages 137–138. Bending the joints is more properly called "lowering the croup."

most obvious way to detect impulsion. Once you have learned from your instructor whether your horse's conformation is such that he tracks up when trotting with impulsion, you have a convenient way to check on it between lessons. An observer can easily tell you whether your horse is tracking up if you explain to him what to look for.

But not all horses that track up have sufficient impulsion—even for First Level. Some free-moving horses track up very easily, even when moving quite lazily. Such horses may have no suspension in their trot stride. (See Figure 37.) They must be driven forward more energetically until they get all four feet off the ground between the beats of the trot. When there is suspension, the horse will overtrack. Another name for suspension is "cadence."

Eventually you will have to learn to decide for yourself, by the way it feels to you in the saddle, whether the hind feet are reaching far enough forward. "Desire to move forward" is one ingredient in this feeling. Another is the feeling you get of "committed forward movement." And, of course, there is the "stretching of the spinal

Figure 37. The horse has lowered his head, flexed at the poll, and is on the bit, but there is no impulsion. Note that all four feet are touching the ground.

column to the bit." In time you will discover how it feels to you when you are on your horse.

In Part I, I discussed relaxation in a preliminary way; here I want to go further into this subject and discuss more specifically *relaxation of the horse's back*. This expression appears in the collective marks as a subhead under impulsion. It is a dressage concept—or at least no one else seems to talk about it. Usually it is synonymous with phrases like "the back is up," or "the back is arched." The opposite condition is described by saying "the back is hollow," or has "sagged" or "fallen." The part of the back referred to is from the point of the croup forward to the withers, and is observed from the side. If the horse has on a Western saddle with a large blanket, you cannot see it. With a dressage saddle and small pad, all you can see is the loin; and it is the slope from top of croup to rear of saddle (the loin) that should be at a minimum. In other words, the loin should be as close to horizontal as possible.

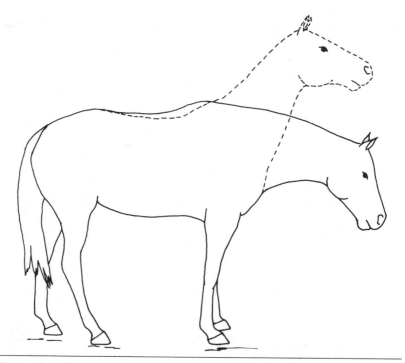

Figure 38. This drawing was made from two photographs of the same horse. Observe the change in the shape of his back when his head is lowered. The loin is flatter, the hollow is smaller, and the withers has changed in shape.

I once had a horse with a slight roach back and was advised to photograph him with his head high to minimize this defect. Figure 38 shows this horse first with head high and then with head lowered. The hollow between croup and withers is actually shallower when his head is low. We say his back is "up." With head high, the hollow is greater and the roach back is flattened. We say his back is "down." The point of all this is that when the back is "down" it is stiff. When it is "up" it is usually relaxed. This is true even though the cervical ligament is tensioned when the head is low. (See page 54.) You can observe the same thing with your own back. When you pull in the small of the back—as when standing at attention—the back is apt to be tense. Relax, and the pelvis tips a little (top of pelvis tips back). The back gets flatter and feels more relaxed.

One reason for getting the horse to lower and stretch his neck (page 52ff.) is that this causes him to relax his back. This makes sitting trot more comfortable and the horse's gaits freer and more rhythmical. Since the conformation of horses' backs varies a good deal, you cannot tell just by looking at the slope of the loin of a particular horse whether his back is up or down. If a high headed horse lowers his neck, however, you can see the change in his back and the rider can feel it. (See Figure 39.)

Since too much of a good thing can often be as much of a problem as too little, it should be noted that it is possible for a horse's back to be *too* arched or *too* relaxed. Seunig warns against both extremes:

> . . . *the horse should always* flex *and* relax *the muscles that are employed for motion in time with its steps and leaps more or less intensively but always elastically and regularly, depending upon the stage of its dressage and the energy that the gait actually requires. . . . It may flex its muscles excessively and relax them hardly at all, so that they are held upwards, that is, they are "tense" as we speak of it colloquially, such as a convulsively arched, tightened back. But the horse can also flex them too little, so that there is practically nothing to relax, as in an inactive, dead, sway-back. In both of these boundary cases the muscles pulsate too little, irregularly, and therefore wrongly. . . . [The back] does not swing correctly.* (Seunig, p. 116.)

One sign of a relaxed back is often a swinging tail. I first noticed this as I watched the Lipizzaner stallions at the Fulmer School of

Figure 39.   The upper drawing shows a student riding. The horse's neck is high, nose poked out, back hollow. In the lower drawing, the instructor has mounted. The horse has lowered his neck, flexed at the poll, and come on the bit. His back is up. Note the difference in the slope of the loin.

Equitation near London (Robert Hall's school). Their tails had a rhythmical side-to-side motion visible from the rear as they trotted away from the viewer. When I asked my instructor about it, she told me this indicated a swinging back. The swinging back, which is easy to sit, is a synonym for a relaxed back. Seunig says:

> Unconstraint [relaxation] is attained when the horse allows the rider to take his place in the saddle without tightening its back and begins its natural, well-timed trot without any action of the reins. The correct . . . oscillation of all its body muscles is also apparent to the observer in . . . the natural carriage of the tail, which swings from base to tip in time with the hind leg that happens to be grounded. (Seunig, pp. 114-115.)

I am told that the swinging tail is not an infallible sign of a relaxed and swinging back, but it is interesting to watch for it. I have only observed a few nondressage horses with swinging tails, and in several of these cases the owner assured me that the horse had an extremely "smooth" trot. In higher-level dressage, when great activity of the hindquarters is required, the horse becomes hard to sit again although the back is still relaxed.

Movements, Figures, and Transitions

Now let us examine the movements, figures, and transitions of the four First Level tests to see what progression in training is called for. First the *movements*. Although the Training Level tests specified working walk, working trot, and working canter, I prefer to think of them at that level as merely a natural walk, trot, and canter performed in a lively but relaxed manner. At First Level, however, a real *working trot* must be shown. The working trot *must* be achieved because you cannot get a good score without it, and it is also the basis for all more advanced work. You cannot do the lateral movements adequately or develop real collection without a good working trot as a foundation.

Indeed, the working trot is quite an accomplishment for the beginning dressage rider. Sometimes it takes a couple of years of conscientious work before a rider can put his horse into a proper working trot at a show without his teacher to watch and help. The working trot is different from any other type of trot required of any other type of American show horse, so its difficulty and importance should not be taken lightly. The requirements will be discussed in more detail when we get to training methods. Working canter and working walk more or less follow from it.

The working gaits are extremely important, but they are tempo-
rary paces. Working walk, working trot, and working canter are
actually *slightly* collected and as time goes on, these gaits are collected a little bit more and a little bit more until they can truly be
called "collected walk," "collected trot," and "collected canter." At
Second Level the trot and canter are considered to be "collected,"
and at Third Level finally, the walk is also. The working gaits are
then no longer called for in competition.

Of course "collection" as shown at Second Level is still very
slight. It should continue to improve and increase all the way up
through the International Levels. Many persons don't like to call the
Second Level trot and canter "collected," especially as they fear
riders will unwisely try to "push the horse together" and merely
create tenseness and lose impulsion. It is really better not to think
about collection at Second Level. If the horse can perform the increasingly difficult figures and transitions well, the collection will be
developing as it should.

Free walk on a long rein is still included at First Level, but at
Second Level it is superseded by *medium walk*, which is a more advanced lengthened walk.

Trot with lengthened stride is required at First Level. At Second
Level it is replaced by the more advanced medium trot. What is
expected at First Level is some lengthening of the stride with as little
change in rhythm as possible. Some horses, when urged to trot
faster, naturally take longer steps without increasing the tempo. If
you have such a horse you are lucky. Most horses, however, when
urged to trot faster, take quicker steps which are very little longer
than before. If your horse does this, you will have to work to
develop a lengthening of the stride.

In First Level Test 3, a *lengthening of the canter* is also called
for. As at the trot, the number of strides per minute should ideally
not change, but each bound should be longer. This requirement
is repeated at Second Level Test 1, and then at Test 2 it becomes medium canter. Any free-moving horse could certainly
lengthen the canter even in Training Level. The reason it is post-
poned to First Level Test 3 is probably because it is felt that by
then a horse should be obedient enough so that even under the
exciting conditions of a show he will remain under control at
a lengthened canter, and come back to working canter willingly.

One movement that has been in and out of tests in the past and which came back in 1979 is still in. This is *leg-yielding*. Leg-yielding is the first lateral movement that one practices and can be done even before the horse is on the bit. Although some trainers do not consider it a proper classical movement, it is fun to do and is a useful preliminary to the more difficult lateral exercises. It occurs in First Level Tests 3 and 4.

Now the *figures*. (See Figure 40.) In general they require increasing suppleness or flexibility—that is, the ability to bend the body

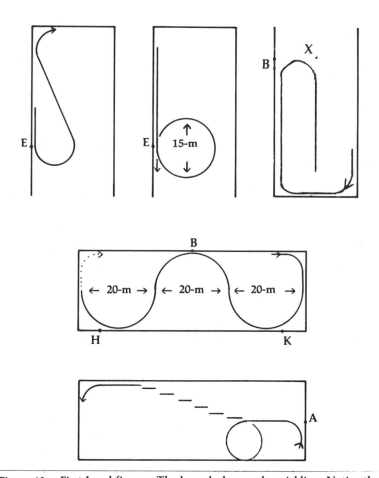

Figure 40. First Level figures. The long dashes are leg-yielding. Notice the sizes of the circles and also notice where the curves of the serpentine touch the track.

of the horse to conform to the arc of the circle. At Training Level only 20-meter diameter (65-foot) circles occur. Although it is not very easy to ride a really *round* 20-meter circle without a track to follow, and might actually be easier to ride a somewhat smaller one, the 20-meter circle required practically no bending—about 2 inches to be exact. (See Figure 41.) A 10-meter diameter circle (33-foot) requires quite a bit (4 inches). Eventually the smallest circle of all (called a volte—6 meters or 20 feet in diameter) requires more than three times as much as the 20-meter circle (6¾ inches). Thus progression to smaller circles requires a more supple or flexible horse.

The four First Level tests are progressively more difficult in this respect. Test 1 reduces the trot and canter circles from 20 meters to 15 meters, thus requiring a little increase in suppleness. Test 2 has a 10-meter half turn and reverse which requires still more bending but is easier than the full 10 meter circles in Tests 3 and 4. These are required in both trot and canter. The serpentine in Test 2 also gives you a chance to show lateral suppleness as you change the bend for each loop. The serpentine should be thought of as three 20 meter half circles.

As for impulsion, it is always harder to maintain impulsion (continue to track up and maintain speed) as the circles get smaller; therefore it could be said that increasing impulsion is required throughout Level One as well as increasing suppleness. It is also easier to maintain impulsion on a half circle as in Test 2, than on a full circle as in Test 3.

The last thing to analyze is the *transitions*. When you add new gaits you add new transitions, of course: working walk to lengthened walk and back; working trot to lengthened trot and back; working canter to lengthened canter and back. There are some challenges here in showing changes that are clear and definite but smooth. Riders are especially lax about downward transitions, being inclined to just gradually get slower. Note that transitions are always made to adjacent gaits—the next faster or slower pace. The only exception is the trot-halt-trot transition which is no longer permitted to be performed through the walk as it was at Training Level. More difficult transitions, such as walk to canter, and extended trot to collected trot, come at higher levels.

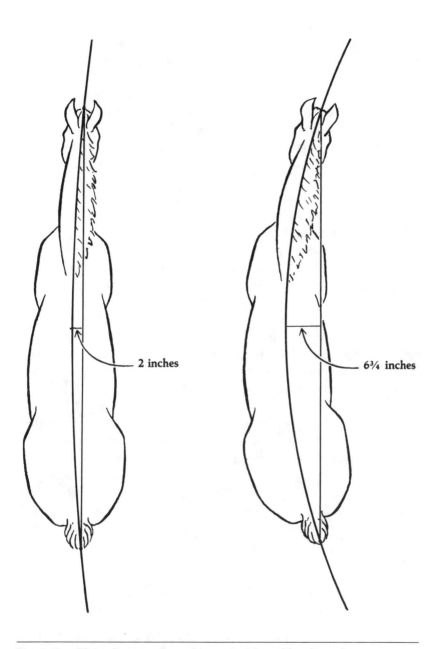

Figure 41. These diagrams show the required lateral bending of
the horse's spine, which varies from 2 inches when performing a
20-meter circle to 6¾ inches when performing a 6-meter circle.

The *place* where trot-canter transitions must be performed shows slightly increasing difficulty as you move along. The easiest place to perform a canter depart is on a large circle, and points "K," "A," and "F" at one end of the arena (and "M," "C," and "H" at the other end) are on ready-made, large, half circles supported by the fence. This is where you begin to teach the horse to canter. At first, canter departs are located on these half circles or the more difficult large circle between "B" and "E," and always at points where you are supported by the fence. Then at First Level Test 1, you are not on a circle but coming out of a circle and starting down the long side at "M."

The change of lead through the trot at "X" is still more difficult. You are definitely on the straight, there is no fence anywhere near, and you are, in addition, supposed to trot only two or three steps before departing into canter on the other lead.

Thus, very gradually, new problems and difficulties are introduced, and the horse's suppleness, impulsion, and obedience must increase along with the rider's skill. When you tackle a new exercise it sometimes seems impossible at first, but a few weeks or months later you will be doing it routinely and wondering whether you and your horse are ready for the next step. Dressage is a never-ending succession of challenges and, with good instruction, achievements. You will even find that your ability to memorize longer and more complicated tests and perform them with confidence will increase with practice.

It should be fairly obvious now that by simply practicing the movements, figures, and transitions of progressively more difficult tests, you have a training program. Even after you can perform a good working trot, you still have a long way to go in learning to maintain it throughout simple figures and then increasingly difficult figures. When you work your horse, you should change the locations of the exercises for variety, but take care that your variations do not unintentionally add extra difficulties with which you are not ready to cope.

The AHSA Second Level Tests

The *purpose* of the Second Level tests is stated to be:

. . . a degree of suppleness, balance, and impulsion. . . . the rider must now add "accuracy" and put the horse on the bit and keep it there without shortening the strides . . . neck relaxed and nose slightly in front of the vertical.

The message here is that accuracy in performing the figures will be expected (the "geometry," as it is often called), and lapses will be more heavily penalized. Beyond that, more suppleness, more impulsion, and improving balance and contact will be required. Balance is first mentioned here and is related to collection.

In the *general requirements for the horse* (the collective marks) "engagement of the hind quarters" and "lightness of the forehand" are added. These are emerging characteristics of collection.

The *movements, figures,* and *transitions* are as follows:

Second Level			
Test 1	*Test 2*	*Test 3*	*Test 4*
	MOVEMENTS		
Collected trot	Medium canter		Half turn on the
Medium trot	Collected canter	—	haunches in walk
Rein back	Travers		Counter canter
Shoulder-in at trot			
	FIGURES		
—	—	10-m figure 8 in trot at X	Around the end in counter canter
		18-m half circle, change, and reverse in canter	
	TRANSITIONS (gaits)		
H-RB-W	Collected canter,	H-RB-T	
W-C	medium canter,	Simple change of	—
Collected trot medium trot, and back	and back	lead (C-W-C)	
Working walk, medium walk, and back			
	TRANSITIONS (places)		
Canter depart at C	Collected trot to	Simple change	Travers to small
Collected trot on 10-m circle to shoulder-in	shoulder-in starting down long side at K or F	crossing center line	circle in collected trot
	Collected trot on 10-m circle to travers	Shoulder-in to medium trot on diagonal	Simple change coming out of small circle at E

Requirements for the Horse

Again we will first discuss the general objectives in order to get an idea of what our training program ought to achieve. How will these advances be manifested: increased suppleness and impulsion, improved balance, correct and steady contact, and in addition, engagement of the hind quarters and lightness of the forehand?

Increased *lateral suppleness* is required by more abrupt changes of direction. For example, in Test 3, the 10 meter figure of 8 necessitates a quick change of bend. There has to be lateral bending to one side, straightening, and immediate bending to the other side. Similarly in Test 3, there is an 18 meter half-circle in canter ending with a simple change of lead and an immediate change of direction on the new lead. The horse must be more supple to do these figures smoothly. Also when doing lateral movements he should be able to bend better through the body than he did at First Level.

Longitudinal suppleness, which refers to the bending of the spine in a vertical plane, has previously only been mentioned. (See page 111.) The principle exercises to improve longitudinal supple-

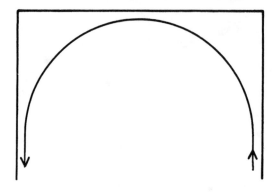

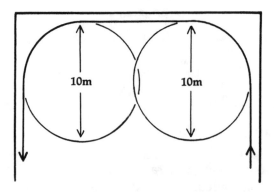

Figure 42.   The top diagram shows how the end of the arena may be ridden on canter departs at Training Level. The bottom diagram shows how it should be ridden at Second Level.

ness are transitions, and there are many of them at Second Level. First there are the transitions from working or collected gaits to medium gaits and back again. Longitudinal suppleness is necessary in the transitions from more collected to more extended gaits or vice versa, in which the frame is lengthened or shortened. Then there is the canter depart from walk and the simple change of lead which is a canter-walk-canter sequence. The walk must be collected a little in preparation for the upward transition, and the canter must be collected a little in preparation for the downward transition. The rein-back is also a suppling exercise, and the rider should sit lightly so the horse can raise and flex his loin easily when he steps back. Longitudinal suppleness is necessary for the "rounder" frame of a collected horse.

Increased *impulsion* or *engagement*—also called greater use of haunches—is necessary as more difficult exercises are added to the tests. The horse simply has to put forth more effort to do them with unchanged rhythm and constant speed. Lateral work, which now includes travers and shoulder-in, requires more effort, and the tests contain successions of turns, circles, and lateral work which are strenuous for the horse. In exercises like these, most horses have a natural tendency to slow down and lose impulsion which the trainer must overcome.

Collected trot and canter also require more impulsion—now generally called engagement because a slight lowering of the croup is a sign of the collection. In fact, some judges will comment "lacks impulsion" at First Level and "lacks engagement" at Second for what is essentially the same failing. Although collection is specified at Second Level, it is really only slightly increased over First Level, and is a natural development of practicing the new movements and figures. It is probably best not to try to actively "collect" the horse.

Balance is first mentioned at this level, and it is supposed to improve further as you progress. This seems like the right place to explain it thoroughly. The term balance seems to me to have two meanings, one rather general and the other peculiar to dressage. The *general* meaning is the common-sense meaning. If the horse is "well-balanced" he does the various movements and figures smoothly and easily without stumbling or lurching and with a steady head. Some horses are naturally athletic and agile; others seem clumsy and awkward and lose their rhythm at the slightest difficulty.

The special dressage meaning of balance refers to the distribution of weight between front and hind legs. Podhajsky puts the dressage definition of balance very clearly:

> *Few horses are naturally balanced, that is to say, carry an even proportion of their weight on forehand and hindquarters. . . . Most horses . . . will carry a greater proportion of their weight on the forehand, a fact which will be still more noticeable when the rider mounts. The hind legs will push the weight more than they carry it, a fault which must be corrected if the paces are to be made as light and elastic as is expected from a school horse.*
>
> *The object of the training will be to correct the balance by making the hindquarters carry a greater proportion of the weight. . . . (Podhajsky, p. 41.)*

Of course, having more weight on the front legs is only "incorrect" if you are doing advanced dressage. At First and Second Levels, and in other types of American riding, there is always more weight on the front feet—but even then, there must not be *too* much. In the general requirements, the word "lightness" (subhead under *Submission*) means not having too much weight on the forefeet. The ordinary American expression which indicates that there is too much weight on the forelegs is "on the forehand," usually meaning that the horse's head is too low and he is heavy on the bit. As a consequence of such a head carriage the burden on the forelegs is increased.

Another expression that you may know is "forward balance." Littauer says:

> *I have already pointed out that the constantly recurring moments of equilibrium lost and again retrieved are a part of the mechanics of the horse's movements. But even in this constant shifting of weight, a certain point of the horse's body can be considered as an average centre of gravity. In the case of a free-moving horse this point is approximately somewhere on the line immediately behind the withers, while in the case of a horse collected up to a certain degree, it is on the line passing through the centre of the body. The first case can be loosely termed Forward Balance and the latter Central Balance.*
>
> *If a rider hunts and jumps on the basis of ordinary gaits (not collected gaits) then his horse moves in Forward Balance. . . . (Littauer, p. 12.)*

There are different degrees of collection. They are the results of varying amounts of the horse's weight being transferred from the forehand to the hindquarters while a greater or lesser impulse forward is maintained. The more the weight is transferred to the rear and the greater the impulse forward, the higher will be the degree of collection. This shifting of the weight manifests itself in the raising of the neck, the bending of the hindlegs in all joints, and the sloping of the back to the rear. As a consequence of this new attitude of the horse the hindlegs diminish their horizontal thrusts forward and increase their vertical thrusts. (Littauer, p. 149.)

I have said that the working trot is slightly collected. The relation of this embryonic collection to *balance* would be that at the working trot there is a little more weight on the hindquarters than there was before. Podhajsky would say that balance is improving. Podhajsky's "correct balance" corresponds to Littauer's "central balance." As circles get smaller (and likewise corners) collection increases a trifle. The neck will be a bit higher, there will be a little more flexion at the poll, and the "impulse forward" will have to increase to maintain speed and rhythm and keep the haunches under the body on the sharper curves, thus improving balance. Circles are among the "collecting exercises." So is shoulder-in which encourages bending the joints of the inside hind leg as it reaches well under the body and takes the horse's weight. Also, true medium gaits show improved balance compared to mere lengthening. More weight is carried on the hind legs, and the forehand is accordingly lightened. This should be happening during the course of Second Level work. If the horse can perform all these exercises well, his balance and collection must be improving. On the other hand, if a judge comments, "too much on the forehand," or "falling on the forehand," this would indicate that the balance was not improving as it should.

Movements, Figures, and Transitions

Now let us examine the table showing the new movements, figures, and transitions required at Second Level. (See page 125.) Most of these have already been discussed in connection with the general requirements for the horse. In fact it seems as though Idiscuss everything several times over before I am finished, but usually each new item has several purposes, and you ought to understand all the ways in which it contributes to your horse's progress.

Shoulder-in and *travers* (haunches-in) are two new lateral exercises. Shoulder-in is universally practiced, but some trainers do not like travers, saying that horses have a tendency to be crooked and carry their haunches in off the track, so why encourage this? It is meant, however, to lead up to two-track. In travers, the front legs continue straight along the track while the haunches are moved away from the rail, and the body of the horse is curved or bent. In shoulder-in, the haunches move straight along the rail while the shoulders bend to the inside. If you can do both exercises, you can move either end of the horse and are prepared for two-track wherein you must move and regulate the position of both ends. In both exercises, the horse must be on the bit and a little collected in order to bend his body around your leg.

Half turn on the haunches at walk is introduced in Test 4. Later, when the horse is doing collected walk, and the turn is done out of collected walk, it is called a pirouette. The difference between the two movements is that in turn on the haunches the horse is permitted to make a very small circle with his inside hind leg. (See Figure 82.) In the pirouette, the inside hind foot should be lifted and set down on one spot. It is very difficult to do this movement well in spite of its apparent simplicity, and many Grand Prix horses do not do it well. There are many difficulties. The horse can lose his bend, come off the bit, fail to maintain the regular walk rhythm, pivot on the inside hind foot instead of raising and setting it down in the walk rhythm, step sideways, or worst of all, step backwards. All of these things can and do go wrong. I think I have spent more hours practicing turn on the haunches than any other one exercise. It certainly does help the rider to develop feel, as one must learn to feel exactly what the hind legs are doing.

Medium walk, *medium trot*, and *medium canter* are introduced at this level and as you would expect, are semi-extended paces. The fully extended forms of the gaits appear at Third Level and from then on, you must do both medium *and* extended trot and canter in every test. As you work for more and more extension it is easy to forget that the horse must become "more collected" at the same time. The croup must begin to be lowered a little at Second Level with more weight being carried on the hind legs and the head and neck must gradually assume a more "collected" position, although some extension of the neck must be permitted to enable the horse to extend.

Two more new movements are *rein back* and *counter canter*. These are easier, in that you probably can already do some sort of rein back, and we all do counter canter unintentionally from time to time. The difficulty lies in doing them correctly. Rein back must be straight and regular. The horse must be willing but must not "rush" back, and his head must remain in position. In Tests 1, 2, and 3, you are permitted to rein back 3 or 4 steps, but in Test 4 you must rein back exactly 4 steps. Rein back is a pace of two time, the legs being lifted and set down in diagonal pairs.

Counter canter is easy for some horses, hard for others. It means, of course, cantering on the "wrong" lead intentionally. I had one horse whose habit of leading with the inside foreleg was so ingrained that I never succeeded in getting him to strike off reliably with whichever leg I asked for. Other horses will change back unasked to the true lead. It is also sometimes hard for the rider to ride confidently at a brisk canter around small curves on the "wrong" lead if he grew up believing that a horse must go on the inside lead or be apt to cross his legs and fall down. Actually horses don't ever seem to trip or fall, but it can be a little scary. On the counter lead, the horse should be bent slightly to the leading leg, that is, to the left if cantering on the left lead on a right-hand circle. The horse must canter in the same frame and tempo as at the true canter. Remember, he is now doing collected canter, so the counter canter must be equally collected.

Counter canter is said to be an excellent suppling exercise. It is also a preparation for flying changes because to do flying changes when and where specified, you must obviously have complete control over the canter lead, and the horse must never change unless asked to do so.

Collected trot and *collected canter* are a very large subject, but will have to wait for full treatment for a book on Third and Fourth Levels. As I have said repeatedly, at this level, collection is a by-product of all your work on all the gradually more difficult movements, figures, and transitions. The most you would do, consciously, now, would be to ask for a *little* more impulsion and engagement with your driving aids while shortening the reins a *very* little bit.

The only really new *figure* is the *10 meter figure 8* in trot. It

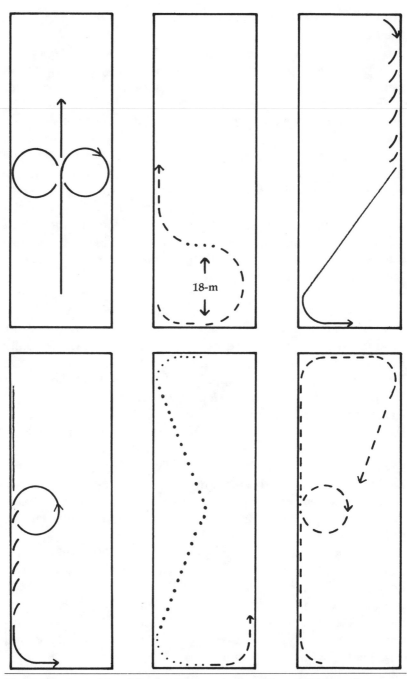

Figure 43.   Second Level figures. The trot is shown by a solid line, the canter by long dashes, the walk by dots. The curved lines represent shoulder-in and travers.

requires a lot of impulsion to keep the rhythm and speed and make a quick change of bend. It is only found in one test.

Walk-canter, required in all four tests, is one *transition* which seldom causes much trouble, probably because we were all used to doing it before we got into dressage. Nearly everyone knows how to collect the walk for a few steps and strike off into canter. Of course, the horse must be straight and keep his head in position. These strike-offs occur at "A" and "C" which means you are on a straight line with no assistance from the large circle. (See figure 42.) The *simple change*, canter-walk-canter, is a good deal harder. There are only supposed to be 2 or 3 walk steps, and, of course, no trot steps must be allowed to slip in. It comes in Tests 3 and 4 and the first two tests of Third Level. After that you must do flying changes.

The maneuver in Test 3 where the horse does an 18 meter half circle in canter, then a simple change, and then a turn in the direction of the new lead is not easy. Neither is the one in Test 4 consisting of a small circle and a simple change into counter canter. These exercises test everything: suppleness, balance, impulsion, and obedience.

There are some *other interesting transitions* at Second Level. The transitions into and out of shoulder-in and travers are meant to be as easy as possible, although they do require a lot of sustained impulsion. These movements are started as you come out of a turn or a circle, and are followed similarly by a turn or circle. The turns are a help, but technically, when one of these lateral movements ends near a corner, for example at "F," you should straighten before starting the turn around the corner. When the movement ends at "E" or "B," however, the lateral movement would merge smoothly into the circle. When you read the chapter on shoulder-in, you will discover that a small circle or turn with proper bend is a good way to lead into shoulder-in. Similarly with travers.

It is well to note that each new movement usually has a coefficient of 2 the first time or two that it occurs in a test. This means that it counts double when the test is scored. So you should be sure your horse is well schooled in each new movement before trying it at a show, if you want a good score.

8 Training Methods — The Working Trot

In this and the succeeding chapters, I intend to concentrate on theories and methods of *developing the horse's trot, straightening and bending* him, and doing *shoulder-in* (plus leg-yielding). These are major objectives, and the mastering of them is very important for all subsequent work. That is why a chapter is devoted to each of them. The other movements included in First and Second Levels will be dealt with together in the following chapter. The half-halt, which is necessary for canter-walk transitions, is discussed in the chapter on rider aids.

Development of the trot—first a good working trot, and then as time goes on, enough collection for Second Level—is a prerequisite for just about everything. In particular, it is necessary for bending the horse and for performing shoulder-in and travers. If the horse is doing only a natural trot, you will be able to bend only his neck, not his body. He will not be "straight" on curved paths, nor will shoulder-in be shoulder-in. Instead it will be only a form of leg-yielding. You cannot develop lateral suppleness without the working trot. That is why this topic is addressed first.

This chapter will probably seem very complicated on first reading. Do not expect to understand it all at once. Many things cannot be understood until they have been felt. There is a summary on page 152 that should come as a relief after struggling through the theories and quotations. You can use this chapter for reference as various topics come up in your work with your instructor, and eventually everything should fall into place. If certain problems do not occur with your particular horse, the discussions of these problems may never seem very relevant to you.

On the Bit with Impulsion—the Working Trot

Assuming that a horse is relaxed, accepts the bit, is moving freely forward, and is obedient enough to get a "passing" score at Training Level, it is time to put him "on the bit" and get him moving with "impulsion." In other words, it is time to learn the "working trot." Sometimes it comes easily and is accomplished in a few weeks; but often, especially with an older horse that has different habits of long standing, it may take a year or even longer. Some riders "get it" quickly, while others, even though they may have ridden successfully for years, find it very, very, difficult.

There is surprisingly little about the working trot in some of the classics, and I have been an observer at many clinics in which it was not even mentioned although the clinic leader often mounted a participating horse and demonstrated his skill by putting the horse on the bit. This can usually be done by an experienced trainer in a few minutes, though if he were training the animal he would, for a time, undoubtedly ride it on the bit only to a limited degree. I think the reason European writers rarely dwell on the working trot is because it is so obvious, so ordinary, and consequently so simple for them. If you had your first lessons on a horse that was accustomed to going on the bit, and if it was almost the first thing you were taught, you would not make a big thing of it either. Furthermore, a young horse in the hands of an expert trainer learns to go on the bit almost without either the horse or rider noticing it. Wätjen, for example, allots less than a page to the topic.

> From the beginning it is essential that the horse learns to react willingly to the driving aids, and to recover its natural balance under the weight of the rider, without at this stage, considering its head and neck position. Very gradually the rider can seek for a contact at the trot. Rising is advisable [posting]. He has to be extremely

careful to put the horse very gently to the bit with increased driving aids. The quietly restraining hands put the horse straight and try to find equal contact with both reins. In this way the young horse learns by a gentle pressure from both legs, helped by the whip, to stretch itself to the bit.

When the horse is gaining strength and becoming more supple in the back, one can start to ride with a slight collection, but only in trotting. (Wätjen, p. 7.)

And there, the horse is on the bit and doing working trot. It is all perfectly simple and clear to the expert.

Seunig, on the other hand, is always thorough. Several quotations can be assembled from his book to give a picture of the working trot.

The working trot is the gait at which most of our future training of the horse occurs. (Seunig, p. 154.)

. . . the working trot must be regular, i.e., well-timed, long-striding, and lively. If the horse's timing is faulty, its feet [do not alight] at uniform intervals of time. . . . (Seunig, p. 155.)

Liveliness of the gait is naturally limited by timing and length of stride. Once the horse advances as far forward as its conformation allows in order to take as long a stride as possible, it can take only a certain number of steps per time interval. If it takes more, it begins to hurry, or it must make them shorter than they should be; if it takes fewer, it is holding back. No matter which it does, it is violating regularity and timing. (Seunig, p. 155.)

Our ability to make vigorously engaged hind legs bend even more during the few instants they are grounded results in an alternately increased extension and flexion of the hindquarters.

This gradually converts the natural trot into the working trot. . . . The horse must allow itself to be driven at the working trot. *This does not mean . . . faster or hastier running. All it means is that seat and controls* must make sure that the rate is always a bit faster than the natural trotting rate spontaneously offered by the horse. (Seunig, pp. 153–154.)*

If the horse allows itself to be driven . . . it lengthens its stride while retaining its timing. . . . (Seunig, p. 150.)

---

*Throughout Seunig's book, the word "controls" is used to mean "aids."

Corresponding to the greater amount of ground covered . . . these oscillations of the leg will be communicated to the elongating back and neck musculature in waves that are more energetic and longer. . . . They will travel as far as the back of the horse's head and result in extension of the poll. This initial extention is a forward stretching of the body to reach the passively awaiting hand, which elastically accepts the weight laid in it by the horse. This constitutes the beginning of the horse's contact with the bit. . . .

When a driving seat is used, the horse's contact with the bit will cause it to come forward to the rider's hands, its mouth, poll, and neck yielding and becoming supple while chewing on the bit. (Seunig, p. 115.)

[The horse achieves] correct contact with the bit, that is, the stretching of the entire spinal column, including the vertebrae of the neck, to reach the bit, which is produced by the uniform engagement of both hind legs. (Seunig, p. 124.)

To summarize, Seunig says that a working trot involves a long stride (tracking up) and as many steps per minute as can be attained with this long stride. Besides tracking up and going at a good speed, the joints of the hind leg should bend when the foot is grounded. You will recall that these two things—a long stride and bending of the joints—comprise "engagement." The improved engagement causes extension of the poll or stretching to reach the bit which is the desired contact ("on the bit"). When all this is right, the horse chews.

The two aspects of engagement are clarified by Littauer:

The word "engagement" is here used to denote the movement of one of the hindlegs forward under the body (at gaits they always engage separately). After engaging, a hindleg goes back and out (disengages) from under the body as much as it went forward an instant before. . . . The greater the engagement, the longer the stride. . . . (Littauer, p. 30.)

. . . there is much loose talk about engagement at collected gaits and claims are often made that it is at collected gaits that the greatest engagement is found. This obviously is not so, because the result of engagement (in the above sense) is speed, and collected gaits, being slow, cannot have great engagement. . . . At the acme of collection at a trot, the Piaffe or trot in place, there is no engagement at all in the sense of the hindlegs moving forward to push the horse ahead. This is why the trot is in place. In this last case the

hindlegs, while marking time almost in place, remain constantly under the croup; they neither go under nor out. The horse rather "sits" on his hocks, his back sloping to the rear and hindlegs bent in all joints. These conditions, in different degrees are typical of all collected movements and today are frequently referred to as "lowering of the croup." However, most of us traditionally still call this also "engagement" and thus confuse the novice. (Littauer, pp. 30–33).

Since working trot is a little bit collected, the bending of the joints should increase with working trot. The principle of bending the joints is shown in Figure 44 which is adapted from Müseler's book. By bending all the joints of the hind leg while the foot is on the ground—the hip, stifle, hock, and fetlock—the hind leg compresses like a spring and the croup is lowered. This, together with the relaxation of the back, takes the shock out of sitting trot. When the legs touch the ground, the spring is compressed and the croup goes down a little. The loin becomes flatter, and the croup slopes more to the rear. A rider on a truly collected horse (lots of engagement of the second kind) can be seen to bounce up and down as the spring (hind leg) expands and contracts.

Figure 44.   Adapted from Müseler's *Riding Logic,* page 99, this well-known diagram shows the bending of the joints of the hind leg, which lowers the croup, and the raising of the neck. The outlines range from a natural halt to extreme collection in the piaffer.

Another quotation from Littauer will add to our understanding of the term "on the bit." He distinguishes very clearly between being "on contact" which was attained at Training Level, and being fully "on the bit."

> *Riding on contact is also called riding on the bit, or being, or moving on the bit, and unquestionably it is. I prefer, however, to differentiate between the two degrees of the same thing, "on contact" being the milder form. Now what precisely is the difference? Unfortunately it is one of those things which are so easy to point out in actuality and so difficult to describe in words. Here is my best attempt: Suppose that after you have established contact between your hands and the mouth of a schooled horse you were to continue to urge the horse forward and you were to do it with increased strength. What will happen then? Evidently the horse will try to increase the speed of the gait. But if, at the same time, you restrain him with your hands just enough to maintain the original speed yet continue to urge, then the horse will accept the bit more firmly, slightly leaning on it. Concurrently, the energy which your legs have created and which your hands have prevented from being transformed into speed will form a reserve of energy inclosed between legs and hands. It will keep the horse in an animated state and he will begin to move more vigorously although maintaining the ordinary trot. The cooperation between your legs and hands will enable you to obtain the maximum unity between the actions of the hindquarters and of the forehand. The horse's gait may become what is called* brilliant. *A movement of a better quality, academically speaking, is characteristic of riding fully on the bit. (Littauer, p. 53.)*

This paragraph is followed by a warning which it may not be amiss to repeat:

> *. . . brilliance of gaits is not an advantage in hunting or in ordinary jumping. It is rather an evil, because a very alert emotional state in the horse tends to border on excitement. . . . The brilliant gaits will not get you there faster and will tire your horse more quickly. . . . The average rider, if riding on the bit in the full sense of the word, will stiffen his horse, harden his mouth, excite him and may turn him into a habitual puller. It requires a technique the mastering of which calls for more time than the majority of amateur riders in the United States have at their disposal. (Littauer, p. 54.)*

We are, of course, engaging in a specialized sport which requires riding on the bit, and we will take the time to acquire, with the help of an instructor, the proper techniques. And we will not put our horses on the bit when riding informally on the trail or across country.

Some writers and trainers use the term "putting the horse to the aids," rather than "putting the horse on the bit," which has the advantage of being a broader term so that the beginner does not unduly concentrate on the reins and hands and ignore the part played by the driving legs. According to Müseler, the horse has been "put to the aids" when it is relaxed and responsive to the combined rein, leg, and back aids. (See Müseler, *Riding Logic*, page 89.)

How is this achieved? Previously, I quoted Müseler's instructions for getting the horse to relax and extend his neck. (See Part I, page 64.) He goes on to "put the horse to the aids." It sounds deceptively simple:

> *As soon as the horse comfortably stretches his neck all the rider has to do is to utilize this forward urge and to let the reins act passively. The horse will then quite automatically lean on the bit and begin to chew it. (Müseler, p. 83.)*

> *The strides will become more and more quiet and, through constant driving and urging, longer. The horse's back will begin to swing pleasantly, it will be rounded with each step, and all muscles will play freely. (Müseler, p. 84.)*

The rider continues to drive the horse forward on a large circle changing direction from time to time. He should make the horse go a little faster than it wants to go, until the horse, bored by the whole thing, goes steadily with neck stretched and a nice feel on the bit.

You obviously cannot do this by yourself, especially as you do not yet have a feel for what you are trying to achieve. Without the aid of a good teacher you will either achieve nothing at all, or else you are likely to end up with some of the undesirable results that Littauer described. Although it almost seems as though Müseler and Littauer are describing different things, they are not; each of the quotations gives us important clues as to what we will be doing when we begin to put a horse on the bit so that he can perform a proper working trot.

While putting a young horse to the aids is so easy for Müseler, he devotes many pages (*Riding Logic,* pages 89–96) to "putting the horse to the aids" when it is an older, spoiled animal, and you might find this interesting reading. Actually, putting the horse to the aids is the German way of referring to the horse's entire elementary training, or in this case, retraining.

Colonel Podhajsky does not use the term "on the bit"* although he discusses straightening the horse and overcoming problems of crookedness in a way that requires the horse to be on the bit. Quotations will be presented when this topic is discussed.

The AHSA *Rulebook* includes a definition of "on the bit." It is not terribly clear or helpful, but here it is:

> *A horse which is on the bit (on the aids) accepts with no resistance a light contact of the rein, is yielding in the jaw and poll, to the rider's hand; moreover, the horse accepts the rider's aids to ride the horse forward into the rein. A horse which is on the bit moves with a supple back, shows no resistance in transitions and remains submissive to the rider. The position of the horse when on the bit depends on the conformation as well as the degree of training of the horse. The light contact of a horse on the bit, or lack of it, can be detected only from the saddle. However, the results of a horse's actions while on the bit or off the bit can be evaluated on sight. Care should be taken to consider the action of the entire horse, and not just his head, when evaluating whether or not a horse is on the bit.* (AHSA, Rulebook, *pp. 172–73.)*

The effect of the "degree of training" on the position of the horse would be that as training progresses and the horse becomes more collected, the neck rises, the poll flexes more, and the face comes closer to the vertical. Thus there is not just one position of head and neck possible when the horse is on the bit. Also, the head and neck position may be consistent with being on the bit, but if the horse is not moving correctly or is not making a proper contact, he is not on the bit. His head could be correct even though he was rushing or, at the the other extreme, doing a jog trot.

---

*I might add that the trainer and instructor, Robert Hall—a pupil of the Spanish Riding School—does not mention "on the bit" either. After six months at his school I had learned to make the school horses do a working trot, but I had never heard the term "on the bit." Nor have I heard it used by Franz Rochawansky, former oberbereiter of the School, who in recent years has been teaching in England, Europe, and America.

Though the position of head and neck is not the whole story, it is very important. So far we have considered mostly the position of the *neck*. The French school emphasizes reactions of the jaw and poll which, of course, mainly affect the position of the *head*. The French do not use the term "on the bit" or "working trot." The emphasis in their early training is on yielding the jaw and flexing the poll. These have also been mentioned by Seunig and Müseler, but only rather incidentally. For the French school, they are the center of attention.

The flexion of the poll is what Americans refer to as the horse's "head set," and the yielding of the jaw is related to "having a soft mouth," or "having a good mouth," or at least not having a "hard mouth." The horse's mouth is crucial, and we would do well to try to be aware of and understand its role.

Let us start by quoting from Decarpentry. General Decarpentry was a member of the Cadré Noir, second-in-command of the French cavalry school at Saumur, an international judge, and president of the FEI Dressage Committee. He died in 1956. His very clear and understandable book is called, *Academic Equitation*. We need to get used to two French terms, *Ramener* (pronounced rah-muh-nay) and *Mise en Main* (pronounced meez-aw-maaa, the last syllable is like the sound a sheep makes but is not prolonged). They mean literally "led back" and "put in hand."

> The "Mise en Main" is the relaxation of the mouth in the position of the ramener. . . .
> The relaxation of the mouth essentially consists in a movement of the tongue similar to that which it does in the act of swallowing, when upper and lower jaw separate only to the extent required to permit the movement of the tongue.
> This movement, a slow and supple one, causes the parotid [salivary] glands to come out of their lodging, induces a slight salivation, lifts the bit or bits which the tongue draws towards the rear of the mouth and then drops as it resumes its place in its channel. As they drop, the bits chink, producing a typical clinking noise. [If the horse is in a double bridle.]
> . . . The head must remain set, not even giving a hint of movement, not even a "yes" nod, while the lower jaw softly relaxes in the small measure necessary to allow the tongue to move. (Decarpentry, p. 63.)
> The Ramener is the closing of the angle of the head with the neck, the poll remaining the highest point of the latter.

The Ramener is said to be complete when the nose reaches the vertical; if the nose comes behind the vertical, the horse is no longer "ramené", he is overbent. (Decarpentry, p. 68.)

The *Mise en Main* is obtained before the *Ramener* (Decarpentry, page 149). According to Decarpentry, however, the *Mise en Main* is not normally taught to the horse. Instead, when everything else is right, the horse offers it.

Once the horse has found the attitude suited to the work demanded of him and can hold it without unnecessary effort, with complete control of his balance and perfect ease of movement; once, to quote the old French masters: "Le cheval se plait dans son air", (the horse is happy in his work), the muscles, which were cramped by the horse's attempts to adapt himself to his rider's demands, relax and their relaxation is progressively communicated and extended to the entire muscular system.

The stage of rather uncertainly directed efforts during which the horse, just as man, had clenched his teeth, is succeeded by a state of harmony in the use of energy, of relaxation, which causes the jaws to unclench and the horse to salivate. . . . (Decarpentry, pp. 63–64.)

The mobilisation of the mouth, which is the essential part of the Mise en Main, *then occurs almost always spontaneously. In order to preserve its character as evidence of the perfect adjustment of energy to movement, i.e. of perfect lightness, it will be enough to avoid interfering with its occurrence.*

The numbness of some horses' mouths, despite the correct distribution of forces that shows in the ease of their movements and the softness of the reactions felt by the rider's seat—nearly always originates in their distrust of the hands, if lack of tact has discouraged their first relaxations. Most of the time, all that is needed to regain the confidence of those horses is a generous "yielding of the hand" at the slightest sign of mobility in the mouth, which one must learn to await with patience and to watch for with unflagging attentiveness. (Decarpentry, p. 65.)

Seunig gives a similar description of "chewing," which is obviously the German equivalent of *Mise en Main.*

When the horse achieves suppleness by stretching out to reach the bit, it comes up to the bit and chews, which is its acknowledgement of the correct action of the reins and of the concert of all the controls and proof that the horse carries itself. (Seunig, pp. 70–71.)

> *There is a* right way of chewing and a wrong one. *In the right way the lower jaw is hardly open, and the lips are closed. . . . These movements of a relaxed masseter muscle . . . convert the saliva into foam, which is visible at the horse's mouth.*
>
> *This chewing is directly produced by a swallowing (rather than chewing) action of the tongue. This movement also increases the secretion of the parathyroid [?] glands, which become more prominent.*
>
> *Chewing that coincides with the gait's rhythm is wrong. (Seunig, footnote p. 70.)*
>
> *Nosebands that are buckled too tight prevent the horse from chewing and cause a dead mouth. (Seunig, footnote, p. 71.)*

To sum up, the horse should prove that everything is all right by carrying out a swallowing activity with his tongue and jaw and producing foam. The horse must reach for the bit, yet hold up his own head and neck ("carry himself") and not expect the rider to hold them up with the reins. When the horse does not carry himself, he is said to use the reins for a "fifth foot."

Now let us see how Wynmalen relates the flexion of jaw and poll to the working trot. He uses French terminology, but seems to have reversed the order in which he obtains the two effects. Remember, as you read the quotation, that the working trot is the first step in the process of collecting the horse.

> *A reasonable degree of "collection" is of course essential to any form of "horsemanship" worthy of that name. . . .*
> . . . .
> *The first step is the attainment of a measure of acceptance of the bit, characterized by flexions of the jaw, accompanied by a measure of flexion at the poll, resulting in a measure of correct head carriage. It is what the French call* le ramener, *which I would like to translate as "obtaining head carriage". Actually the literal translation is "bringing the head back into position". And, unfortunately, that is more often that not the manner wherein this head position is obtained, with fatal results to the horse's further progress.*
>
> *However, done properly, this position of the* ramener *constitutes already some degree of collection; we might perhaps call it "collection of the first degree." This time the accent is on "done properly", namely by riding the horse forward, towards his head and not by pulling the horse's head back towards his body. (Wynmalen, p. 112.)*

> *. . . whatever the head carriage may look like, it can be of no value unless it is based on increased energy of the quarters, resulting in free and improved forward movement. (Wynmalen, p. 113.)*

Improved forward movement (impulsion, tracking up) plus some flexion of the poll so that the horse does not "poke his nose out," and possibly some flexions of the jaw (chewing) is a pretty good summary of a working trot.

Wynmalen then speaks of "collection in the second degree," which he says is known in France as "going in hand" (*la mise en main*) and in England as "collection." This more advanced form of the trot which he then describes is called "collection" in our dressage tests, too, and is not required until Third Level.

There is, or at least there was, a difference between French and German dressage. The French emphasized the sensations reaching the rider's hand from the horse's mouth as an indicator of the correctness of the horse's gaits, while the Germans emphasized the sensations reaching the rider through his seat from the horse's back. This difference is pointed up in a footnote by Decarpentry's translator:

> *. . . germanic equitation in its present state . . . increasingly ignores the mobility of the mouth, even when it does not actually condemn it, while on the contrary Baucher [a French master] made it the subject of his first lesson. . . .*
>
> *. . . Baucher's pupils did not attach sufficient importance to the value of the impression received through the seat. . . .*
>
> *. . . in countries where Baucher's influence was small or nonexistent—in Central Europe for example—the value of the mobility of the mouth as a proof of lightness is often neglected, while the one given by the feeling in the seat is carefully observed, often to the exclusion of everything else. (Decarpentry, a note by the translator, p. 13.)*

I should add that Decarpentry tried to convince each side of the merits of the other. In fact, since his book was published, the differences in Europe have become less distinct as members of each school have observed and have learned from the other. I mention these complex matters in an elementary book, because your instructor may lean one way or the other; if I mentioned only one school, you would be confused if your instructor belonged to the other.

The warning given by Wynmalen—that to obtain the flexion of the poll the horse must be driven forward to the bit rather than the bit being pulled back closer to the body—is repeated in many places. For example, Froissard writes:

> It must be achieved by an advance of the body toward the head, not a retreat of the head toward the body; for although you can obtain the same result by both procedures, the consequences of the resulting head carriage are diametrically opposed. With the first procedure, the horse goes into this head carriage by forward movement, capital element never to be lost from sight. The least of the evils resulting from the second would be to teach him to yield to a traction of the bit by retracting head and neck. Rarely can the trainer's skill arrest the retraction at this point, which usually spreads all along the spine and arrives at the retraction of the entire body, the feet remaining at their place—the backward flow of energies. It therefore is preferable to choose the slightly longer, but safer road. (Froissard, p. 66.)

It was not clear to me what this and similar warnings meant, and I was never sure what the distinction between "the body advancing toward the head" and "the head retreating toward the body" was, exactly, until I found the following discussion in Decarpentry:

> But the intrinsic advantages of the Ramener are accompanied by serious drawbacks when it is obtained by drawing the head and neck towards the trunk, because the Ramener then necessarily communicates this backward movement to the trunk itself. To start with, the feet remain in the same position, the limbs incline backwards from the feet up; the horse tends to squat on his haunches. Then, to avoid the instability of this awkward position, the horse moves his hind legs backwards; he becomes stretched out with a hollow back, ("il se campe") whereas the whole progression of dressage aims at driving the horse forward into the opposite attitude of collection.
>
> When the Ramener is obtained by means of progressively tighter side reins worn in the stable, the horse almost inevitably assumes one or the other of these two faulty attitudes. If the horse is walked in hand, or lunged with side reins, those dangers can be partly avoided if the trainer is very skilled and vigilant.
>
> However, even in those conditions, the practice of flexions of the poll, amounts nonetheless to teaching the horse the art of coming

behind the bit, of escaping its contact by drawing away from it as little as may be, whilst in all the previous course of dressage the aim has been to "push him on to his bit", by making him "go into his reins", and "draw his cart". At the very best, there will be a reversal of direction in the conduct of dressage, and the slightest fault against impulsion committed by the trainer will completely contradict the whole of the horse's previous education. It is therefore prudent to give up methods that aim at drawing the head back towards the body, and to avoid trying to obtain the Ramener on a stationary horse. (Decarpentry, pp. 68–69.)

Here the French position is clear: Decarpentry and Froissard are opposed to obtaining the Ramener on a stationary horse! This is what is called, in America, "bitting up." Bitting up is a common procedure to improve a horse's head carriage. The reins are fastened, possibly by putting them around the back part of the saddle, so as to pull the horse's nose back into position and hold it there. Or fairly short side reins are attached to the bit—the horse being left to himself for a time in his stall or other enclosure to figure out the nature of this restraint and learn to yield to it. It is the practice of obtaining flexion of the poll on a horse that is standing still which is condemned.*

Teaching flexions of poll and jaw (*Ramener* and *Mise en Main*) is sometimes also done, as Decarpentry mentioned, by the trainer working on foot and the horse either standing still or walking forward. Instead of waiting for them to appear spontaneously, the trainer obtains the flexion of poll or jaw by manipulating the reins which he holds near the bit. This method was practiced by Baucher, a Frenchman who lived in the first half of the Nineteenth Century and who had great influence in Europe at the time. Decarpentry concedes that Baucher's method, when very skillfully used, may be satisfactory. I myself have never seen his method in practice.**

For all practical purposes, if you obtain flexion at the poll while riding the horse forward, you need not worry. You will be "driv-

---

*Wynmalen goes into detail about the ruinous effect of bitting up with a dumb jockey in his book *Equitation*, pages 52–53. He illustrates the two faulty positions described by Decarpentry.

**You can read about a similar technique in which the trainer works on foot to obtain flexions in James Fillis, *Breaking and Riding*, pages 32–39. So far as I know, no writings by Baucher are available.

ing the body forward toward the bit." You will have to drive the horse forward to maintain speed, otherwise the horse will slow down when he feels the restraining rein. If there is anything that dressage trainers seem to be unanimous about, 100 percent, it is their opposition to "bitting up."

Lieutenant Colonel Chamberlin, who studied French methods, very clearly details three phases in developing head carriage. His system, like Wynmalen's, is obviously derived from the French, but he has given it his own slant and the flexions have quite a different purpose. In phase one, the horse merely accepts a steady contact with the bit, carrying neck and head in a natural extended position. I have already quoted this on pages 69-70. In phase two, the flexing of jaw and poll occur together with lateral flexing of the neck. The third phase is collection proper, or raising the neck, which Chamberlin recommends only in a very limited degree. At this point I would like to quote Chamberlin's description of phase two:

> . . . there are three steps to be accomplished in the second phase. . . .
> The three steps involve: first, relaxing the muscles of the lower jaw
> so that, in response to any continued tension stronger than the nor-
> mal support on one or both reins, the mouth opens (called flexion of
> the jaw); second, softening and bending the neck laterally, par-
> ticularly in the upper third of its length, by use of the direct rein;
> third, flexing the neck at the poll very slightly as a result of increas-
> ed tension on both direct reins [in halting or reducing the speed].
> The lateral flexion teaches the horse to bend his neck slightly and
> yield promptly in turning about and changing direction. The soften-
> ing and relaxation of the jaw and poll are for the purpose of
> developing spring-like actions which, as the horse learns to concede
> readily to the demands of the rider's hands, lessen the irritation of
> the bit to his mouth. The flexion of the poll is taught after the flex-
> ion of the lower jaw has become a habit, and must be cautiously
> and tactfully demanded. (Chamberlin, p. 57.)

> . . . when relaxing the jaw, the mouth should open easily, but only
> part way; there should be no continuous, wide gaping. As the
> rider's hands reward the jaw's relaxation by instantly releasing the
> additional tension momentarily, the mouth should close and chew
> softly once or twice as the bit's pressure diminishes. (Chamberlin,
> p. 58.)

Chamberlin's poll flexion is not what is required in the working trot. We want a slight change in head carriage with the head being continuously in a more vertical position so that the nose is not poked out. Nor have I heard elsewhere of the sort of yielding of the jaw that he recommends.

Chamberlin's methods hardly seem likely to result in overflexion of the poll, but his warning about the dangers of overflexion should not be ignored.

> *To the great detriment of the horse, poll flexion easily may be over-done, causing an exaggerated rounding of the neck. This brings the horse's face to a position back of a vertical plane so that his nose is near the neck or breast. Poor or inexperienced horsemen frequently obtain this faulty over-flexion, which is not produced at the poll, but in the middle and lower half of the neck. (Chamberlin, p. 57.)*

Flexion behind the poll, also called the "wrong bend," is serious and must be dealt with immediately if it should appear. (See pages 64–66.) It may or may not be accompanied by getting behind the bit. Seunig says:

> *If the horse shortens its neck downward in trying to escape from the contact with the bit . . . we get a so-called* wrong bend *between the second and third cervical vertebrae. . . .*
> *A horse with a false bend is not responsive, since it uses this as a valve, enabling the controls [aids] that should be allowed to pass through the entire spine to escape. (Seunig, p. 124.)*

It is interesting to know that for a time, Baucher, advocated this overflexion or wrong bend. Old pictures of Baucher and his followers frequently show horses in this position, as do equestrian statues and paintings of the period when his methods were popular. In the latter part of his life, Baucher changed his ideas and ceased to overflex his horses. So long as the poll is the highest point of the neck, the horse is not overflexed. It is easy to observe this from the saddle.

It is time now to *summarize the working trot.* The requirements of a correct working trot have been extracted from the previous quotations. One writer emphasizes one thing, and another writer emphasizes something else, so we must consider all of them to get a complete picture of what is to be achieved. I have listed the requirements in the order in which they might well be obtained, starting with the objectives described in the earlier chapters in connection with preparing the horse for Training Level competitions.

1. Neck in a low, extended position, back is up.

2. Slow, regular rhythm, result of relaxation and lowering the neck (about 156 steps per minute at trot).

3. Accepting the bit with steady head and no objection to a light contact.

4. Going freely forward at a good rate of speed without increasing the rhythm.

5. Some continuous flexion of the poll so that the nose is not poked out.

The horse is now on the bit.

6. A little more energy is demanded by driving leg or whip. The hind legs work more energetically, the horse stretches onto the bit with a little firmer contact, he tracks up or overtracks. A certain amount of energy is "imprisoned" between the rider's leg and hand.

Now the horse is on the bit with impulsion. (See Figure 45.)

The feeling of going "on the bit" with "impulsion" is what you must learn to recognize. There is a sensation of surging forward, or committed forward movement—or however it seems to you. My experience is that the horse also goes anywhere you steer him, on or off the track, without change in the sensation of purposeful advancing. He will perform a test in a dressage arena—where the almost nonexistent "rail" offers little or no guidance—much more accurately than before. Another thing you may notice when the "engine starts working behind" is sweating of the stifle area or, if it is winter, steaming of this area as well as of the shoulders.

It is often said that dressage improves obedience and that a horse that is on the bit is obedient. This is true in a certain sense. The horse does go where he is steered and does respond better to the aids when he is on the bit. But he can at any moment become

Figure 45.   The working trot. On the bit with enough impulsion
for the First Level. Poll area level. Left diagonal lifted well above
ground. Tail carriage also indicates increased impulsion. Compare
with Figure 37. Neck is stretched more forward in this instance
(stretching into the bit).

naughty or rebellious and come off the bit and be disobedient.
There is nothing necessarily automatic or permanent about the
horse's increased obedience, although he should be naughty less
often as training proceeds.

If all goes well, you will have two other dividends somewhere
along the way. First, the horse's back will relax and start to swing,
and it will at last be *easy* to sit the trot. This is because of the correct play of the back muscles and increased spring action in the
joints of the hind legs. It is, however, easy to be misled and think
that the back is swinging when it is not, for whenever impulsion
slackens and the horse stops "working behind," it is *also easy* to
stick to the saddle at the sitting trot. In fact, in the early stages
before the back relaxes, beginners are tempted to go at a lazy trot
because sitting an energetic trot is such hard work. The other divi-
dend is the yielding or mobilization of the jaw, which you may
notice and should reward by a brief relaxation of the fingers.

Problem	Detection	Remedy
Neck not down	Can see that poll is too high	Ask down, or walk horse with head in correct position and then push horse into trot
Nose poked out	The first six inches of the neck from the ears back slope down instead of appearing level	Gradually shorten reins while keeping horse going well forward with legs
Rushing	Rhythm (or rhythm and speed) too fast, easiest to detect at rising trot—posting is too fast	If horse is tense, slow his speed till rhythm improves, then drive on If horse is lazy, go faster to lengthen stride, then slow down
Impulsion lacking	Horse is not stretching into the bit (observer can see that horse is not engaging—you must know if your horse tracks up or not)	Drive on with leg or whip till he stretches, or go faster, or do some canter or lengthened trot to wake up the horse
Jaw hard, resisting	Horse is pulling or mouth feels dead	Jaw relaxes and horse chews when everything else is right (French). Vibrations or "asking" help
Back not relaxed	Trot is hard to sit	Relax yourself, relax thighs—horse's back swings when everything else is right (German). Post—horse not ready for lengthy periods of sitting trot

Other problems		Suggestions
Horse does not carry himself	I have not experienced these THANK GOODNESS	Loosen rein, refuse to hold up head Lifting type (French) half halt
Horse is overbent		Push up head with legs if horse is slow Lifting type half halt

Observers will see the dripping foam that accompanies it. Old horses may not develop the "chewing" or Mise en Main spontaneously. Decarpentry discusses remedies for this in his book beginning on page 139.

To perform a correct working trot you really must experience all six of the requirements listed. When my horse and I were learning the working trot it seemed as though a different thing was wrong at each lesson, so that the instructions I was receiving were always different. Eventually it all "came together," and I learned to notice and correct whatever deficiency the horse was exhibiting at the moment. That horse was a middle-aged Thoroughbred gelding, a former race horse and junior hunter.

Some dressage objectives seem clear and easy to understand; you feel that you know what you are looking for and that when they come, you will recognize them. "Stretching into the bit" was not one of these. It was one objective that seemed mysterious to me. You may feel as I did, that only very special horses and riders could be expected to achieve something so exotic. Well, although it was elusive at first, it really did happen. It was the noticing and remembering and reproducing of this sensation that finally made the working trot a reality for me. That horse's back did swing—although his tail did not. He did stretch forward into the bit, but only very occasionally did he produce any foam at all.

Although it is not my intention to try to teach readers how to teach their horses the working trot, the following chart may be helpful in conjunction with lessons from a good instructor. I compiled the list and showed it to my teacher when I had finally grasped all the elements of the process and had realized the purpose of the various instructions I had received. I am sure there are additional problems that I did not happen to experience, as well as other good "remedies." The methods of detection may differ, too. For instance, you have to learn just how your horse's poll and neck look to you from the saddle because conformation of horse and height of rider vary. This chart is not meant to be all-inclusive.

9 Training Methods— Straightness and Bending

A good deal has already been said about straightness and bending, so by this time you know pretty well what they are. To sum up briefly, the objective is to make the horse straight while traveling on straight lines, and curved when traveling on curved lines—in both cases to cause the hind feet to follow directly behind the forefeet. There are two problems: to straighten the horse if he is crooked, and to bend him, particularly his body, on turns, circles, and serpentines. He must also be bent when doing shoulder-in. This is called *lateral suppleness.*

As we approach this somewhat intricate subject let us ask first how crookedness is manifested and detected, then what causes it, and finally how it can be overcome. There is a great deal in the literature about it, so finding descriptions, explanations, and remedies is not difficult. As Seunig says:

> There is probably no subject in the whole realm of horsemanship about which there has been so much mysticism as crookedness, and I am inclined to believe that more has been written about this subject than about the same problem in human beings. (Seunig, p. 123.)

One crookedness problem that has been mentioned is the horse that canters with his haunches in. (See Figure 46.) There are

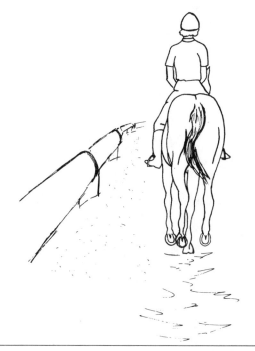

Figure 46.   Crooked canter—all four feet are visible. The leading (inside) forefoot is on the ground. The outside hind foot is on a path between the two forefeet. To be straight the haunches would need to be about six inches to the left. This is not bad for First Level, however.

really two aspects of this form of crookedness. They are shown in the illustration. It is not natural, actually, for the horse to canter with his spine perfectly straight. Normally it bends a little, and is concave on the leading side. In both drawings the spine is curved, consistent with the right lead. In the upper drawing the horse is cantering with haunches in. In the lower drawing the shoulders have been brought in front of the hindquarters and the horse is straight enough for lower-level dressage. (See Figure 47.) Judges watch for and expect this degree of straightness.

Straightening the *spine* for the higher levels is unnatural, and asking a horse to be straight at the canter is one unnatural thing that dressage trainers expect. The purpose of straightening the horse's spine at the canter is to make repeated changes of lead possible. A single flying change does not require a straight horse, but repeated changes every one, two or three strides do.

Figure 47.   Cantering horse with spine curved consistent with
right lead. In the upper diagram the horse is crooked— his
haunches are carried in. In the lower diagram he is straight
enough for lower levels—his hind feet are tracking his forefeet.

It is not hard to find out the degree to which your horse carries
his haunches in at the canter. If someone stands behind you as you
canter away from him, it will be easy to see whether the hind feet
are in line with and conceal the forefeet. Have the observer note
whether crookedness is more pronounced on one lead than on the
other. It usually is.

Another form of crookedness occurs at the trot, but with the
body straight rather than curved. Figure 48, taken from Podhajsky's book, illustrates this problem. In the lower sketch, although
the horse's spine is straight, he is "crooked" because his hind legs
do not follow his forelegs. Podhajsky elaborates as follows:

> *Horses are narrower through the shoulders than they are through
> the hips. If the outer side of the body is parallel to the wall, the
> hindquarters are carried further into the arena than the forelegs.*

Figure 48.   The lower horse is straight in the spine, but
"crooked." His hind feet do not track his forefeet. The upper
horse is curved in the spine, but "straight." His hind feet are
tracking his forefeet. Adapted from Podhajsky's *The Complete
Training of Horse and Rider,* **page 50.**

> *Also, by pushing his shoulder against the wall the horse can evade
> the guidance of the rider and cannot be turned so easily. On the
> other hand, which is a matter of greater consequence, he will be
> able to avoid, by this crookedness, the bending of the joints of the
> hind legs, thus escaping the gymnastic training of the hindquarters
> that is so necessary for balance and physical training.*
>
> *With a straight horse the spine must be parallel to the wall, that
> is, the distance from the outside shoulder to the wall must be greater
> than that of the outside hip.* * *(Podhajsky, p. 91.)*

*No doubt you have noticed that in the upper sketch the spine is not straight. Podhajsky
says on page 50, "A slight bend to the rein on which the horse is being ridden should always
be demanded from a trained horse in an arena even when on a straight line." This develops
gradually and almost unnoticeably. As one bends the horse for each corner, in time the
bend tends to persist between corners. Nevertheless, the horse is said to be straight because
the hind feet follow in the path of the fore feet.

With both types of crookedness mentioned so far, the horse is crooked to one side when traveling on the right rein, and to the other side when traveling on the left rein. There is a third type of crookedness, however, in which the horse is crooked always to the same side, either right or left, no matter which direction he travels around the ring or which lead he is on at the canter. This problem is the most often discussed and the most troublesome. It can be referred to as the problem of the *stiff and hollow sides.*

In this situation the neck bends easily to one side (described as the hollow, soft, concave, or difficult side) and resists bending to the other side (the stiff, convex, or constrained side). Podhajsky describes it in this way:

> . . . *a horse may not accept the bit evenly on both sides. He will make himself stiff on one side and will follow the slightest action of the rein on the other by turning his head. He will take a firmer contact and only reluctantly follow the action of the rein on the side on which he is stiff. On the other side he will anticipate the action of the rein and bend this way; that is to say, he becomes hollow on this side. (Podhajsky, p. 43.)*

In another place he describes it thus: (See Figure 49.)

> *Every horse will accept the reins in a different way when they are applied by the rider. The contact itself will be uneven: on one side it will be firm; on the other side soft or even non-existent. In equestrian terms the horse makes himself stiff on one side and hollow on the other. At the same time the hind leg on the stiff side (that on which the contact is firm) will be less bent than the hind leg of the hollow side (that on which the contact is soft) which will move more to that side so the track of this hind foot will be outside that made by the corresponding forefoot. This accounts for the* crookedness *of the horse. Nearly every horse tends to be crooked, but the degree will vary with the individual. It must be the rider's main object to overcome this fault and to make the contact with the bit equal on both sides of the horse's mouth. This object must be the rider's constant endeavour throughout the entire training. It is easier to overcome the crookedness in the young horse than it is in one that has not been made straight in his early training. (Podhajsky, p. 100.)*

Podhajsky's remark that straightening is a never-ending process is well taken. I recall once watching someone help a friend "unbend" her crooked horse. The helpee asked, "How long must I do this?" and the helper replied, "Forever."

How do you determine which is the hollow side of your horse? Here is one way as it is explained for the Pony Club:

> In order to ascertain which is the stiff side, the rider should walk the horse on a loose rein, then pick up the left rein only and if the pony answers immediately by turning his head to the left and moving off in that direction, it is almost certain that this is the soft side. If the rider now drops the left rein and picks up the right rein and he finds that the pony will not turn his head to the right but moves in that direction with a stiff jaw and neck, keeping his head straight or even turning it slightly to the left, then the right side is the stiff side. (Training the Young Pony, pp. 59–60.)

This procedure, however, does not always reveal the stiff side. I used to wonder why neither of my horses had a stiff and a soft side when the books said that all horses, or very nearly all, did have them. Not only did my horses turn equally well, but the contact with the bit was not stronger on one side than on the other. Finally the significance of a statement by Podhajsky sank in:

Figure 49.   The problem of the stiff side and the hollow side as described by Podhajsky.

> *When the reins are applied evenly the horse will bend his neck to the hollow side, on which he will not accept the rein. The rider will be able to recognize this as the rein will not touch the neck on this hollow side, whereas it lies close to the neck on the side on which the horse makes himself stiff. . . . (Podhajsky, p. 43.)*

In other words, while riding straight ahead I could take up the reins with an equal contact on each side, but then the horse's neck was *not quite straight*. When this is the case, you can see more of his bridle and eye on his soft side.

Another manifestation of the soft and stiff sides is apparent when you ask the horse to circle. Here I quote from the monthly publication of the California Dressage Society, *Dressage Letters*, Vol. III, No. 1, p. 4:

> *Another indication of the same problem is that a horse traveling on a circle in the direction of its hollow side will tend to drift out on a larger circle in trot, but will tend to decrease the circle at the canter. Why? The horse thus avoids bending the joints of that hind leg on the hollow side. Traveling in the other direction, just the reverse will be true, for the same reason. The symptom may be most noticeable to the horseman who is trying to establish a specific circle for his horse on the longe line. ("The Inside Hind Leg," by Melanie Lofholm, in collaboration with Hans Moeller.)*

I have found these effects very noticeable under saddle, too. For example, when doing a figure eight, one loop will get larger than desired and the other loop will get smaller.

Seunig has a different definition of straightness which emphasizes weight distribution:

> *Even loading on the near and off legs, no matter whether the forehand is more or less stressed than the hindquarters, is the distinguishing feature of correct . . . flexion.*
>
> *Any horse that satisfies this condition of even loading on the near and off legs, whether its body is actually a straight line or exhibits a certain flexion of the ribs, is straight. (Seunig, p. 119.)*
>
> *Impulsion and purity of gait can be maintained, even on two tracks, only if the off hind hoof carries the same share of the load as the near one.*
>
> *The only exception to this rule is work on a circle, where the natural tendency of the horse's body . . . to lean inward, obeying*

the law of centrifugal force on curved lines, places additional load on the inner pair of legs and thus causes greater bending of the inside hind leg. (Seunig. p. 119 footnote.)

Seunig is saying that if the horse is straight, his near and off legs will strike the ground with equal force and bear equal weight. This is true, he says, in lateral work and regardless of whether the horse is in forward or central balance, but it is not true on the circle.

With this criteria of straightness in mind, let us read Seunig's definition of crookedness:

Crookedness is produced by one hind leg's evading the uncomfortable job of even loading by not advancing straight ahead under the horse's body but somewhat to one side. One result of this evasion is a bending of the horse's body that departs from the direction of motion. This is manifested to the rider by the horse moving against the leg on the side of the evading hind hoof and against the rein on the other side and falling heavily on the corresponding shoulder. (Seunig, p. 121.)

I take this to mean (see Figure 50) that the horse was hollow on the side of the evading hind leg, did not yield to the rein on the other side (stiff side), and also had too much weight on the foreleg

Figure 50.   Seunig's description of a horse hollow on the right or "crooked from right to left."

on that side. Seunig's explanation puts the emphasis on the action of the hind leg, not on the rigidity of the neck or jaw.

Additional manifestations of crookedness are mentioned by Jackson:

> *You will probably have noticed that at the rising trot your horse goes more comfortably when you ride on one or other of the diagonals . . . and will often try to throw you back on to it by a stride or two at the canter. . . . That is due to the horse's natural asymmetry. . . . (Jackson, p. 87.)*

A horse will also sometimes (intentionally?) stumble. This also will have the effect of putting the rider back on the preferred posting diagonal. Jackson has a long list of symptoms of "asymmetry," as he calls it: (See Figure 51.)

> *Some of the symptoms of asymmetry to the right [hollow right side], for instance, are:*
> *(1) The horse does not fully accept or tension the right rein; and he resists the action of the left rein.*
> *(2) He carries his right hind quarter to the right and slightly ahead of his left, with his head and upper neck curved to the right, and the base of his neck to the left.*
> *(3) His off hind leg is stronger than his near hind, he favors the left diagonal (off hind—near fore) and he engages his off hind more than his near, when trotting, but does not distend it in a full stride behind the vertical, so that the near hind—which depends for its engagement on the distention of the off hind—cannot fully engage forward in front of the vertical.* He delivers his impulsion in the direction of his near shoulder, on to which he is impelled when going in a straight line, and particularly when circling to the left.*
> *(4) His strides are unequal. . . .*
> . . . .
> *He finds it difficult to lead on the off fore at the canter or gallop and often cannot change on to it in an emergency. (Jackson, p. 144.)*

One final thing which occurs if you are working alongside a solid wall: you may notice that the outside stirrup frequently bumps

---

*What Podhajsky, Seunig, and Jackson say about the deficiencies of the two hind legs is not exactly the same if you compare the quotations carefully. Their analyses differ somewhat. So does the article quoted from *Dressage Letters*.

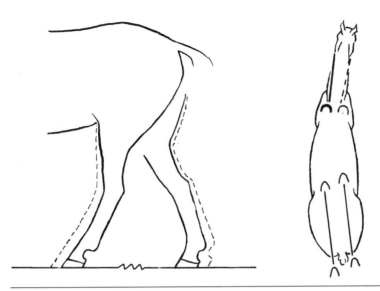

Figure 51.   Jackson's description of a horse hollow on the right side. The left-hand diagram shows what he means when he says that the right hind does not distend far enough to the rear and consequently, the left hind cannot engage as far forward as it should.

against the wall when going in one direction but not in the other. The stirrup would bump when the stiff or convex side was on the outside next to the wall.

The next question is *why* the horse should be crooked. A subsidiary question is: Do all horses tend to be stiff on the same side? A variety of interesting suggestions and theories have been put forward, and you can take your choice. There seems to be no proved and universally accepted explanation. I will simply quote a number of them.

> *Most green horses, especially if they are naturally balanced, will be straight. That is to say, the hind feet will follow the tracks of the forefeet. Under the weight of the rider, when working in the arena or when incorrectly collected, the horse will show an inclination to be crooked; the hind feet will no longer follow the tracks of the forefeet but step to the side, and the horse will not have an even contact on both sides.*
>
> *It has often been said that the crookedness of the horse is caused by the position of the foal in the womb, but this theory remains to be proved. On the other hand, the fact must be recognized that the forehand is narrower than the hindquarters and that the horse will*

be crooked if his shoulder is allowed to be taken too close to the wall. (Podhajsky, p. 46.)

Seunig has the following suggestions to account for crookedness:

The reason for a horse's one-sidedness is interpreted variously. No entirely conclusive explanation has been found as yet. Many attribute crookedness to the position of the foal in the womb, bent over to the right, but forget that multiparous animals, such as dogs, are also crooked. In any event it is a fact that asymmetrical conformation is a factor that greatly favors the tendency to execute certain primitive movements chiefly with the stronger and nimbler half of the body . . . and this is true of the horse as of all other living creatures. It has also been proved that socalled "left-handed" riders, the left halves of whose bodies are much better developed than the right, unconsciously "make" a horse that turns out from right to left, but when mounted by all right-handed riders it does exactly the opposite, so that it becomes stiff on the right side. This seems to indicate that the horse's defense against the unconscious use of greater force by one half of the rider's body is a factor in the development of crookedness. (Seunig, p. 121.)

Seunig believes that it is most often the left hind that is stronger and nimbler, and hence it is the right hind which evades to the side. Thus, in his view, the right side would most often be the hollow side.* He comments on page 121, ". . . remember the greater frequency with which the near stirrup hits the wall."

Jackson also finds most horses hollow on the right. He says:

Most horses prefer you to ride on the left diagonal—that is to sit down into the saddle as the left diagonal touches down. . . . That is due to the horse's natural asymmetry. . . . When working on circles at the trot most horses tend to fall unduly on to their left shoulders when circling to the left and often resist bending their necks to the left, in the direction of the movement. (Jackson, p. 87.)

He has this explanation to account for crookedness:

*In my opinion, Seunig is inconsistent. He seems to say that when trained by a left-handed (and left-legged) rider, the horse becomes stiff on the left. Since left-handed trainers are in the minority, it would seem that "left-stiff" ("right-hollow") horses should be in the minority too. However, I may not interpret him correctly. His whole discussion is almost impossible to understand, and he (or his translator) uses the term "outside" hind continually without clearly indicating which is the "outside." Possibly he meant "off-side."

> *The horse, like the human being, is born stronger, more dextrous, more adroit, on one side than on the other. Most authorities agree that the majority are naturally asymmetrical to the right, just as most humans are right-handed. The muscles of the right side of the horse are flexed while those of the left are extended. . . . (Jackson, p. 143.)*

In Müseler's opinion, however, horses are not asymmetrical to the right:

> *By nature all horses are a little one-sided. It is generally assumed that the reason for this is the position of the embryo while the mare is in foal. Just as most people are right-handed, so most horses are bent a little towards the left. (Müseler, p. 96.)*

Froissard agrees with Müseler:

> *The naturally straight horse is nonexistent; horses are usually bent to the left. (Froissard, p. 62.)*

General Decarpentry has a somewhat different analysis of the cause of crookedness than those that have been so far quoted:

> *However, all horses have a spinal curvature. The spinal column forming the axis from head to tail . . . is not exactly in the middle of the body. One part only of this axis, approximately half-way along its length, is centrally situated. Its extremities are more or less deflected and always to the same side.*
>
> *Whether standing or in movement, the horse finds it difficult to alter this attitude, either to straighten himself or to bend in the opposite direction.*
>
> *If the curvature is pronounced, and when the skeletal development of the horse is complete, this fault which is incompatible with academic correctness is extremely difficult to rectify adequately and above all with long-lasting results. (Decarpentry, pp. 112–13.)*

Well, enough is enough. It is not really important whether asymmetry to the right or to the left is more prevalent. Nor do we have to know *why* the horse is crooked. What is important is to be aware of your own horse's crookedness and how it is manifested. Since most of the manifestations are unpleasant, it is necessary to take steps to minimize them. The remedies proposed by various writers are, as you might expect, designed to overcome the problem as each writer sees it. I will present quotations giving an assortment of remedies, which should help you to understand the instructions your teacher gives and the reasons behind them. And if the asymmetry of your horse is not very pronounced, you may even be able to control it yourself well enough so that he does not have to concern himself with the problem.

Seunig has some preliminary suggestions as to how to cope with the soft-stiff problem before the horse is on the bit. His advice is for a horse hollow on the right, or, as he calls it, "crooked from right to left." If your horse is hollow on the left, you will have to reverse everything. Figure 52 puts Seunig's suggestions in graphic form. First, while riding straight ahead:

> On the assumption that the horse is crooked from right to left, the inside [right] rein, shortened somewhat to provide steadier control, will turn the forehand far enough to the right and forward, with light "opening" tugs towards the side and away from the neck, for the outside hind foot to track the outside forefoot, so that a line connecting the two is parallel to the trace [track].
>
> If the inside [right] leg is not yet able to maintain even loading by its sustaining action, crookedness and the resultant tendency to put a greater load on the near shoulder will reappear once this lateral action of the opening rein ceases. (Seunig, p. 186.)

On turns to the right (the hollow side) he instructs the rider:

> What happens is this: the rider's inside leg [right] behind the girth, acting laterally, will direct the outward-turning off hind leg against and in front of the outside [left] hind leg, with the circumspect support of the inside [right] rein.
>
> The outside leg on the convex side, applied as far forward along the girth as possible, will take care of the forward drive. . . . (Seunig, p. 187.)

This means that the inside leg pushes the haunches to the outside, and a "mere hint of an inside rein" is used to execute the turn. The aids used when turning toward the stiff side (in this case, to the left) are as follows:

> . . . the inside [left] hand will remain alongside the neck and confine itself to giving the barest hint of the change of direction by an absorbing closing of the finers. The right rein, which is now the outside rein, supports the stretching of the outer side of the neck as before by going forward, but it will also try to prevent a hasty turn by acting as an opening rein, this time from the inside towards the outside.

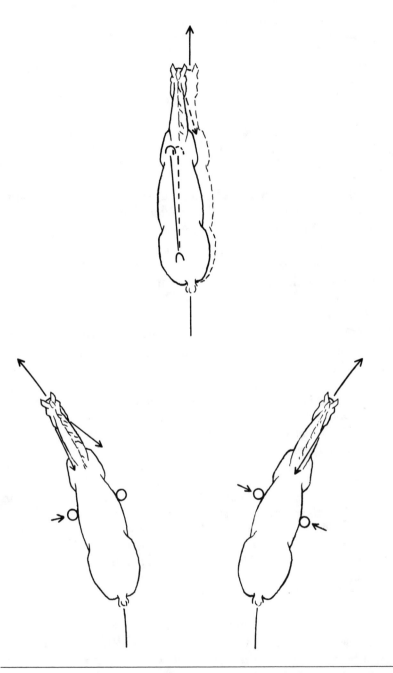

Figure 52.   Seunig's suggestions for coping with a horse hollow on the right.
The horse is shown turing right, turning left, and going straight
ahead.

> *The left leg, which is now the inside leg, will exert lateral pressure just behind the girth in order to keep the horse from hurrying the turn. . . .*
>
> *Any driving action of the outside leg at this time would force the horse's body even more to the near shoulder and the near rein. . . .*
>
> *The right leg [therefore] . . . behind the girth [acts] . . . as a restraining control. . . .*
>
> *. . . the rider will have to distribute his weight as symmetrically as possible on the two sides of the horse's body, using a light . . . seat. (Seunig, p. 187.)*

This all sounds pretty complicated but really is not when you try it, and it will help minimize the problem and make the horse feel straighter. On the turn to the left (the stiff side) it appears that both legs have a "restraining" effect. I interpret this to mean that if the haunches tend to fall *in* because the horse turns too sharply you restrain with the inside leg, while if they tend to swing *out* you use the outside leg.

The other remedies which will now be cited require that the horse be on the bit. First, here is Podhajsky's solution to the problem of the horse that makes his outside parallel to the wall of the arena: (See Figure 53.)

> *. . . the forelegs must be brought in front of the hind legs, which means that the shoulders of the horse must be taken away from the wall so that the hind feet will step into or in front of the corresponding footprints of the forefeet. . . .*
>
> *Both reins must be employed to take the horse away from the wall, while both legs push him forward. The action of the reins without the corresponding use of the legs would make the horse reduce his speed and the exercise would have no effect, for the horse can only be straightened if the speed is maintained during this correction. The rider must not try to bring the forehand in with the inside rein without holding the outside rein, as this would lead only to an increased position of the head and neck to the inside, not to a straightened horse. (Podhajsky, pp. 91–92.)*

You must "keep" the outside rein to hold the neck straight and then use the inside rein to move the shoulders over. The horse must be on the bit before the shoulders can be moved over using both reins in this way.

Moving the shoulders over is not the same problem as equaliz-

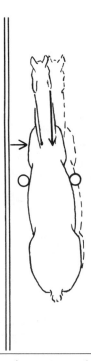

Figure 53.   Podhajsky's suggestion for coping with a horse that carries its
shoulder too close to the fence. In this diagram, the horse is on
the right rein, and the rider moves the shoulders to the right.

ing the hollow and stiff sides. Podhajsky has a different remedy for
that: (See Figure 54.)

> *When the reins are taken up most horses will adopt more position to*
> *one side than to the other—generally, but not always, to the right.*
> *In this case the rider must now hold the right rein, that is to say the*
> *rein on the hollow side, and try by short actions of the left hand,*
> *like squeezing water out of a sponge, to give the horse the correct*
> *position. This may be described as a* unilateral half-halt *through the*
> *left side. . . . Before and during the half-halt the horse must be*
> *pushed well forward with the seat and legs in order not to lose im-*
> *pulsion or allow the pace to slacken. If the horse does not react*
> *immediately to these short actions of the reins on the stiff side they*
> *must be repeated, but on no account should a steady pull be main-*
> *tained. As soon as the horse answers by relaxing the muscles of the*
> *throat and a nodding of the head as if he were to say: "yes, I under-*
> *stand," the action of the rein on the stiff side and the pushing aid*
> *must immediately cease, and for a short time the rider will direct his*

Figure 54.   Podhajsky's suggestions for straightening a horse hollow on the right. The remedy is a unilateral half-halt through the left side.

> *horse with the rein of the hollow side only. . . . If the rein of the hollow side is not held, the value of the exercise will be lost for the horse would be made to relax the contact of the stiff side and would not be made to accept the contact on the hollow side.*
>
> *The proof that the half-halt has succeeded will be recognized by the fact that after the half-halt through the left side the horse will, having accepted the contact on the right side, maintain the position to the left. (Podhajsky, pp. 100–101.)*
>
> *The half-halt can be practiced only if the horse follows the unilateral action of the rein by lowering his neck, but should he raise it and produce a bulge in the lower side of his neck he is not yet ready for this aid. . . . (Podhajsky, p. 102.)*

A little later on he relates the two problems, the problem of the shoulder being nearer the wall and the problem of the stiff side and the hollow side:

> *. . . there will always be a tendency for him to incline the forehand to the wall. . . . It will be easier to take the forehand towards the side on which the horse is stiff, because on this side he accepts the*

rein. On the other side he will try to follow the action of the rein by bending his neck in order to spare himself the inconvenience of being straightened. . . . The half-halt by the outside rein [the stiff side] must teach him obedience and must make him carry the whole forehand in and not only the neck. (Podhajsky, p. 103.)

In this last sentence he is talking about a horse that is hollow on the right and going around the arena on the right hand. The trainer does a unilateral half-halt through the left side to straighten the neck and achieve a contact on the hollow side, and then moves the forehand to the right. Podhajsky does not say how to do this. It could be either by a traction on the right rein (he speaks of directing the horse for a short time with the rein of the hollow side only) or by moving both hands to the right without any change in the contact. The latter is a method I was taught at one time. Going around the arena to the right is the "hard" way when the horse is hollow on the right. It is easier to correct the problem, as he says, when going to the left (the horse's stiff side). In that case, all you have to do is use a little left rein. (See Figure 55.)

How do you straighten the canter, that is, bring the front feet in front of the hind feet? Podhajsky's method for the trot, as just described, will also work with the canter. Going around the arena leading on the stiff side, it is easy. When going around the other way with the lead on the soft side, you have to start with a unilateral half-halt through the stiff side.

Of course, if your horse is stiff on the right and hollow on the left you will have to reverse all the directions. By reading "hollow" and "stiff" instead of "right" and "left" it is easier to follow the instructions. My own theory as to why a horse may be hollow on the left is that usually horses are led on the left side and turned to that side from infancy. It seems as though this would tend to bend the spine to the left and stretch the muscles on the right side. If a foal is born crooked to the right it might have the effect, in the couple of years before he is ridden, of straightening him out or even bending him a little to the left.

Seunig's solution is quite different, but follows logically from his contention that the problem is in the hind leg of the hollow side, which does not carry its share of the load.

. . . the really difficult side *is the hollow off side, where the horse is moving not with but against the leg and is not responding to the*

reins. Once the rider succeeds in getting the hind legs on the difficult (wrongly hollowed) side to engage forward in a straight line under the load and to have that side of the body come up to the bit, the constraint on the constrained side disappears by itself. Now the impulsion of the two hind legs, which are reaching forward equally, reaches the corresponding reins uniformly. (Seunig. pp. 122–23.)

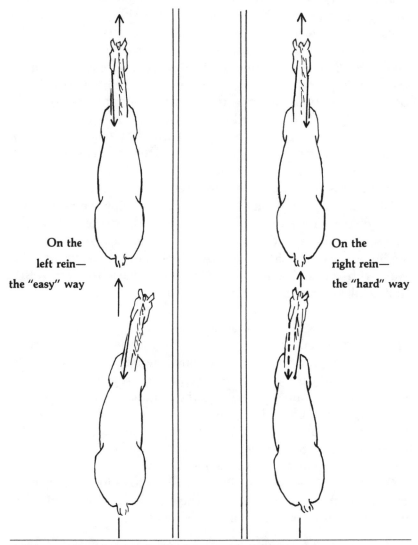

On the
left rein—
the "easy" way

On the
right rein—
the "hard" way

Figure 55. Podhajsky's suggestions for correcting a horse that carries its shoulders too close to the wall and is also hollow on the right.

> *[The trainer] . . . develops impulsion and allows any resistances to escape forward, straightening the horse by driving the hind leg of the difficult side underneath the load. . . . (Seunig, p. 123.)*

General Decarpentry, who found the underlying cause of crookedness to be a congenital spinal curvature, has methods of straightening in keeping with this theory:

> *. . . if the curvature is not too pronounced and if the horse is still young, it is possible to straighten the spine to a partial extent by holding it flexed in the opposite direction more or less frequently and for varying periods of time; above all, appropriate gymnastics can provoke an asymmetric development of the muscular system which favors an opposite flexion. This asymmetric development of the muscular system, opposed to the skeletal asymmetry, will partly counteract the latter and enable us to obtain a "relatively straight position". (Decarpentry, p. 113.)*

In other words, do circles with the horse bent against his natural curvature. If he is hollow on the right side, do circles to the left, bending him, and thus making the left side hollow. Froissard also recommends circling as the chief remedy, with the horse "adjusted" or bent to the circle.

These rather conflicting views are systematized by Jackson, who explains that in regard to straightening there are two schools of thought—the Flexionists and the Impulsionists.

> *The Flexionists try to flex the left side of a horse asymmetrical to the right [hollow on the right side], and thus to stretch the muscles of the right side and secure equality of extension of the right side and the left. (Jackson, p. 145.)*

The exercises used include small circles to the left, shoulder-in to the left, and haunches-in to the left. Decarpentry and Froissard are Flexionists.

> *The Impulsionists aim to develop not only the extension, but the active distension, of the muscles of the right side, which they regard as partially atrophied. They aim to make the horse fully distend his off hind as well as engage it, so that he can deliver impulsion over a full stride, behind the vertical as well as in front, and thus enable him fully to engage his near hind forward under him as the off hind distends more fully backwards.*

To achieve this the Impulsionists try, as their first objective, to put the horse frankly 'in front of the legs' in strong impulsion, whether straight or bent. . . . Next they aim to put the horse strongly on the bit. . . . Only when they have their horse going freely forward in strong impulsion and frankly on the bit do the Impulsionists attempt to begin to straighten his forehand. (Jackson, p. 146.)

The exercises he lists for straightening the forehand are so complicated, involving complex rein effects and circles on two tracks, that I will not detail them here. You can read about them if you wish in Jackson's book. He concludes:

I should here explain that I myself use the methods of both schools, according to the characteristics of the particular horse I am riding. For horses that go freely forward with good natural impulsion, which often includes Thoroughbreds, Arabs, and Anglo-Arabs, I use mainly, although not exclusively, Flexionist methods.

In practice, with all but very asymmetrical horses, I find the shoulder-in the most useful single exercise to straighten the horse, because by doing shoulder-in one can effectively stretch the muscles of the horse's contracted side.

I find the indirect rein of opposition generally the most useful aid, for with this rein one can effectively straighten the horse when he is moving forward by putting his shoulders in front of his quarters. These two usually suffice to straighten free forward movers sufficiently for the ordinary purposes of cross-country riding and polo.

For horses that lack impulsion—often the heavier types—I prefer the methods of the Impulsionists, because in developing their impulsion to correct their asymmetry one can solve so many other problems as well. (Jackson, p. 148.)

I might add that shoulder-in and the indirect rein of opposition should be sufficient also for low-level dressage.

Until recently the Germans worked mostly with rather heavy and cold-blooded horses, so they would naturally develop the Impulsionist methods. The French used Anglo-Arabs, so their Flexionist methods are logical. Shoulder-in will be taken up in the next chapter. The use of the rein of opposition sounds similar to Podhajsky's technique for moving the shoulders over, which I have already quoted.

We will now bring this chapter to a close by studying the means whereby the horse can be bent or "adjusted" to the circle. Froissard has a clear presentation:

> *There are two manners of adjusting your horse on the circle:*
> *—with the horse's barrel tangent to the circle, press the forehand and hindquarters onto the circle. Thus the horse bends around the rider's inside leg;*
> *—with the entire horse inside the circle, only the head and hind legs tangent, your inside leg presses his barrel outward in order to place it on the circle, while your outside leg and your hands keep the two ends on the circle.*
>
> *Let us only consider the first case. Track to the left, you lead the forehand onto the circle by a light left opening rein and right neck rein, the right leg slightly retracted, acting from front to back so as to place the hindquarters on the circle, while the left leg at the girth—around which the horse's barrel is bent—maintains the impulsion. Slightly advance your right (outside) shoulder to keep facing in the same direction as the horse, adjusting yourself on the circle [See Figure 56.] Limit your first demands to a few steps on a circle of large diameter, exercising first the rigid side (the one not incurved by nature).*
>
> *This work on the circle will not only more or less perfectly straighten the spine, but supple it and bring about a more pronounced engagement of the inside hind. (Froissard, pp. 62–63.)*

Figure 56.   Froissard's first method of adjusting (bending) the horse on the circle.

Decarpentry has some useful additional suggestions:

> When circling to the left, the left rein will act by moving slightly to the left. . . . The trainer will also use the aid of the right rein if the horse, as he usually does, attempts to localize the flexion in his neck by "breaking" it in front of the withers instead of allowing the flexion to extend from one end of his body to the other.
>
> It will usually be found that the most effective way of counteracting the "break" that allows the horse to escape total flexion from withers to tail, is to oppose it with the right rein held against the base of the neck. . . .
>
> As always . . . it is only by trial and error that the rider will be able to discover the correct use of his aids, and to modify them according to the various resistances of his pupil. (Decarpentry, p. 117.)

A few words of explanation are now in order. Of course you do not prepare to bend your horse by positioning his barrel either tangent to the circle or inside the circle. This figure makes the action of the aids in bending the horse very clear but should be taken as an explanatory device only. What you really do is start with a straight horse and then attempt to curve his body either by bending the ends in or else by bowing the middle out. On my horse, the method that works is to bow his body out by using the inside leg quite vigorously on the girth. I always have to do it—every time he turns and in both directions. As Decarpentry says, trial and error will determine which works for you. In either case you must prevent the neck from bending more than the body ("breaking") by using the outside neckrein—or as Jackson would call it, the indirect rein of opposition—against the base of the neck. This is a problem mostly when turning to the hollow side.

The method Froissard uses in applying the outside leg may be unclear. When using the leg, some trainers roll the calf against the horse's body: forward when driving, and backward when pushing the quarters laterally to the side (or preventing them from moving against the leg). This is what Froissard means by the leg acting "from front to back."

Limiting your demand to a few steps on a large circle can be done by bending only when turning the four corners of the arena at first, and making the turns on a large radius. Some trainers would disagree with the advice to work at first on the side which is difficult—turning to the left if the horse is hollow on the right.

There are those who advocate working more in the difficult direction, and there are others who insist that everything must be done equally to both hands (in both directions) and who would do it the easy way first to help the horse understand. Of course, going around the arena with the hollow side to the inside is the easy way, though you still have to ask for the bend of the *body* and be especially careful that the neck does not bend too much. Bending is done at all three gaits, first at the trot and then at canter and walk.

Getting the horse on the bit and then succeeding in bending the body—I found to be a rather exciting accomplishment. The bending of the body was easy to feel; the horse went around turns and circles in a more upright position, the hind legs did not fall in or out, and the curves felt smoother and rounder. You can tell that the horse is bent because the outer rein will touch the neck, and the inner rein will be off the neck in turns and circles. Before the horse bends you have to carry both hands further to the outside, as shown in Figure 57, and the inside rein will touch the neck. An observer can see whether the hind legs are following in the tracks of the forelegs or falling in or out. As you become better at bending and keeping the horse bent, whatever manifestations of

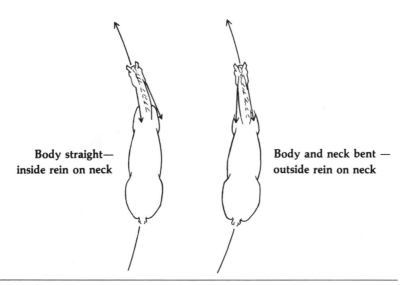

Body straight—
inside rein on neck

Body and neck bent —
outside rein on neck

Figure 57. Bending the body on turn or circle. If the horse's body is bent, you will be able to "steer" by moving both hands to the inside and the outside rein will touch the neck.

crookedness have been bothering you should become less and less troublesome.

Before leaving the subject of lateral suppleness, I should add that there are those who maintain that the horse's spine is so stiff and has so little lateral flexibility that the horse really does not bend at all. It has been suggested that the apparent bending is not the result of the joints between the vertebrae but rather of muscular adjustments, especially in the shoulder area, for the shoulders are not attached by bony joints to the spine, but by muscles and ligaments only. About all we can conclude is that the horse *looks* as though he bends and *feels* as though he bends, and that is what we are after. A horse started in dressage when young can become truly supple. An older horse, if he is stiff, can at least be made to "bend," which makes riding more pleasant.

10 Training Methods — Shoulder-in

The term *lateral movements* is the general term covering all exercises in which the hind feet and the forefeet of the horse proceed on different paths. Another name for this class of movements is *work on two tracks*. Although "two tracks" is a common designation, it is not a very accurate one. It refers, of course, to the fact that the fore and hind feet do not move on the *same* track. Actually the two tracks may overlap, which is often described as *three* tracks. If the two tracks are entirely separate it can be said that there are *four* tracks, each foot following its own track. (See Figures 58 and 59.) The French term that is the equivalent of "lateral movements" is "side steps" (*pas de côté*). The lateral movements, which are illustrated in Figure 60, include:

1. Leg-yielding,
2. Shoulder-in,
3. Counter shoulder-in (or shoulder-out or head to the wall),
4. Travers (haunches-in),
5. Renvers (haunches-out, tail to the wall), and
6. Two-track (half-pass).

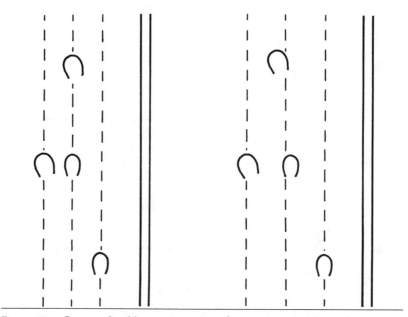

Figure 58. Correct shoulder-in. Footprints from one stride of shoulder-in done on three tracks and on three and one-half tracks. Notice that the forefoot prints point away from the fence, while the hind footprints point straight along the fence.

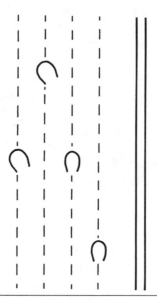

Figure 59. Footprints of one stride of shoulder-in performed on four tracks.

Such a variety of terms is very confusing. I will therefore use only the names which appear in the AHSA tests: Leg-yielding, shoulder-in, travers, and two-track. Notice that the expression "two-track" is used in a general way (work on two tracks) and also specifically for one particular lateral movement (the half-pass). Turn on the forehand and turn on the haunches are also movements in which the fore and hind feet do not move on the same track and hence can also be classed as lateral movements.

Although some consider *shoulder-in* basically a training exercise rather than a final goal, it is important enough to be included in First Level Test 4, and also in each subsequent level. There is virtually nothing about *leg-yielding* in the classical literature. It will be discussed briefly later in this chapter. *Turn on the forehand* can be done as a preliminary to leg-yielding and shoulder-in to teach the horse to move his haunches sideways away from one leg, but it is not in any test and most trainers do not do it. It will not be discussed. *Turn on the haunches* is discussed in Chapter 11.

Shoulder-in is done mainly at the trot. Some trainers also do it regularly at the walk, while others do it briefly at the walk to help the horse understand what is expected, and then, once the horse has learned to do it at the walk, practice it only at the trot. Some say it cannot be done at the canter; others say it is useful for straightening the canter. Shoulder-in helps to straighten, supple, and collect the horse. Of course it can accomplish these desirable results only if it is done correctly, so let us start by getting a good idea of just what it is and just how it ought to be done. Here are excerpts from two AHSA definitions:

> The horse is slightly bent around the inside leg of the rider. . . . The horse is looking away from the direction in which he is moving. (Rulebook, p. 155.)

> The hindlegs travel straight on the track, the inside hindleg stepping well under the weight of the horse. The outside shoulder of the horse is placed in front of the inside hindquarter. (Supplement to Rules, p. 12.)

Taken together, these give a pretty good description. When the outside shoulder is in front of the inside hindquarter, the outside foreleg and the inside hindleg will tread on the same track. If the hind legs move straight along the path, the footprints will point straight ahead. If the horse's body is curved as it should be, the forefoot prints will turn in. (See Figure 58.)

The FEI in its 1975 revision declared that the horse must move on three or three-and-one half tracks, not on four tracks. Figure 58 shows the footprints of one stride of shoulder-in on both three tracks and three-and-one-half tracks. In the latter case the inside hind and outside fore are not centered on one track, but neither are they separated enough to be on separate tracks. If they were separated, the exercise would be on four tracks as shown in Figure 59. In that case, the horse's body would have to be more bent and placed at a greater angle to the wall, which is no longer considered correct by the FEI.

The direction of progress is along the side of the arena. The horse's spine is curved, with the *convex* side leading; hence the

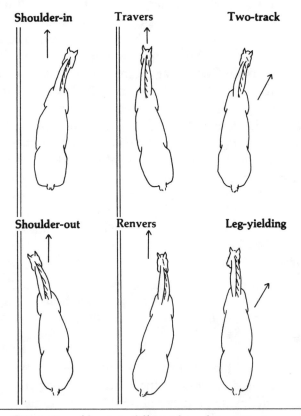

Figure 60. Orientation of horse in different lateral movements.

Figure 61.   A properly bent shoulder-in. The hind feet are
pointing straight ahead while the front feet are pointing in off the
track, proving that the body is indeed curved. The horse is on 3½
tracks, which would be clear if he were viewed head on.

horse is looking *away* from the direction he is going. (In haunches-
in and haunches-out, the *concave* side leads and the horse looks
toward the direction he is going. See Figure 60.) The *hind* legs do
not cross but move straight ahead on the track. The forelegs cross.
(See Figure 61.)

You will often hear people say that the legs do or do not cross in
a particular exercise, but it is not always easy to tell what they
mean. In determining whether the legs cross, the horse must be
viewed on a line perpendicular to the hips, if you are talking about
the hind legs, or perpendicular to the shoulders if you are talking
about the forelegs. (See Figure 62.) When shoulder-in is correctly

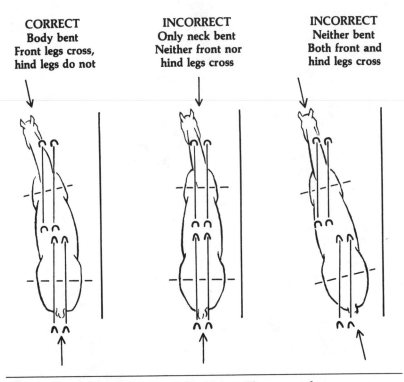

Figure 62. Crossing of the legs in shoulder-in. The arrows show the direction from which the horse should be viewed when determining whether the legs cross or not.

performed with body and neck uniformly curved and moving on three or three-and-one-half tracks, the front legs will cross and the hind legs will not. If *both* front and hind legs cross the body is not bent, and the horse is doing leg-yielding rather than shoulder-in. If *neither* cross, the horse is not bending his body but only his neck.

Figure 63 adapted from *Training the Young Pony*, depicts the correct movement in a different way. The pony is on three tracks. From the point of view from which these sketches were made, you can easily assess the action of the forelegs. They can be seen to cross correctly. From this angle, however, it is hard to tell whether the hind legs are crossing. They appear to be, although, of course, they should not actually do so. You would have to get squarely behind the pony (viewing on a line perpendicular to his hips) to judge the hind-leg action easily.

Figure 63. **Shoulder-in on three tracks. Adapted from** *Training the Young Horse and Pony,* **page 67.**

Besides doing shoulder-in along the side of the arena, it can be done on the center line. This is called for in some higher level tests. It can also be done on circles. At the Spanish Riding School the young horses are first taught the movement on the large circle. Finally, it can be done right around the arena including the corners. Wynmalen clearly describes and illustrates these latter figures in *Equitation* (pages 158-9). Neither is in current tests.

Sometimes shoulder-in is still done on four tracks. Podhajsky states that this was its original form as described by de la Guérinière and that it is still performed in this way at the Spanish Riding School. He also maintains that only when done in this way can all its benefits be achieved. The AHSA *Rulebook* pictures the horse on three tracks, but then says that the horse should be at an angle of 30° to the wall. This would require four well-spaced tracks, and would require more bending than could be expected of a Second Level horse. The horse would have to be supple enough to do a volte in order to be bent enough to move on four tracks.

The mechanical aspects of performing shoulder-in and the benefits to be obtained from practicing it are elaborated on by all the writers. I will quote several:

Sideways progression is not natural to the horse. In a state of freedom, he only accidentally uses it, and then in leaps, to get away from a sudden cause of fright.

Lack of natural practice makes this mode of lateral progression difficult for the horse, both as regards the disposition of his body as a whole and the movement of his limbs.

The practice of "side-steps" will eradicate his awkwardness, and will improve the horse's ability to preserve or modify his balance, or to recover it rapidly if necessary. It will improve his agility and his ease of movement.

. . . The muscles of the topline, especially in the region of the loin, are particularly stimulated, suppled, and strengthened.

With regard to the limbs, the stimulation of the adduct and abduct muscles commanding lateral movements, which are practically inoperative in straightforward progression, will have to be co-ordinated with the simultaneous efforts in flexion and extension of those which determine forward movement in the direction of the long axis of the body.

The resulting modifications in the activity of the locomotor system are very favorable to the development of the gaits required by academic equitation. . . . (Decarpentry, pp. 121–22.)

Within the leg, the joints work only in a fore-and-aft plane and it is practically impossible to rotate the leg or to bend part of it outward or inward. The leg is a rigid machine for carrying weight and for moving forward. What side motion is possible comes from the shoulder and hip joints. (Wynmalen, pp. 153–54 quoting Horses, by Dr. G. C. Simpson.)

. . . the shoulder-in improves the bending of all three joints of the hind legs and makes them carry a greater proportion of the weight. This bending improves the suppleness and the activity of the hind legs, and gives more freedom to the shoulders, which improves the paces and favours a lighter contact with the bit. (Podhajsky, pp. 138–39.)

. . . the inside hind leg will move more in the direction of the centre of gravity of the horse. This will make the hind legs carry a greater proportion of the weight, thus relieving the shoulders and allowing the forelegs to step forward more freely. (Podhajsky, page 134.)

. . . in the shoulder-in we demand a much increased effort, since the inner hindleg . . . is obliged to tread sideways very far underneath the body in order to receive the load. This entails increased flexion

Figure 64. Shoulder-in. Front feet pointing toward the viewer, hind feet pointing straight ahead on the track—proof that the body is bent. Rider's shoulders parallel to horse's shoulders. Unfortunately the horse has come off the bit. Compare height of head with Figure 45. Rider's toes are turned out because she is using legs vigorously.

> *of the hock and a measure of lowering the [inside] haunch. (Wynmalen, p. 156.)*

Recall that increasing the weight carried by the hind legs improves balance; bending the joints of the hind legs and lowering the croup (haunch) is necessary for collection; and bending the spine is lateral suppleness. We will want to obtain all these benefits so we will work diligently to do the movement well.

Besides the mere correct positioning of the horse, there are many difficulties to overcome before an entirely correct execution of the shoulder-in is possible.

> *To commence with, the horse is unable to deliver this action; he cannot help evading it; he tries to follow the action with the hindleg in question, instead of initiating it. Hence clumsiness, loss of rhythm and loss of impulsion, the main difficulties in all work on two tracks. (Wynmalen, p. 156.)*

> *. . . look to see whether the exercise is executed in the same manner on both reins. If, however, the horse has little position on one rein [three tracks] and as much as de la Guérinière demands on the other [four tracks], then neither of the two versions is adhered to but the exercise is presented just as the horse thinks fit, which is wrong and useless. A horse will always take his shoulder-in better on the rein of the side on which he accepts the bit [the stiff side] and try to avoid the discomfort of the exercise by overbending his neck on the other, the hollow side.*

> *The speed should never be allowed to slacken when practicing shoulder-in, which is so often the case, nor should it be increased with hasty steps as many horses have the inclination to do. (Podhajsky, p. 135.)*

> *The horse must execute lateral work joyfully and be completely relaxed, free from any tension or constraint, and maintain his position, that is, the angle of his body to the wall, without faltering until his rider brings the exercise to an end. (Podhajsky, pp. 137–38.)*

> *. . . the rider must be quite certain that the pony is . . . not just bending his neck. No force must be used in this exercise and it must not be performed if the pony's head is too high. The head and neck must remain still and in the correct position.* (Training the Young Pony, p. 67.)

All the things these writers warn about will happen when you begin to do shoulder-in. The head will come up, the horse will slow down, he will be tense and rigid, he will feel clumsy, and the degree to which he turns in from the rail will waver and vary. If he evades with the inside hind, his whole body will come off the track, not just his shoulder. If he evades with the outside hind, the body will remain straight so that when the shoulders come in, the haunches fall out. Your instructor will notice these things, call your attention to them, and tell you how to correct them until you can notice and correct them yourself.

There are several ways of adopting the shoulder-in position. These are shown in Figure 65. Podhajsky describes one method:

> *In the* shoulder-in *the forehand of the horse is brought in about half a yard, thus describing a separate track parallel to the original track on which the hind legs must continue. (Podhajsky, p. 134.)*

Wynmalen describes another way. The rider starts by riding the horse on a circle to the left:

We select a suitable point whereat we desire to leave the circle; probably the point where the circular track meets the side of our school; when our horse's quarters have arrived at the selected point, we push him away, sideways, along the tangent to the circle, probably along the side of our school. (Wynmalen, p. 155.)

From a straight position   **From a circle**

From a corner

As though starting a circle

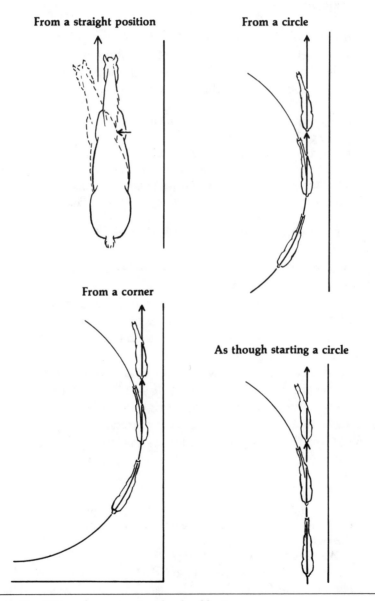

Figure 65.   Ways of commencing the shoulder-in.

A third way, also described by Wynmalen, is a sort of combination of the first two:

> Assuming we are riding on a straight track along the side of the
> school; we commence a circle and as soon as the quarters reach the
> spot where the forehand has left the track, we begin the shoulder-in.
> (Wynmalen, pp. 158–59.)

A variation of Wynmalen's first method, and possibly the most
common method of all, is to start the shoulder-in immediately
after completing a corner, that is, after doing a quarter of a circle.
Podhajsky also describes this:

> It is of great advantage to begin this lateral exercise directly after
> passing through a corner. The horse is led into the corner as if he
> were going to execute a small circle. As soon as the forehand has
> begun the arc of the circle and moved half a yard away from the
> wall, the pressure of the inside leg is increased and the outside rein
> takes the horse in shoulder-in along the wall. (Podhajsky, p. 136.)

Thus, by one means or another, the shoulder is brought in off the
track. The movement must *not* be started by pushing the hindquarters out. If that were intended, the exercise would not have
been called "shoulder-in."

Some instructors like to explain the aids for each new movement
to their pupils. Others expect the student to know the aids and be
ready to apply them whenever he is asked to try a new movement.
You will have to be ready with a knowledge of the aids if your instructor expects it, and it would not be a bad idea to have some
idea of the aids even if he does not. If you learn a set of aids in advance, however, they may not be right for your horse, and you
may have to alter them as training progresses.

What are the aids for shoulder-in? As usual, the descriptions
vary somewhat. First, Wynmalen, starting again from a circle to
the left:

> . . . the aids are simple enough; we push him away with our inside
> leg, aided by our hands and reins, which we carry slightly towards
> the right.
>   We push the horse away in the flexed position of the circle; we do
> nothing to alter that flexion, on the contrary we do our best to
> maintain that flexion intact. Accordingly, the sideways pressure to

the right, effected with our reins, does not hinder the horse's movement; actually it assists it, since the left rein, acting as rein of opposition to the haunches, helps in pushing the quarters to the right. (Wynmalen, pp. 155–56.)

Podhajsky starts with the horse straight on the track:

> *The shoulder is taken into the circle with the inside rein, while the outside rein must prevent the horse from bending his neck too much. The inside rein maintains the position and the outside rein defines the degree of the position and leads the horse in the desired direction. The rider's inside leg, with a deep knee, is applied on the girth and maintains the inside bend of the horse's body evenly from head to tail. It also causes the inside foreleg to step over that of the outside and the inside hind leg to step well under the body. The object of the outside leg behind the girth is to prevent the hindquarters from falling out, and to maintain the fluent forward movement. (Podhajsky, p. 135.)*

> *The rider's weight must be shifted on the inside seat bone. (Podhajsky, p. 136.)*

Froissard also starts from a circle and describes left shoulder-in:

> *The aids applied are:*
> The left rein:
> *fifth effect [indirect rein of opposition behind the withers—see page 247] acts on the entire body of the horse, who bends;*
>
> The right rein:
> *limits the inflexion of the neck and is at the same time the guiding rein which keeps the forehand on its track;*
>
> The left leg:
> *around which the horse is bent, acts close to the girth from back to front;*
>
> The right leg:
> *keeps the off hind from deviating;*
>
> The body weight:
> *is rationally distributed with a slight accent on the right. (Froissard, pp. 70–71.)*

Note that the rein aids described are not alike. Wynmalen wishes the horse to cease circling and move along the track, so the reins act to the right (to the outside). Podhajsky has the reins act to the left (to the inside) to bring the shoulder in off the track. Froissard uses the "fifth effect." (See Chapter 12 for a description of the French classification of rein effects.) There is also a difference as to body weight. Podhajsky emphasizes the inside seat bone, and Froissard the outside. (See Figure 66.)

Actually what you must do is use aids to cause the horse to do shoulder-in and to overcome anything that is wrong. Sometimes you may have to do something quite different from these descriptions. For instance, one of my horses evaded inward with the inside hind. In other words, when I took the shoulder off the track the whole horse tended to come in off the track. I was instructed to use my inside leg behind the girth, and shift my weight to the inside seat bone to hold the hindquarters on the track. The inside leg, even though behind the girth, also had the effect of driving the horse forward and keeping up his speed. I had no need to use the outside leg behind the girth because the hindquarters did not fall out. My principal rein aid was the outside rein against the base of the neck which moved the horse's shoulder in, and at the same time kept the neck from taking on any additional bend. (See Figure 67.)

I have also found that I cannot take the forehand off the track and *then* start to push sideways with the leg. I have to give all the

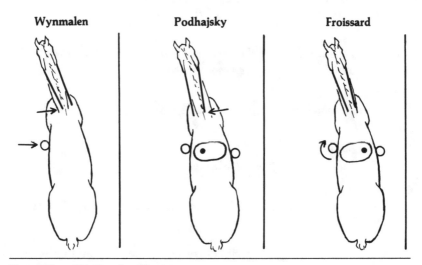

Figure 66. Aids for shoulder-in.

Figure 67.   Still other aids for shoulder-in.

aids simultaneously to get a smooth transition and keep the hind-quarters advancing on the track. I mention these points merely so that you will not consider the aid descriptions as sacred and never to be violated. Aids are to aid the horse, and you must do whatever will aid him to do the right thing.

At first you will not continue shoulder-in for more than a few steps. There are various ways of ending the exercise. (See Figure 68.) Podhajsky advises:

> . . . a few steps of shoulder-in will be sufficient in this stage of train-ing before obtaining fresh impulsion by riding briskly forward. (Podhajsky, p. 136.)

Froissard says:

> . . . request a few steps of shoulder-in, then cease the movement while finishing the circle element you have begun. (Froissard, p. 70.)

Podhajsky has these additional suggestions:

> . . . it will be of great value to interrupt this exercise occasionally by a small circle on a single track.
> The inside rein leads the horse into the circle and is supported by

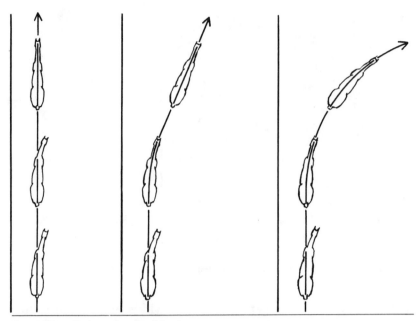

Figure 68. Ending the shoulder-in.

> *the inside leg pushing forward on the girth. The outside rein gives just enough to enable the horse to leave the wall and begin the circle. . . . Another very good exercise . . . is to interrupt this lateral movement by going forward on a single track, that is, by going forward on a diagonal line to the opposite wall, thus following the direction of the horse's head. (Podhajsky, pp. 136-37.)*

Before leaving this subject, we must say something about *leg-yielding.* Leg-yielding is a different lateral movement which is done either along the side of the arena like shoulder-in or travers, or across the arena on the diagonal like two-track. (See figure 69.) It is the latter form that is required in First Level Tests 3 and 4. It should really be called "yielding to the leg." This exercise can be practiced at the very beginning of dressage training. The AHSA *Rulebook* defines it as follows:

> *The horse is quite straight, except for a slight bend at the poll, so that the rider is just able to see the eyebrow and nostril on the inside. The inside legs pass and cross in front of the outside legs. The horse is looking away from the direction in which he is moving.* (Rulebook, p. 155.)

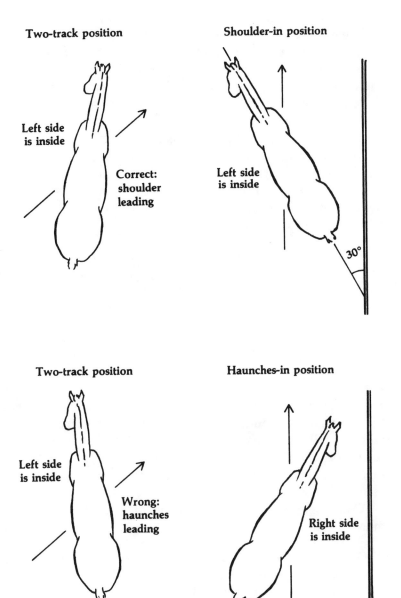

Figure 69.   The various forms of leg-yielding. In two-track position, the body
should be parallel to the long side or with shoulder leading a
little. Shoulder-in position, shown here at 30 degrees, should not
exceed 35 degrees. This form is started by bringing the shoulder
in. Haunches-in form is started by pushing haunches in.

In the classics I find it mentioned only by Podhajsky, and his brief comments are not sufficient to define it clearly. He describes yielding to the leg at the halt, which is "turn on the forehand." He then says that at the Spanish Riding School it is next performed at the walk, but not at the trot. He does not describe just how it is done at the walk because it is done only briefly as a learning device and is never included in a performance. Some trainers, like Podhajsky, do leg-yielding only as a preliminary to other lateral movements; but many consider leg-yielding important as an exercise in its own right and do it both as a preliminary to shoulder-in and two-track and also for its own peculiar benefits throughout the training. The AHSA Dressage Committee evidently takes the latter view:

> . . . *together with the more advanced movement shoulder-in, it is the best means of making a horse supple, loose and unconstrained, for the benefit of the freedom, elasticity and regularity of his paces and the harmony, lightness and ease of his movements.* (Rulebook, p. 155.)

Leg-yielding along the track in shoulder-in position is not a very well-defined movement and is not included in any test. In general, I would say that it should be done on four tracks at a little more angle than shoulder-in. (See Figure 70.) The *Rulebook* says that the horse's body should be at an angle of not more than 35 degrees with the rail. The horse's body is straight, and he looks a little to the inside. You can start the exercise by pushing the haunches out or by bringing the shoulders in. In spite of its name, the latter seems to be preferred.

When doing the other form of leg-yielding on the diagonal as required in the test, the *Rulebook* specifies:

> . . . *the horse should be as close as possible parallel to the long sides of the arena, although the forehand should be slightly in advance of the quarters.* (Rulebook, p. 155.)

Figure 69 shows him correctly with shoulders leading and also in the incorrect position with haunches leading. The leading end of the horse is the end that will reach the fence first.

The exercise is practiced by "turning early" and, as soon as the horse has completed the turn and is parallel to the long side,

Figure 70. Leg-yielding. The horse is on four tracks and the body and neck are straight. Hind feet as well as forefeet point in off track. If viewed from directly behind, the front legs and the hind legs would be seen to cross. Trot is not quite regular. Left fore and right hind should leave track simultaneously.

pushing him toward the track with the inside leg. (See Figure 71.) If you do it in this way you will automatically have the horse looking in the correct direction (away from the way he is going) and it will be easy because the horse wants to get back on the track. Gradually turn sooner, so that you will have farther to go, until you can turn down the center line and go all the way to "B" in the large arena or "M" in the small arena. You must keep up the impulsion, keep the horse on the bit, remain parallel to the long side, and move smoothly on a straight line towards the correct letter. The speed and rhythm should not change.

By way of contrast, two-track is started by turning down the center and pushing the horse back toward the side he has just left. This gives the correct bend for two-track. Two-track can be done correctly with the horse looking the way he is going only after he is

Two-track   Leg-yielding

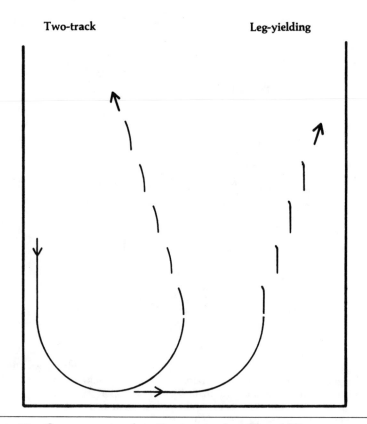

Figure 71.   Common ways of starting two-track and leg-yielding.

doing a good working trot and is a little collected. *Any* horse can do leg-yielding, however, because bending the head or neck *away* from the way the horse is going (for instance to the left) induces the haunches almost automatically to yield to the opposite side (in this case to the right). This is because the horse tends to be stiff.

Years ago when I had no instructor and was trying to do dressage by myself, I thought I was doing two-track with the "minor" fault of turning the head in the wrong direction. Little did I know that with the head turned the wrong way it was simply *not* two-track. It is important in leg-yielding that the horse move sideways away from the *leg*, not sideways away from the neck rein. Western reining horses move away from the rein. Let us remember that the exercise we are doing is called "leg-yielding."

11 Training Methods – Other Movements

This chapter will deal with the walk and canter, lengthening at trot and canter, halting, rein back, travers, turn on the haunches, and counter canter. I have grouped these particular movements together mostly because they were not discussed at great length by the classical writers. Nevertheless, for one reason or another, they are all important.

Developing the *walk* and *canter* are an indispensible part of training that must not be neglected. Canter and walk together almost always account for half or more of the points on a test. At Fourth Level they take up considerably more than half. Unfortunately there is very little discussion by the masters of the basic requirements for walk and canter.

Lengthening the stride at the trot and canter is important to work on because more and more extensions are required as you advance. There are two trot extensions in First Level Test 1, and in addition, two canter extensions beginning in First Level Test 3 and continuing throughout Second Level. Then, beginning at Third Level, there are medium trots and extended trots as well as medium canters and extended canters in each test. The importance of extensions reaches its peak in Third Level Test 1. Extended trot and canter are new at this point and have coefficients with the result that one-third of the test consists of extensions.

The *halt* occurs twice in each test in connection with the salutes at the beginning and end, and all the First and Second Level tests contain an extra halt with or without a rein-back before moving off again. Thus, it is fairly important pointwise.

Although nearly every horse can do *rein-back*, doing it correctly in a dressage test is quite difficult and requires practice. It is introduced at Second Level Test 1 and appears in every test thereafter.

Travers occurs in Second Level Tests 2 and 4 only, and is probably the least important of this group of exercises. Its value is as a suppling exercise rather than as a point-getter.

Turn on the haunches and *counter-canter* are first performed in Second Level Test 4. They are required in nearly every test thereafter, counter canter in the form of a serpentine, and turn on the haunches in the form of the more demanding pirouette.

Working Walk

Working walk is defined as follows:

> *A regular and unconstrained walk. The horse should walk energetically, but calmly with even and determined steps with four equally spaced beats. The rider should maintain a light and steady contact with the horse's mouth. (Rulebook, p. 150.)*

This statement, emphasizing regularity, briskness, and contact, is all right so far as it goes, but it does not mention being on the bit which is a definite requirement. As at the working trot, this means a suitable head and neck position and a definite contact. The neck must be fairly low and flexed a little at the poll, but the nose is still well in front of the vertical. With this head and neck position and a definite contact, the horse must go freely forward, overtracking and walking with four equally spaced beats. To have a steady contact, the rider must follow the natural movement of the horse's head with his hands.

Previous AHSA tests included "free walk on a *loose* rein" at Training Level, and "free walk on a *long* rein" throughout First and Second Levels. Exits after the final salute in all AHSA tests were ridden at free walk on a *loose* rein. (See Figure 25.) Now free walk on a *loose* rein has been entirely eliminated. All exits are in free walk on a *long* rein. In the body of the tests, free walk on a *long* rein occurs in Training and First Levels, and medium walk at Second Level. The result is that the free walk must now have a very slight rein contact, and the lengthened form of walk in Second Level must now be "on the bit."

It is not always easy to persuade the horse to walk freely forward on the bit. If you start from a free walk on a loose rein with long, purposeful, regular (four even beats) strides, take up a little contact and ask for a little flexion at the poll, most horses will immediately slow the rhythm, shorten their steps, and raise their heads. But the working walk is "unconstrained" and therefore it is important to have steps almost as long as at the free walk. Over-tracking six inches is good. If, when you ask for trot, your horse sometimes speeds up his rhythm at the walk and lengthens his steps instead of trotting, he is probably walking the way he should walk all the time at working walk. But he must not get bouncy. The working walk is a flat-footed walk.

The AHSA said in the old *Notes* that the walk should be at the rate of four to six miles per hour. Four miles per hour equals 107 meters per minute. This is approximately the distance once around the small arena the way one would normally proceed with rounded corners. Try measuring the distance your horse covers at the walk in one minute. You will probably be disappointed. A really good, active, purposeful walk is hard to obtain but very desirable.

Wynmalen recognizes the difficulties. By "carriage" he means flexion at the poll.

> . . . attempts at achieving "carriage" by the use of the walk alone will fail, because the pace does not lend itself to the creation of compressed energy. Instead, a semblance of results will be achieved by shortening the forehand, pulling the head into the body and not by driving the body up to the head. That, as we have seen already, results in a closing of the shoulder, in the destruction of the free forward movement, in a mouth behind instead of on the bridle and more often than not, in the destruction of the pure four-time gait. High-couraged horses may be induced to jog at the slightest provocation, or else the horse may tend towards the amble [pace]. The demanded increase of energy, which it is difficult for the horse to deliver at this gait, may induce him to approach the hoof-beats of each lateral pair of legs. Instead of the absolutely regular intervals, 1-2-3-4, of near-hind, near-fore, off-hind and off-fore, the horse may tend to near-hind and near-fore close together, a little interval, followed by off-hind and off-fore, such as 1.2-3.4. (Wynmalen, p. 182.)

How does one overcome these difficulties? In the first place, one should not start working walk too soon. For a long time the horse should do only free walk on a loose rein.

> At the walk, one has to ride the young horse on a long rein without contact, until it has learnt to accept the bit at the trot and at the canter. . . . (Wätjen, pp. 7–8.)

Then comes free walk on a *long* rein in which the merest hint of contact occurs without any attempt to flex the poll. (See Figure 72.) Seunig advocates the following procedure for use *before* the horse is on the bit:

> The free walk with surrendered reins *has been exercised ever since the first day the horse was mounted. Sometimes it was turned into a free walk with relaxed reins. If the sequence of steps remained uniform and long-striding, we then tried for a temporary slight contact with the bit. This contact with the bit was automatically established when the young horse was halted after trotting [reduced to walk?]. The faster gait's impulsion and posture kept the young horse in hand, with the rider's legs in supple contact. But we required this initial gathering at the walk for no more than very short stretches so as not to disturb the free and easy regular advance. We immediately gave the horse full freedom of the reins whenever its strides grew shorter and hastier. (Seunig, p. 212.)*

I have not noticed the rhythm becoming "hastier" when impulsion fails, but rather I have noticed it become slower. Either would be an undesirable change in rhythm.

Wynmalen and Seunig both go on to discuss developing the working walk (they use the expression "ordinary walk") from the working trot. What this means is that you change from a good working trot to a walk, pushing the horse forward into the walk so that his steps do not lag, and easing the rein to allow the neck to extend a little but trying to keep the head carriage of the working trot as much as possible. Of course you must change from the steady hand position of the trot to the give-and-take flexibility required to follow the horse's head at the walk. Wynmalen describes it thus:

> Fortunately, all these difficulties can be avoided quite easily by allowing carriage, energy, rhythm and collection to develop at the trot and from the trot and, in conjunction with it, at the walk also. .

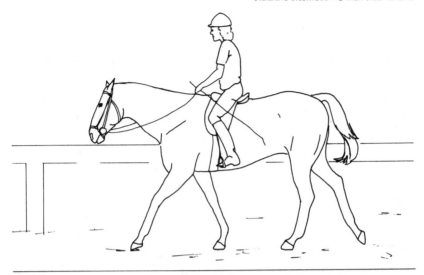

Figure 72. Free walk on a long rein. The rein sags a little and there is no flexion at the poll. Poll may be lower than withers. Note overtrack as shown by the greater distance between forefeet than distance between right fore and left hind.

> *Suffice it to say here then that the slight approach to carriage and collection required in the ordinary walk will develop automatically and without any special schooling during the early stages of a horse's career as a direct result of his work at the ordinary trot [working trot]. (Wynmalen, p. 182.)*

Seunig describes the process in this way:

> *As posture and flexibility improved at the trot and the gallop, a somewhat more positive bit contact, with shortened reins, developed automatically in these walking lessons after about a year's training. The horse's hind feet advanced more or less beyond the hoofprints of the forelegs depending upon its natural locomotion machinery. This was the ordinary walk [working walk]. . . . (Seunig, p. 213.)*

In spite of the problems encountered in trying to develop the working walk from the free walk, sometimes it is easier to proceed in that way. When the horse is doing a good, free walk, you shorten the reins a little while keeping up the speed and rhythm with legs and whip. The rhythm need not become irregular (1.2–3.4–1.2–3.4) if you are careful not to demand too much. If the horse tends to break into the trot you may have to punish him.

The neck can be kept down, if it tends to come up, by "asking down" as at the trot; and then, when the head comes down, one must either give a little rein or take a little, depending on whether the horse needs to extend his nose or flex more at the poll. Be sure to notice how the poll area looks to you when your instructor says your horse is on the bit at the walk. Usually this area (the first six inches of neck behind the ears) looks level when the horse is on the bit, but its exact appearance depends on how tall you are, the conformation of the horse, and the way the mane lies. If it is supposed to look level, you will know that when it slopes up toward the ears the head is too high or the poll is not flexed; if it slopes downward toward the ears, the horse is overbent. (See Figure 73.)

Whether you find it easier to obtain the working walk from the working trot or from the free walk, the AHSA tests require you to do it *both* ways. At Training, First, and Second Levels there is a variety of walk sequences based on the pattern: trot, working walk, free walk (or lengthened or medium walk), and then working walk again. Sometimes this sequence is followed exactly. First you pass from working trot to working walk. Then, after a long

Figure 73. **Working walk. Horse is on the bit. Reins straight and poll flexed. Poll area level. Good overtrack.**

stretch of one of the longer striding forms of walk, you must shorten the reins and proceed at working walk again. Sometimes there is an intervening halt which makes it a bit more difficult to recapture the forwardness of the preceding movement.

You may be puzzled by the distinction between the free walk and the medium walk. The latter can be viewed as showing an improvement in balance. Starting from the "almost collected" position of the working walk, the horse must be able to lengthen his stride while remaining on the bit and extending his neck only a little. He would then have a slightly shorter frame and better balance, i.e., more weight on the hind feet, than at the free walk.

Working Canter

The working canter is not a semiextended gait, although it may seem so compared with the slow, pleasure-horse canter to which many of us are accustomed. In spite of its briskness there are two faster canters, medium canter and extended canter.

At the *working canter* the horse must again be on the bit and going well forward. (See Figure 74.) Translated, this means that the head and neck position and contact should be approximately the same as at working trot (neck probably a little higher) and that the horse must be going fast enough. You may have to "ask down," just as at the walk and trot, if the horse tends to come above the bit. He must flex at the poll as for the trot. Note the slope of the poll area as usual.

You may have to drive energetically when you perform the transition to the canter in order to make the horse go distinctly faster than at working trot and with a definite contact. The gait must be in three time and never degenerate into a four-beat rhythm. (See Figure 75.) The four-beat rhythm cannot be felt as such from the saddle, it merely feels lazy. It can be observed easily by someone on the ground. The easiest way is to watch from behind, fixing the attention on the diagonal (inside hind and outside fore) that makes the second beat of the canter. When the gait is in three time, the shoes on these feet should simultaneously appear and disappear as the feet are lifted and then touch down again.

The canter must also be made straight. This is discussed in the chapter on straightness (see pages 168–171, and 174). An observer behind you is in a good position to notice whether the horse is

Figure 74.   The working canter. The neck is lowered, the poll is flexed, and the horse is on the bit. It is not a very impulsive canter, however. The hind legs should be more under the body. This drawing shows the third beat of the canter when the leading forefoot is on the ground. A blanket of this size gives extra padding without keeping the rider's calf from contacting the horse's side. Rectangular dressage pads are now available.

Figure 75.   Horse above the bit, a lazy canter. This is marginally a four-beat canter. The left fore is touching down before the right hind, although an observer behind the horse probably could not detect it. This is the first beat of the canter when the outside hind is in support.

straight or not. You can also see for yourself, by looking back over your inside shoulder, to see where the croup is. The canter is usually straightened by moving the shoulders away from the wall so that they will be in front of the haunches. You will have to remember to do this every time you start down the long side, and probably it will be more of a problem on one lead than on the other.

The working canter is best developed from the working trot by trying to keep everything unchanged when making the transition, that is, the rider's body and arm position, length of rein, and position of the horse's head and neck. Hence the transition should be made from a good working trot when everything is right at the trot. The horse must continue to step well under the body with the hind legs at the working canter. As soon as the canter commences, the hands should start to follow the natural movements of the horse's head. These movements should seem to the rider to be forward and back rather than up and down. Up and down "hobbyhorse" type of head and neck movements are undesirable.

Lengthening the Stride

Extending, or lengthening, is basically just a matter of urging the horse forward until he brings his hind feet further under him, pushes off more strongly, and goes faster with longer strides and a longer period of suspension. The problem is that as you push, the horse may respond by merely moving his legs faster and taking more steps per minute but not longer steps. Some horses lengthen without any reluctance. Others do not seem to know how to do anything but speed up their rhythm. Fortunately most can be taught to lengthen, at least to some degree.

The *AHSA Rulebook* says this about *lengthening the trot:*

> *Lengthening the stride is an exercise in transitions and longitudinal suppling of the horse. In the working trot the horse should be able to lengthen its stride, without rushing. The horse should move forward to the bit and lengthen its frame. In turn, after the lengthening of stride, the horse should make a definite transition to a shorter stride, without loss of regularity and rhythm in the trot.* (Rulebook, *p. 150.)*

Most of these expressions should be clear to you by now. Rushing, as you know, is an increase or speeding up of the rhythm of the trot. It is, of course, undesirable. Longitudinal flexion or longitudinal suppleness is the bending of the spinal column in a vertical plane. (Lateral flexion is bending it from side to side.) Thus far in the training, the raising of the back (see page 116) and the flexing of the poll when the nose is brought nearer to the vertical involve a small degree of longitudinal suppling. Now there will be longitudinal extension when the frame of the horse is lengthened a little as extension of the trot takes place, and longitudinal flexion at the end of the period of extension.

"Lengthening the frame" means that the distance is increased from the nose to the hocks. Seunig says it is the distance from the nose to the point of the buttock (page 158 footnote in *Horsemanship*). Both are illustrated in Figure 76. What happens is that the neck is extended a little ("move forward to the bit") and the hind legs (including the hocks and the points of the buttocks) are distended a little further toward the rear at the end of each step. You should extend your hands a couple of inches as the horse lengthens and takes the extra rein. (See Figure 77.)

It might seem that there would be no reason to lose regularity or rhythm when making the transition downward to the working trot

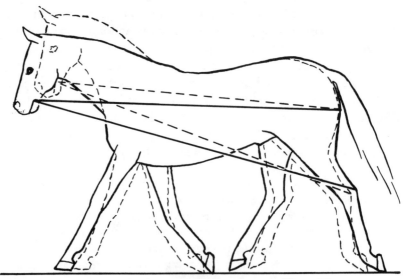

Figure 76.   Lengthening the frame—extending the trot. The solid lines show the longer frame according to both definitions. The dotted lines show a more collected horse and measure the shorter frame.

Figure 77.   Lengthened stride at the trot. Compare with Figure 45,
which shows horse at working trot. Observe that when the stride
is lengthened the nose is extended a little and the hock and
buttock are distended farther backward—thus the frame of the
horse is lengthened.

after the lengthened trot. It often happens, however, especially if
the horse extended a little too much, that he is not in entire command of his balance when he comes to the end of the diagonal and
has to shorten his frame, slow down, and bend to go around the
corner. In that case there may be some uneven strides, and the
rhythm and regularity will not be perfect. The rider can easily
notice this if it happens. Irregular steps may also occur during the
period of extension, and judges are quick to notice and censure.

Before going on, this sentence from the definition of the extended trot should be added:

> The fore feet should touch the ground on the spot towards which
> they are pointing. (Rulebook, p. 151.)

The forefoot should not stretch forward and then be drawn back
before coming to the ground. This fault is often seen, even in
presumably exemplary photographs of the extended trot. (See
Figure 78.)

Figure 78.   Incorrect extended trot. Forefoot extended too far, too soon. It will be some time before the right hind touches down. Remember that the hind foot must overtrack the right forefoot. While the hind foot is coming forward, the left fore must hover and then be drawn back as it is put down. Ideally the fore and hind canons should be parallel.

Now let us see what can be found about extension in the other sources. Wätjen tells us what he expects and gives some hints on how to achieve it:

> At the extended trot the horse should move forward, gaining ground with long elastic strides, while being well on the bit. Self-carriage and balance are the two important factors.
>
> The extended trot should be developed from the ordinary [working] trot, and should only be practiced for short periods. Proper transitions from the ordinary [working] to the extended trot are very important, and the rider should make full use of the long sides and the diagonal of the riding school to teach his horse to lengthen its strides. By engaging the hindlegs with increased driving aids, the rider induces the horse to use his forelegs freely from the shoulders. The artificial cramped stretching of the forelegs, whereby the strides do not gain sufficient ground is wrong and unnatural. The hindlegs must follow the diagonal without stepping sideways or moving too

much apart. The increased driving aids, together with the restrain-
ing influence of the hands, teach the horse to increase the pace with
an elastic back and a supple head and neck position. (Wätjen,
pp. 21–22.)

A number of important points are made here, some of which you
might easily overlook, so I will try to expand on what he says.

The horse should be doing a good working trot, on the bit,
before being asked to lengthen. He must be on the bit before he
lengthens so that he can stay on the bit as he lengthens his stride.
To keep the horse on the bit, the rein must be given as the horse
extends his neck, but must not be allowed to go slack. There must
be some restraint, and the rider should feel the neck stretch forward and downward. If the hind legs start moving wide apart
(spraddling) instead of tracking close together, the horse is being
asked for too much. The rider should be satisfied with a little less
extension for a while. Some writers say that the dressage arena is
not large enough to develop the extended trot, but Wätjen apparently feels that it is. Actually, I have never seen any trainer attempt a longer period of extension than the diagonal of the big
arena—about 175 feet. By "cramped stretching of the forelegs,"
Wätjen probably refers to the same thing just quoted from the
Rulebook. The forefeet should not be poked forward and then
drawn back before touching down. Trainers of Arabian horses call
this "dwelling" and desire it, but the action is frowned on by
dressage people. Each forefoot should touch the ground when at
its greatest forward extension. Podhajsky says:

> *It is also a fault when the horse does not bring his hind legs suffi-*
> *ciently under the body and appears to make a longer stride with his*
> *forelegs, which accordingly have to be withdrawn to equal the*
> *stride of the hind legs. In terms of riding the horse promises more*
> *in front than he can show with his hindquarters. (Podhajsky, p. 34.)*

Podhajsky also stresses the maintenance of rhythm:

> *The difference between the various tempos—the ordinary [work-*
> *ing] trot, the collected trot, the extended trot—does not lie in the ac-*
> *celeration or the reduction of the pace, but exclusively in the*
> *lengthening of the stride or the elevation of the steps while main-*

taining the rhythm. This rule cannot be impressed too often or too strongly on the rider because it is so important to realize that this is the goal we are trying to reach throughout our training.

. . . in the extended trot he will increase the length of his stride and, therefore, stretch his legs more. (Podhajsky, pp. 108-09.)

When increasing the speed the rider pushes the horse forward with both legs but only gives sufficiently with the reins to enable the horse to make longer strides without losing his position and collection. (Podhajsky, p. 113)

The admonition not to lose "position and collection" may seem puzzling as one usually thinks of extension and collection as opposites. A paragraph from Littauer throws light on this point. Littauer calls the first stage of lengthening a "semi-extended" trot.

The semi-extended trot is not necessarily as fast as the normal fast trot; but during it the extension of the forelegs is greater than at the fast trot because a certain amount of weight has been switched to the hindquarters, thus somewhat lightening the forehand. On the other hand, due to this switching of the weight to the rear, the hindlegs, bending in the joints somewhat more than at the merely fast trot, don't engage as much. . . .

While, to obtain a fast trot with lengthened strides the rider merely urges the horse forward, well on the bit, with the hands keeping the action of the hindlegs and of the forelegs united (connected), thus preserving a rhythmic gait and preventing possible breaks in the trot, in order to obtain the semi-extended trot the rider should intermittently check with the reins (half-halts) while constantly urging the horse forward. The combination of these two signals, if tactfully executed, switches some of the horse's weight from the forehand to the hindquarters, and the lightened forelegs begin to exhibit greater and somewhat higher extension. (Littauer, p. 157.)

Perhaps Littauer would call our lengthened trot merely a "fast trot with lengthened strides," but when it is obtained from a good working trot on the bit, it should begin to show some of the features he describes, which you will easily recognize as being aspects of collection. In fact, Littauer calls his semi-extended trot "a close relative of collection." This is what is supposed to be happening by Second Level which calls for *medium trot* instead of merely a "trot with lengthened strides." The stride should be getting longer as the horse's training progresses, but also, with the horse more on the bit—that is, with poll a little more flexed—more weight will be carried by the hindquarters and the forelegs will be lightened. As for Littauer's half-halt technique, I have not seen it used in this way.

Podhajsky says that the shoulder-in can be used to improve extension, and this quotation also shows a relation between collection and extension:

> . . . the shoulder-in improves the bending of all three joints of the hind legs and makes them carry a greater proportion of the weight. This bending improves the suppleness and the activity of the hind legs, and gives more freedom to the shoulders, which improves the paces and favours a lighter contact with the bit.
>
> All this makes the shoulder-in a valuable auxiliary in obtaining a more expressive extended trot. From a brisk energetic shoulder-in, place the horse straight alongside the wall and immediately ask him to go forward in extended trot. Or discontinue the sideways movement of shoulder-in by sending the horse in the extended trot diagonally to the opposite wall on a single track, thus following the direction of the position of the horse's head. In both these exercises it will be found that the steps in the extended trot will be longer and more energetic. (Podhajsky, pp. 138–39.)

Here again is mentioned the shifting of weight to the rear, a characteristic of collection. By now it should be clear that the extension we are striving for is somewhat different from what might be called "pleasure-horse extension." I have watched English pleasure horses doing the extended trot. They do lengthen their stride and overtrack, but they also markedly speed up their rhythm and are usually above the bit.

Chamberlin has this advice to offer:

> In extending the trot correctly, the horse takes a progressively stronger support on the bit as his speed increases. The hands must provide this support smoothly and elastically, as the strides lengthen in answer to the energetic action of the rider's legs. With practice, the trotting strides become gradually longer, until after several months a maximum extension for the particular horse is attained. Depending on the individual, there is necessarily more or less increase in the rapidity of the strides, but their lengthening is the objective. The rider feels that the strong impulsion demanded by his

legs is allowed to escape through his hands in a regulated, cadenced manner. He also feels that the horse's balance depends largely on the steady, elastic support of his hands. . . . The support is never a heavy pull.

. . . At first it should be practiced on straight lines, later on large curves, serpentines, and circles. . . .

Since the extended trot is very strenuous, it should be used for short distances and only on soft, level footing. (Chamberlin, pp. 102-03.)

Chamberlin says there will be some increase in the rhythm. This is, as you well know, undesirable; but I have never heard a judge at First or Second Level criticize a *slight* increase in rhythm so long as there was actual lengthening of the strides. Sometimes, especially with horses that extend naturally, it feels to the rider as though the rhythm has actually slowed down.

Since lengthening is the prime consideration, how can you be sure that the stride is longer? This is easy for an observer to see—it is simply a matter of whether and how much the horse overtracks. The hind footprint should be definitely in front of the corresponding fore footprint. Or, to be more exact, when a horse does a lengthened trot the hind print should be *farther forward* than when that particular horse does the working trot. If he overtracks at working trot, as some horses do, he should overtrack *more* when he lengthens. Lengthening is one of the easier things for the rider to feel. Once your instructor or an observer has watched you a few times, and told you what is happening, you should be able to tell for yourself. I think what one feels is the period of suspension, which gives a very pleasant sensation like flying.

If you do not have the help of an observer, you can also tell by examining the horse's footprints in soft damp soil. The fore and hind prints can be distinguished because the hind feet are narrower and the forefeet are rounder. (See Figure 79.) Or count the number of strides (easier when posting) between two particular fence posts.

Chamberlin and Wätjen differ in the use of curved tracks. Chamberlin advocates extension on straight *and* curved tracks; Wätjen does this work on straight tracks only. There are no extensions on curved tracks in the AHSA tests at present, although there have been in the past. There are curved tracks in FEI tests. Never extend another person's horse around a corner unless in-

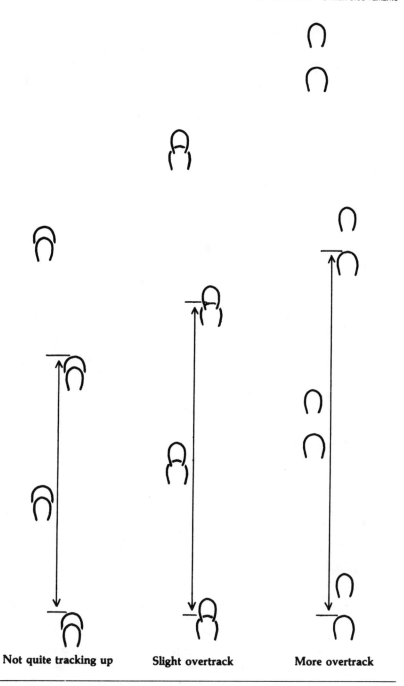

Not quite tracking up   **Slight overtrack**   **More overtrack**

Figure 79.   Length of stride at trot. The arrow shows the length
of one stride.

structed to do so; some trainers and instructors are very strongly opposed to this. There also seems to be a difference as to the amount of support that the horse takes on the bit. Wätjen says the horse must "carry himself," that is, hold up his own head and neck. Chamberlin seems to expect a stronger contact. Actually the latter may be describing an "ordinary fast trot" rather than a "semi-extended trot" à la Littauer.

Wynmalen has a technique that I will quote briefly. He alternates extension and collection, developing both simultaneously. I have never seen this method in use.

> *The horse . . . finds it easier to quicken rather than to lengthen his strides; and that we wish to avoid at all cost!*
>
> *So this is how we proceed.*
>
> *We have our horse nicely settled at his ordinary trot with a soft contact on the mouth. . . .*
>
> *We now close our legs gently, just enough to make him accelerate, just enough to do so distinctly but no more. The energy for this acceleration is delivered by a hindleg, which pushes with increased strength from a position behind the vertical. This action can have no other effect than to lengthen the next few strides. But only through the momentary effect of acceleration! That effect ceases as soon as the horse settles to his increased speed; the increased speed in itself does not really help our purpose; on the contrary it may very well spoil it; it may cause the horse to run fast with short strides, which is a disastrous form. It is for that very reason that we demand only momentary acceleration which must, as we have seen, produce a few lengthening strides. We demand this acceleration by action of the legs alone, without action by the hands.*
>
> *But as soon as we have obtained a few longer strides, the hands receive the horse gently on the bit, the legs cease driving, the horse is brought back quietly to his ordinary trot.*
>
> *And here, in a nutshell, we have the entire principle for the development of the diagonal gaits [trot], extension, collection, retardation! We extend the stride, we receive the increased energy on the bit (collection), we retard. (Wynmalen, pp. 196–97.)*

Wynmalen devotes several pages to the elaboration of the technique whereby he alternately extends and collects the horse, developing both forms of the trot.

Decarpentry suggests the use of sloping ground to encourage extension.

On upward grades, the horse instinctively throws the whole of his mass forward to give it the best disposition for the economical use of the thrust of the hind legs. He loads his shoulders by unloading his hind quarters, thereby increasing the propulsive power of the latter. His neck lengthens. His forelegs are lifted in more rapid succession, they develop their elevation and augment their extension after touching the ground. The top is tensioned along the whole of its length, the loin becomes firmer so that it can transmit without waste the efforts of the hind legs, which for their part flex their joints better, extend more energetically and come to the ground in more rapid succession.

Lengthening of the trot, in these conditions, as long as it is obtained with prudent measure in progression and duration, and on carefully selected gradients, provokes a flexing and stretching of the locomotive system far superior to any that could be obtained from the horse, for an equivalent leg action, on level ground. Through the repetition and the judicious progression of these efforts, the horse will get into the habit *of using more muscular energy in response to a set degree of impulsive action of the legs. (Decarpentry, p. 106.)*

While the shifting of weight to the forehand is not desired as an end product, this may be a useful training procedure. Decarpentry also mentions trotting in heavy going, trotting when going toward home, and trotting alongside another horse with a more extended gait, as useful techniques.

Finally there is the problem of the horse that breaks into the canter instead of extending. Decarpentry comments:

The main difficulty in the work of developing the trot is the horse's propensity to break into the canter when asked to increase his speed, and this propensity can turn into a resistance if one does not take care.

In the first place one should avoid provoking a breaking into the canter due to abruptness when demanding increased speed, or to lack of firmness or suppleness of the seat, or in general to any asymmetries in the rider's position, movements or aids. It may even by necessary to discontinue using the legs in alternate sequence.

If the horse does break into a canter, he must be stopped without brutality, but quickly and firmly so that he can associate this sort of reprimand with its object, i.e. breaking into the canter. Without raising his voice, the rider will thereupon utter the command: "trot", and will repeat this procedure every time the horse commits the same fault. (Decarpentry, pp. 109–10 including note.)

This is not a great deal of advice for such an important movement as lengthening the trot. Advice on *lengthening the canter*, however, seems to be completely nonexistent. Perhaps this is because the extended canter was not formerly stressed in dressage training. Also, extending the canter comes naturally to most horses. When a horse is trotting and wishes to go faster, he changes to the canter; he does not naturally extend the trot. When he is cantering, however, and wishes to go faster, he extends the canter. But there are problems. Some horses quicken without lengthening, just as they do at the trot. Some tend to run away and are hard to keep under control, and some become very crooked.

I should mention that the dressage rider does not lean more forward at either extended trot or extended canter. He maintains his regular dressage position with seat "down" in the saddle and body vertical. At first it may seem that sitting the trot when the horse lengthens is impossible, but when the horse extends "with supple back" it becomes reasonably comfortable. The supple back should come naturally as a result of correct trotting on the bit.

Wynmalen suggests in one place that if the rider starts to rise at the trot when he wants extension, that this can become a signal or aid for extension. Since tests at this level call for lengthening both rising and sitting, this might lead to problems when you show your horse.

The Halt

There are two problems in obtaining a proper halt. First, the horse must be brought to a standstill. At this stage it may be a direct halt from the trot, or there may be intermediate walk steps. At Training Level a few walk steps are permitted, but not at First and Second Levels. Second, an attempt must be made to get the horse to "square up" and stand still, on the bit, before moving off again. We will take up these problems one at a time.

The standard writers offer some advice about the correct way of bringing a trained horse to a good halt, but give little help on how to teach the horse. If you have difficulties you will have to rely on your instructor for guidance. In general, the halt is considered a rather difficult and advanced transition!

The Pony Club manual has this to say about early halting when the rider is just getting the horse on the bit:

At this stage, the pony must be asked to reduce his pace from trot to walk very carefully and slowly. If he is hurried in any way, up will go the head again with the same false bend of the neck, causing a great deal of resistance in the mouth and back. . . . In order to get a smooth reduction of pace, the rider closes both legs, sits very deep in the saddle, whilst he lightly resists with the hands and 'asks' with the right hand and right leg [if the horse is stiff on the right side] . . . for a relaxation of the jaw; as the pony responds, the rider must instantaneously be still with his hands and gently push the pony into a walk with his legs. The secret lies in 'asking' and rewarding by the immediate relaxation of the aid when the pony has responded.

From a walk, the pony must be brought back to a halt, using exactly the same aids as when going from a trot into a walk. (Training the Young Pony, *p. 62.)*

The effect of "asking" is to remind the pony (or horse) to keep his head down. I have found it effective.

At the beginning of training, the horse is not halted very often and not much attention is paid to how he stops so long as he does not stop abruptly and toss up his head. Podhajsky says:

So far halts have been practiced only at the conclusion of the daily work or between working periods. (Podhajsky, p. 152.)

This would mean only about three or four halts per day in the early stages of training. Similarly Froissard warns:

The halts *should during early schooling be used with the greatest moderation, because they tend to enervate the horse. (Froissard, p. 63.)*

When has the time come to work on the halt as an important transition? Froissard says:

A profitable introduction to the halt can only be undertaken after a tentative suppling of the hindquarters and a partial straightening of the horse. (Froissard, p. 63.)

Podhajsky would possibly delay even longer than Froissard:

Practise in lateral work, the exact execution of exercises, and the changing of pace and tempo will increase the balance, suppleness, and the action of the rein going through the horse's body so that now he will be ready to learn the halt. . . . *A correct halt belongs to the more difficult exercises and needs appropriate preparation. (Podhajsky, p. 152.)*

He then gives the aids for a correct halt, assuming it is from a collected trot and without intermediate walk steps:

To produce the correct halt the horse must be pushed forward with both legs on the girth and held in a lively collected trot. The impulsion procured in this manner will then be absorbed by repeated short actions of the rein and the braced back of the rider in order to ensure that the hind legs step well under the body and to obtain a halt in the direct line of the movement. Experience has taught that if the action of the rein is too prolonged and too firm, it will have a restraining effect on the hind legs, thus making it difficult, or even impossible for them to step well under the body. . . .

The rider will obtain a near perfect halt if he succeeds in bringing it about mainly by bracing his back. The rein on the hollow side should remain applied with a slightly firmer contact supporting the action of the rider's back, while the rein on the stiff side, by repeated short actions, prevents an increased position of the horse's head to the hollow side, thus helping the movement to end correctly.

When the horse has come to a halt, the pressure of the legs and the action of the reins must cease. (Podhajsky, p. 153.)

Podhajsky and the members of the German school believe in applying the legs and reins simultaneously when halting, and ascribe much importance to the use of the braced back. Podhajsky sums it up:

When reducing the pace to the halt, the transition should be smooth, fluid, and level, which is possible only if it is brought about by the correct application of the rider's back, leg, and rein aids, thus ensuring that the horse does not lose his balance. (Podhajsky, p. 39.)

Müseler is another example of this view:

If the [rider's] back comes into action the whole horse is shoved together and pushed forward. He runs up to the bit and there, if the reins don't give, finds sufficient resistance to stop him. It requires a minimum of pressure on the bit to make the horse understand that . . . he should stop. (Müseler, pp. 13–14.)

Seunig's description is a little different:

> After suppleness has been achieved, the transition to the walk
> and then to the halt will no longer be the result of letting the horse
> come to a stop, but rather a slowing down of the horse with a seat
> that does not follow the movement as much, . . . the hand absorb-
> ing the impulsion and avoiding any backward action if at all pos-
> sible. (Seunig, p. 157.)

Froissard represents the French school where the attitude is quite
different. A cardinal principle of this school is never to apply the
legs and reins at the same time. It is felt that the legs say "go forward" while the reins say "don't go forward" so that they contradict each other. And, of course, the braced back is not part of
the French system of aids:

> To shorten the pace, cease leg action and increase rein tension by
> alternate pressures of the fingers. Exert pressure with the fingers of
> one hand without letting those of the other act, then slightly relax
> those which have just acted and exert pressure with the others as if
> you wanted to squeeze the juice from a lemon in each hand alter-
> nately. Each increase and decrease of pressure lasts but a split sec-
> ond. This simple hand action suffices to obtain the shortening of
> the pace, provided you keep your elbows close to the body and
> your shoulders drawn back. When the desired slowdown is at-
> tained, cease hand action but keep your reins a little tauter than
> before and make your legs act anew.
>
> To halt obtain first of all a shortening of the pace, then close the
> fingers of both hands at once over the reins. Keep your elbows close
> to the body, shoulders resisting. Once the halt is obtained, cease the
> hand action which has prompted it, your lower fingers relaxing
> very slightly, reins kept taut. (Froissard, p. 130.)

> . . . your elbows must be kept close to the body and your wrists in
> straight alignment with your forearms, so that the tension of the
> reins can only be altered by the action of your lower fingers. If you
> want to add force to this action, have recourse to your shoulders
> which may choose to "permit," by yielding, or to "create a wall," by
> blocking themselves as long as required to oppose an initiative
> taken by the horse. . . . The shoulders are, so to speak, the extreme
> end of the reins and their slightest contraction is felt by the horse's
> mouth. (Froissard, p. 131.)

You will notice that Podhajsky, Müseler, and Froissard

specifically mention that when you wish to halt you first obtain a little more collection. Podhajsky speaks of a lively, collected trot. Müseler notes that the stride becomes shorter and higher. Froissard tells the rider to shorten the pace. This increase of collection is often called a "half-halt." The half-halt (in this case the German, not the French half-halt) will be treated in Chapter 12.

Moving on to Chamberlin's comments on the halt, it is apparent that he shows French influence, for there is no mention of legs or back in this paragraph:

> After the horse's mouth is made, as will be explained later, the fingers close and the hands are fixed in position once only, to decrease the gait or halt. At the instant the halt occurs, the fingers and elbow relax to reward the mouth. (Chamberlin, p. 98.)

Wynmalen recommends using the legs to stop. This surprises me as he is usually so "French."

> . . . the correct way to stop a horse, is to close both legs on the girth and simultaneously to effect a light but steady pull on the reins. It is surprising how very few people use the legs to stop a horse, or for that matter know that the legs can and should be so used. Yet where the properly schooled horse, who has learned to understand the meaning of this signal, can be stopped in an entirely effortless manner, it sometimes requires almost herculean strength to bring the unschooled variety to a halt! (Wynmalen, Equitation, p. 56.)

Many writers warn the rider not to "pull" on the reins to stop the horse, but instead to "fix the hand." Müseler, Chamberlin, and Wynmalen, although they do not agree about the use of legs and back, agree in advocating a "fixed hand." Here I quote Wynmalen, beginning with sentences from his chapter on leading the horse in hand.

> . . . we offer the maximum passive resistance whereof we are capable, letting the horse do all the pulling. In that way, and in that way only, the release of strain will be automatic and immediate the moment the horse moderates or ceases his pulling. . . . (Wynmalen, pp. 41–42.)

> [Thus] the principle has been explained in [the chapter] dealing with the horse led from on foot.

> *. . . from the saddle, the hand's action should be exactly the same. But, as we now sit in the saddle on the horse, we can obviously not alter the speed whereat our body is being carried forward by the horse. That is true, but there is, or at any rate there should be, considerable independence between our hands and that part of our body which is sitting in the saddle. Whilst we cannot prevent the seated part of our body going forward with the horse, we can see to it that our hands, forward of the body, slow up their movement and finally stop it altogether. In other words we let the horse carry our body closer to our hands and we do not retract the hands towards the body. It is a fine distinction but an important one.*
>
> *As a result of this action the horse will notice that he himself is causing tension on the rein, because he is going faster than his rider's hands; exactly as when being led; and exactly so, and for the same reason, he will stop. The idea of pulling will not occur to him, because he is not being pulled at. (Wynmalen, pp. 70–71.)*

The distinction is indeed a very fine one, and I am not sure that I (or the horse) can follow it as put forth in this quotation. There is, however, a definite distinction between a "fixed" hand and a "pulling" hand. Actually, in both cases you may *start* by pulling. The difference is in what happens when the horse begins to yield. The pulling hand continues to pull, moving back toward the rider's body, until the horse stops. The fixed hand, however, stays in one place relative to the horse's body and consequently reduces its pull as the horse begins to yield, and ceases to pull when the horse ceases. In my opinion, if you tie a horse to a post, and the horse pulls, the post pulls back—but, of course, only so long as the horse pulls. Whether it seems to the horse as though the post pulls, I do not know. The fixed hand is like a post, but it is mounted on the horse and goes along with him. When the horse is pulling, the hand, in my opinion, has to pull in order to remain stationary (in relation to, say, the withers).

Chamberlin, however, puts it this way:

> The hands resist, in contra-distinction to pulling, *so that when the colt concedes, they do not fly in toward the body, but instead, instantly relax and move forward to reward obedience. (Chamberlin, p. 82.)*

Wynmalen says:

> *For the hand to be unyielding we have to tighten the joints, wrist, elbow and shoulder so that the limb becomes difficult to move. (Wynmalen, p. 40.)*

So, however we may describe it, on occasion we should all be able to employ a fixed hand.

In evaluating these varying suggestions for halting, one must bear in mind that the type of horse one is dealing with makes a world of difference. Some writers sound as though you never pull on the reins. This is fine, if the horse wants to stop. Some horses must be driven forward continually to maintain a good working trot. Merely stop driving such a horse, and he is happy to be allowed to stop. The problem may be to prevent too abrupt a halt, and it may be important to push him forward into the slower pace or halt. But other horses, notably young Thoroughbreds, want to go, not stop. At this stage of their training fixing the hand, either with or without use of the legs and back, would probably fail entirely to convey to them that they were supposed to stop. Your instructor will help you. Do not be surprised if his suggestions sound a little less than ideal.

If you are instructed to close your legs when halting, the difficulty is to do so without simultaneously lifting your seat out of the saddle, for I believe your instructor will expect your weight to be on your seat when closing the legs to halt. This can only be done if you squeeze with the calves of your legs and not with your knees. Gripping with the knees causes the thighs to grip, and when the thighs grip, the muscles of the thighs get rounder and this lifts the weight off the seat bones.

For a long time I have been curious as to when and by whom the braced back was invented, for I have never seen an account of its origin. It is not mentioned by the French school, but is constantly referred to by the Germans. Although they mention it so often, they seldom try to explain it. So when a writer mentions bracing the back, or pushing the small of the back forward, or using the loins, the reader does not know exactly what is intended. I think that in some European countries beginners must be taught the technique very early and it is so well understood that there is no need to explain it.

When mentioned in the quotes in this chapter, I believe it means *either* that you follow the movements of the saddle *more* closely with your seat, digging the seat bones into the saddle at each stride, *or* that you stiffen your back and cease to follow so that your seat bumps somewhat. A third tactic is for the seat to cease to follow the trot movement, relaxing and settling heavily and solidly into the saddle like a sack of sand. This last may be what is meant in the Pony Club manual by the expression "sit very deep." If your instructor is a "back man" you will have to try to find out from him exactly what he wants you to do. Since I have had very little experience with such instructors, all I can do is suggest the various things which they might mean. The whole concept of the seat as an aid will be taken up in Chapter 12.

Now let us consider the second problem in obtaining a good halt. Besides just stopping, you must be concerned about how the horse stands when he has come to a halt. He is supposed to be straight and square and immobile. The only advice I have ever heard for stopping straight is to hold the horse straight with legs and reins when stopping. Podhajsky mentions this in the quote on page 220. It is easy to see from the judge's position at "C" whether the horse comes down the center line straight and remains straight while stopping. Judges are very strict on this point.

Writers mention the importance of halting with the weight evenly distributed on all four feet or stopping in a balanced manner. Both these expressions merely mean that the four feet shall be at the corners of a rectangle, and that the rear canons shall be approximately vertical, that is, that the horse shall neither be stretched nor standing under. This is stopping "square." When the legs are so placed, the weight is of necessity evenly distributed on the near and off sides. (See Figure 80.) It will not actually be evenly distributed between fore and hind legs, however, until the horse is a good deal more collected with the neck higher and the nose vertical. As yet you should not try to achieve this.

Bringing the four feet to the corners of a rectangle is called "squaring up" and often involves teaching the horse, especially when halting through the walk, to take a final half step with the foreleg that moves last to bring it up to its mate, and a final half step with the hind leg on the *other* side to bring *it* up to *its* mate. (See Figure 81.) The horse is apt to bring up the forefoot himself. You can tell which foreleg takes the last step by watching the shoulders. If the *right* shoulder, for instance, moves last, then the

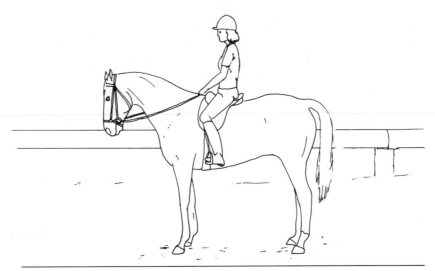

Figure 80. A square, balanced halt. At this stage the head should
be a little in front of the vertical.

left hind will have to take a final half step. Wynmalen has the only
thoughts I have found on squaring up:

> Whilst going forward the horse moves his limbs in a definite se-
> quence of movements. To complete a stride, or several strides, the
> horse must be able to complete the entire sequence of the
> movements of individual limbs which go to make up such a stride or
> strides. Now a good halt means a square halt, implying that the
> horse be allowed to round off his stride naturally and fluently and
> be not interrupted in the middle of it. This then implies a further
> refinement in the use of hands and bridle.
>
> . . . Therefore, the hand should not stop, at any rate not com-
> pletely, until the horse has stopped square, which he will do
> automatically provided he be given the chance. . . . as soon as the
> horse has slowed up sufficiently to indicate that he is about to halt,
> the fingers will let the faint final impulsion slip through unhindered,
> so that the horse may round off his stride. (Wynmalen, p. 71.)

It is very easy to try this. Maybe it will work for you and your
horse. In my experience, the horse is more apt to square up of his
own accord when stopped in a collected manner from a working
trot than when stopped gradually through the walk.

You may have to lean over and look at your horse's hind feet
after he has halted to see if they are side by side. (Not when riding

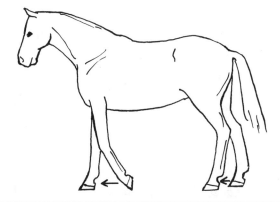

Figure 81.   Squaring up at the halt. After the forefoot comes up beside its mate, the opposite hind foot must be brought up.

a test, of course!) If the last hind foot has not been brought up, try nudging with your heel. If the horse does not understand what you mean, you can try tapping the hind leg with your whip.

Always square up by moving a leg or legs forward, never backward—not even one leg! Judges do not accept this. One horse that I had eventually sometimes took a full step with the final hind foot. This could have been corrected only by moving the other three feet forward. I was advised, however, that it was better not to do this, but to be satisfied with less than perfection.

How do you induce the horse to stand immobile and on the bit? To be on the bit at the halt means that the head and neck position should be the same as when the horse is on the bit in motion, and that the horse should keep a contact, neither trying to pull the reins out of your hand nor tucking his head in toward his chest and dropping his contact. The ideal is that you halt, ease the reins a little, relax the legs—merely keeping them against the horse's sides—and sit perfectly still.

Aside from this, about all that can be suggested is to pay attention to whether you shift your weight. Frequently riders shift their weight about more than they realize. The reins should be taken in one hand during the salute with as little effect on the bit as possible and no effect on the rider's weight. The nodding of the rider's head (if a woman) or removal of the hat (if a man) should be the rider's only movement and should be done with minimal effect on the weight distribution on the horse's back.

Rein back

The *rein back* must be preceded by a distinct halt from the preceding trotting movement, but you should not make an effort to square up. The Pony Club Manual contains some good advice:

> The rider brings his pony to a halt and, whilst his legs are still acting, the hands resist so the pony, finding he cannot go forwards, goes backwards due to the impulsion created by the leg aids. . . . The pace is in two-time. He must rein-back by lifting each diagonal pair at the same time.
>
> He must not be pulled back, or he will throw up his head and hollow his back so that he could not step backwards correctly. He must keep his head still and step back perfectly straight. (Training the Young Pony, *pp. 79-80.*)

At first you are allowed to back 3 or 4 steps, but then in Test 4, you must back exactly four. To control the number of steps you will find that you must ask for the new forward movement while the horse is still stepping backward. With a little experimentation you will know exactly when. The horse should remain on the bit and be "thinking forward" and ready to move off again even while moving backward. Rein back should not be practiced very often.

Travers

This movement is included in few tests and is not liked by some trainers. Podhajsky, for example, says it is only used at the Spanish Riding School in rare instances and then it is done on the horse's stiff side only. We are required to do it to both sides, however, and most trainers consider it a useful preliminary to two-track.

The *Rulebook* states: (See figure 60 for illustration.)

> The horse is slightly bent around the inside leg of the rider. The horse's outside legs pass and cross in front of the inside legs. The horse is looking in the direction in which he is moving. (Rulebook, *p. 143.*)

Actually, since the forehand moves straight ahead on the track, the front legs do not cross, but the hind feet point slightly outward toward the rail and do cross if the horse is well bent.

Wynmalen and Decarpentry recommend starting travers as you resume the track after riding a small circle. If you do it this way, the horse is already bent and you start the horse along the track when the forehand has just reached the track but the haunches are still on the circle. In other words, the horse comes off the circle a few moments sooner than he would for shoulder-in. You can easily see where this point would be in Figure 65. In Test 2, travers is started at the conclusion of a 10 meter circle, and this is probably the easiest way, although it can almost as easily start at the conclusion of a turn rather than a circle, and that is also a good way to practice it. The rider's outside leg keeps the haunches in off the track, the inside leg, around which the horse is bent, maintains impulsion, and the reins guide the horse along the track. The outside rein must keep the neck from bending more than the body. You can also start the movement as in Test 4, by simply pushing the haunches in with your outside leg while keeping the forehand on the track and thus bending the horse's body. The horse is bent the same amount as for shoulder-in and must be slightly collected in order to maintain the bend. When done correctly, you get a distinct impression of moving sidewards. Of course, the horse must remain on the bit and not change rhythm or speed. As with other exercises, everything will go wrong at one time or another, and you will have to learn to notice and correct each deviation and eventually to keep them from happening.

Turn on the Haunches

The *Rulebook* defines the *turn on the haunches* as follows:

> *This movement is a schooling exercise which can be executed from a halt or walk and is preparatory for the pirouette, which is executed out of a collected gait. The horse's forehand moves in even, quiet and regular steps around the horse's inner hindleg while maintaining the rhythm of the walk. In the half turn on the haunches, the horse is not required to step with its inside hindleg in the same spot each time it leaves the ground but may move slightly forward. Backing or loss of rhythm are considered serious faults. This movement may be executed through 90°, 180° or 360°. (Rulebook, p. 145.)*

Figure 82 illustrates the turn through 180° which is a half turn or

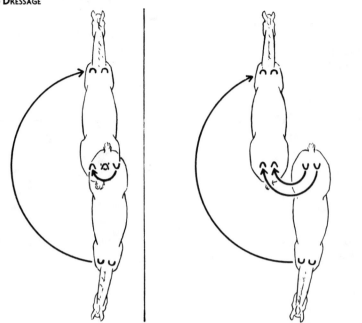

Figure 82. Half turn on the haunches to the right. The diagram shows both the lower level half turn, with the inside hind foot making a small circle, and the more advanced pirouette, in which it steps on one spot.

half pirouette and is the required form in the AHSA tests. The diagram shows the inside hind, which is the pivot leg, taking small steps forward and thus making a small circle. At Third Level when it is done in collected walk, it is called a half-pirouette, but the only difference, aside from the horse needing to be more collected throughout, is that the horse should preferably *not* make a circle with the inside hind, but instead step up and down on the spot. In either case, the horse should not halt first but move fluidly into the turn, he should remain on the bit, be bent a little in the direction of the turn, and keep stepping with all four feet in the walk sequence. Finally, he should not offer any resistance, nor change his rhythm from the walk he was doing, nor tip his head to the side.

While all this sounds relatively easy, especially as the horse is moving slowly and it seems as though everything would be under control, it is really incredibly difficult to get everything right, and even Grand Prix horses often do not do it very well. I think I have spent more time practicing turn on the haunches than any other one movement.

Podhajsky describes the aids and they sound simple enough:

The inside rein leads the forehand into the turn; the inside leg on the girth maintains the correct position, ensures that the movements of the legs are not interrupted and, together with the outside leg, prevents the horse from stepping back, which would be a bad fault in this exercise. The outside rein, lightly applied defines the degree of the position of the horse's head and prevents the horse from falling into the turn or from hastening the movement. The outside leg, behind the girth, demands the turn around the inside leg and must push forward the moment the horse shows any sign of stepping back. (Podhajsky, pp. 158-9.)

The difficulty is partly that you have to learn to feel what the horse's hind legs are doing. Is he lifting his inside hind or is it "stuck?" Is he stepping in place, or slightly forward (which is all right), or is he stepping a little sideways or backwards (which is not)? It is also difficult because there are so many things to notice all at once: rhythm, bend, head position, and relaxation of the jaw, as well as the movements of the legs. Finally, horses usually do not respond as Podhajsky's description of the aids would lead you to expect. The inside leg on the girth does not always "maintain the correct position" which is a bend to the inside. The legs do not always "prevent the horse from stepping back." The outside rein does not do all the things it is supposed to do, and so on. Your instructor will probably start by having the horse make quite a large circle with the hind legs which will be gradually decreased as you gain control over all aspects of the movement.

Counter Canter

All that is required at *counter canter* in Second Level is a canter depart on the "wrong" lead in the middle of the long side which should not cause much trouble once the horse has learned to do a simple change of lead. The counter canter is then maintained around the end of the arena which may be ridden as a large half circle. The *Rulebook* says:

The horse maintains his natural flexion at the poll to the outside of the circle, in other words, is bent to the side of the leading leg. His conformation will not permit his spine to be bent to the line of the circle. (Rulebook, p. 140.)

So you will permit your horse to flex a little to the *outside* and try to keep the gait otherwise just like his regular canter. It should not be any slower and should be balanced and on the bit.

12 Riding Techniques

In this chapter, I want to discuss several of the more advanced aspects of seat and aids. The first of these is *bracing the back*. This technique apparently is of German origin and is a translation of the German expression, *"Kreuz anziehen,"* which means literally, "small-of-back tightening." It is a rather controversial subject. Some riders brace the back; other riders do not. And as usual, both groups generally believe that they are absolutely right. The subject is variously referred to as bracing the back, driving with the seat, weight aids, action of the loins, and pushing the buttocks or pelvis forward. All these expressions refer to the same—or at least very similar—phenomena.

Another subject that occupies a good deal of space in many books is *rein aids*. They have a bewildering variety of names: direct, indirect, opening, leading, opposed, and so on and on. I think they can best be understood *after* one has learned to execute the figures and movements described so far in this guide. After you can do shoulder-in, for example, it clarifies things to put a name to the rein aids you are using, and only then can you appreciate the effects the aids are having. It does not help much to learn the aids and their names and then attempt to use them and obtain the described results. If, however, you are already using a particular technique and achieving a certain result, it is nice to know what it is that you are doing.

This is also the place to discuss the *half-halt*. It becomes more important when you work to increase collection as you approach Third Level, but you will surely be expected to use it in your Second Level work. This will be the German half-halt (or half-parade) which is used as a call to attention before commencing a movement or figure as well as to improve collection. There also are some other meanings of the term which will be explained.

Then there is the crucial matter of *feel*. The importance of "feel" in achieving the working trot has already been touched on (see page 150). Rising on a desired diagonal without looking at the horse's shoulder or foreleg, checking your lead at the canter without looking down, and squaring up at the halt are some other areas where you need feel. Finally there are a few odds and ends having to do with seat or aids. These include weight shifts, collapsing the hip, and the aids going through.

Bracing the Back

The logical place to start learning about this complex subject is with a quotation from Müseler, since he devotes more space to the subject than any other writer. To begin with, he distinguishes three variations in the position of the rider's back which he calls "normal," "braced," and "hollow." The diagrams in Figure 83, which is adapted from his book, show the three positions of the back.

> When 'bracing the back' the lower end of the spine and the rump-bone (os sacrum), which connects the spinal column with the pelvic bones, are pushed forward. The pelvis is thereby pivoted, being raised at the front and lowered at the rear, thus preventing the body from tilting forward. (Müseler, p. 17.)

Referring to Figure 83, in the central diagram, the back is braced. Note that the pelvis is lowered at the rear (curved arrow); the lower back feels as though it moves slightly forward (straight arrow); the back is flatter (less hollowed in at the waist); and the shoulders are to the rear of the hips (shown by the relationship of the shoulders to the vertical line passing through the hip joint).

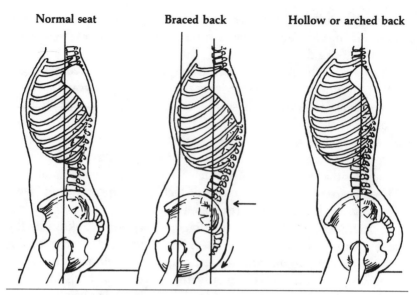

Figure 83. Bracing the back. Adapted from Müseler's *Riding Logic,* **page 16.**

This is the position a child in a swing takes to make the swing move forward. The swinger then assumes the "hollow" position as the swing swings back. When it reaches the farthest backward point, he assumes the "braced" position, and then accentuates this position as it swings forward.

Expressions meaning the same thing include bracing the back, back muscle action, bringing the back into action, tilting the hips, action of the loins, driving with the seat, pushing the pelvis forward, and pushing the tummy forward. Bracing the back is also referred to as using back aids, seat aids, or weight aids. These expressions are fairly self-explanatory. The "tummy," it seems, must be thought of as being entirely below the waist. Another term is "pushing the small of the back forward." The "small of the back" must also be thought of as being below the waist, what I would call the "lower back." Referring again to the diagram, and comparing the "braced" position with the "normal" position, notice the position of the lower spine in relation to the shoulder blade. A vertical line through the shoulder blade has been added in the "braced" position to make this comparison clearer.

D'Endrödy also describes the braced back. The following paragraph is from his book:

> *Braced position: the rider, by bracing certain parts of his back, waist, and the muscles of the loin, creates in the structure of his seat a certain elastic tension. By leaning slightly backwards, he pushes forward the lower part of the spine, so that the buttocks become set forward, whereas the seat-bone presses strongly into the saddle. This tension of muscles cancels the slight concave position of the waist, and makes the spine take up a straight form. (d'Endrody, p. 66, footnote.)*

He says this is a "combination of the French relaxed position and the German braced position," but to me it sounds exactly like Müseler's braced back.

Seunig describes the braced back very similarly, calling it "the seat that provides increased drive." He starts from a "normal seat" like Müseler's normal seat.

> *. . . in the normal seat the upper body rests chiefly upon the two seat bones (the ischia, which are shaped like sled runners), . . . the load may be shifted to their front edge (the crotch seat) by tilting the hips slightly forward. Similarly the load can be shifted to their rear edge (the seat that provides increased drive) by a similar tilt of the hips backward. (Seunig, p. 55.)*

> *Now if the pelvis is pushed forward by a greater elastic contraction of the small of the back, the rear edges of the seat bones carry a greater load than in the crotch seat. The hips slant backwards more or less, depending upon the degree to which the small of the back is contracted, and the normal seat's vertical line from the ischium to the hip slopes to the rear like the pelvis. (Seunig, p. 61.)*

It is easy enough to carry out this action and assume the two positions: normal and braced. The diagrams in Figure 84 should make it even clearer. Try it as you sit in your chair. So, now that you can "brace the back," when and why should you do it? I believe that the way in which the braced back is used and the purposes sought vary somewhat from writer to writer, and I will attempt to list the various applications. In summary they are:

1. Sticking to the saddle,
2. Increasing impulsion,
3. Promoting engagement, and
4. Reducing the pace.

One application to which Müseler devotes a good deal of space and comes back again and again is *sticking to the saddle* or *following the movement of the horse.* In this version the rider tilts his pelvis, and the small of the back becomes flatter, in a completely relaxed way. In fact, it seems to me to be accomplished by relaxing certain back muscles, almost by slumping. Having done this, one simply stays in the new position, remaining flexible, and follows the walk, trot, or canter *in this position.* A passage from Müseler makes this plain:

> . . . this back-muscle action pushes the rider's buttocks . . . forward, and the lower end of his spine rests firmly in the saddle. . . . This makes for a very close contact between rider and horse without necessitating any tiresome muscular exertions. . . . By bracing the back more or less firmly one can sit tighter or looser in the saddle. (Müseler, p. 14.)

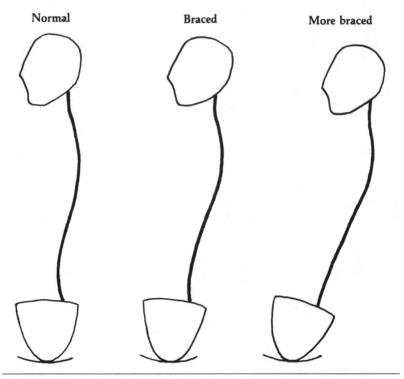

| Normal | Braced | More braced |

Figure 84.   Increased bracing of the back. The tilting of the pelvis and the change in the shape of the spine are shown.

The term "braced back" seems a little inappropriate in this context. It suggests muscular exertion or tension, which obviously is not what Müseler is talking about. He says again and again that one cannot stick to the saddle without bracing the back, and that one must be supple and no muscular effort should be involved. I would go along with him to the extent that it does seem to me that I can follow the saddle closer (sit deeper in the saddle) by adopting a slightly braced position.

Seunig, on the other hand, describes following the horse's movement while in the "normal" position. Read the following description from his book:

> The upper body is kept straight and naturally upright above the vertical line from the seat bones to the hips, so that the spinal column, which has the shape of a rather flat S, is not impeded by cramped tension and can follow or sustain movement as required and swing with it. This swing serves the purpose of absorbing the shocks of the gait that cannot be taken up by the knee, the shoulders, and the elbows alone, so as to guarantee a deep seat that does not leave the saddle.
>
> By means of very minute oscillations of his spine, hardly perceptible to the eye, the rider who has a "soft" seat is able to "sit out" the movements of his horse, that is, to stick to the saddle. (Seunig, p. 56.)

You may wish to experiment if your instructor does not have strong views on this subject. The bracing of the back can be so slight that it is not visible to the onlooker. Following the movement in the braced position involves more flexion (give and take) in the hip joints than in the spine.

The second application of the braced back is *driving with the back (or seat)*, gaining more impulsion. Judges will often comment when impulsion is insufficient: "Drive the horse more forward with back and legs." This means to make the horse go faster (with proper rhythm, of course) by using the driving leg and also bracing the back, which the horse feels as an increased forward and downward pressure of the rider's seat in the saddle. Yet there is disagreement as to whether the horse can really be driven better in this way than by the leg alone. First, let us hear from exponents of the braced back as a driving aid. These include Müseler:

> By 'bracing the back', . . . it is easy to move a swing, and in the same way we can make a horse go forward.
>
> If the rider in 'moving on' not only uses his legs, but also brings his back and loins into play, he will find that he obtains the desired result with a minimum of leg pressure. The more use the rider makes of his back the less leg pressure will he require. (Müseler, p. 13.)

How does the rider "make more use of his back"? By tightening the back muscles more strongly in the braced position and even leaning a little backward. Look again at Figure 84. To walk or trot on, therefore, one would brace one's back somewhat more while increasing the leg aids and giving with the reins.

Seunig is not as all-inclusive as Müseler in his advocacy of the braced back, or "weight control" as he calls it here:

> The leg is the control [aid] that produces the motion of the horse, setting it in motion and maintaining it. Neither the hand nor the rider's weight can take its place.
>
> Only after the horse is in motion, unresistingly using its muscles to move forward and carry the rider, can the rider drive it forward, slow it down, or make it change direction by distributing his weight. But these weight controls will achieve their purpose only when supported by leg and hand, that is, when all three controls work together. (Seunig, p. 63.)

He does not advocate the use of the "weight aid" at all times:

> . . . every control [aid], including the leg control, is supported by the increased forward push of the pelvis. When no control signal [aid] is given, the small of the back should be thrown forward only enough to keep the hips vertical. (Seunig, p. 63, and footnote.)

So when not aiding, one reverts to the "normal" seat, according to Seunig, with the pelvis vertical rather than tipped either forward (crotch seat) or backward (braced).

Podhajsky is not entirely clear to me on this subject, but I think he advocates a lesser degree of bracing than Müseler.

> The rider's back must be upright with the small of the back braced. The spine must not be hollow and the back must remain supple and flexible. This is necessary to enable the rider to follow all movements of his horse as if he were part of his own body. The back must remain firm and upright. . . .

> *Here we have another example of how much contrasts combine to make harmony. The rider should sit upright but not stiff, and he should be completely relaxed without slouching. This harmony can only be the result of a long and systematic training. . . . (Podhajsky, pp. 212–13.)*

Just how the small of the back is to be used as an aid he does not explain. He remarks that if the hips tilt forward so that one sits on one's fork, "any pushing aid of the weight would be impossible." But he does not describe the pushing aid of the weight. The crotch seat or fork seat would be represented by the third diagram in Figure 83, the one Müseler designates as "hollow" or "arched."

Wynmalen, in the French tradition, does not advocate the driving seat. He discusses Müseler at some length (see pages 95–99 in *Dressage*) but really does not seem to understand him. He is not convinced that bracing the back can make the horse move forward, and concludes that bracing the back as advocated by Müseler does not make a whole lot of sense. Yet oddly, in one place in his book (page 119), Wynmalen speaks of a "sustained drive by legs and seat." I have long wondered how this slipped in. It is completely out of keeping with the rest of his book. He does make what may be a wise suggestion:

> *. . . movements such as bracing the back, and many other movements of the rider besides, can, even though they are not truly aids in their own right, become "aids by association."*
> *. . . The simplest example, probably, is the aid of the spur; this, provided the rider knows his job, is always preceded by a gradual tightening of the calf of the leg against the horse's flank; quite obviously then, the schooled horse will not wait for the arrival of the spur, but will act on the approach of the calf; or on any action usually even preceding the approach of the calf, such as for instance "bracing the back". (Wynmalen, p. 98.)*

Seunig does not advocate bracing the back in the early stages of training, and when he explains how it is brought into the training program he says something that is consistent with the idea of "aids by association." After the horse has learned to respond to the leg, he says:

> *The only thing left for us to do is to combine the forward-driving action of the seat with the action of the legs in the horse's brain. It is*

easy to do this because the pressure of the seat bones from back to front that is exerted when we push our pelvis forward also exerts a forward thrust upon the horse's back. (Seunig, pp. 152–53.)

If this seems to indicate an "aid by association," however, it is only fair to add the following quote, also from Seunig:

The increased tightening of the small of the back when the pelvis is pushed forward and the upper body is carried upright—the characteristic feature of the seat that provides increased drive—pushes the horse forward to the hand, puts it "in hand". (Seunig, p. 61.)

I say "increased drive" because the normal seat itself, without any contribution on the part of the rider, sustains motion and thus acts like a driver as the result of the correct action of the rider's weight upon the motion of the horse. (Seunig, p. 66.)

These quotations indicate that Seunig ascribes a genuine driving effect to the correct action of the weight.

Long ago I once had a couple of lessons on a horse schooled in this way, and I could scarcely induce the animal to even walk forward because I did not understand what to do with my back and seat. The instructor said "push your tummy toward your hands," which did not make much sense to me at the time. I would like to have another opportunity to ride that horse today.

The third use of the seat is in *promoting engagement.* Remember that engagement has two aspects: stepping well forward under the body (tracking up) and bending the three joints of the hind leg when it is grounded (lowering the croup). The driving leg of the rider brings about the long stride, and the driving seat or weight aid is said to induce the bending of hip, stifle, and hock. I quote Seunig again:

. . . when the small of the back is pushed forward without the rider's upper body leaning backwards perceptibly, the increased forward-driving seat enables the horse to bend its hindquarters more because of their increased load. . . . (Seunig, pp. 67–68.)

Pushing the small of the back forward shifts the weight of the upper body backwards, so that the hindquarters, which are engaged under the horse's body because of the driving leg control, are bent even more at their joints, thus stretching out more elastically and rapidly, like tensed springs. As soon as the rider feels that the weight control has had the effect of temporarily increasing the burden on the hindquarters, he must immediately resume the normal seat, which follows the movements of the horse, in order not to prolong the burden and achieve the opposite of what he desires. If he did not do so, the horse would escape the uninterrupted pressure by ceasing to engage its hindquarters. (Seunig, p. 153.)

Sometimes a more aggressive following of the movement of the horse in a more braced position is advocated. Along this line, Wätjen says:

The weight aid is nothing more than a stronger bracing of the back, or following the movement of the horse. (Wätjen, p. 30.)

When it is desired to increase engagement in this way, the rider does not follow the horse's motion by flexing in the small of the back, but rather by flexing mainly in the hip joints with the waist held firm. More about the use of the seat in engagement will have to wait for a discussion of collection.

The fourth application of the braced back is in *reducing the pace and halting.* These are also called "downward transitions." I will present several quotations and then explain a bit more:

The driving seat control. . . is essentially the same, whether used to accelerate the rate or to interrupt it. The end result is determined by the co-operating rein control. (Seunig, p. 153.)

The restraining aids must influence the horse by an increased bracing of the back and a firmer action on the reins by the rider's wrist and forearm, the upper arm remaining in contact with the body, thus influencing the back muscles of the horse. (Watjen, p. 30.)

At first it will be the action of the reins that brings about the transition but, later it is done by the bracing of the back. When changing to the walk the horse will be pushed forward with both legs, in the same way as when reducing the speed at the trot, and brought to the walk by repeated actions of the reins together with a braced back. . . . The result that the rider seeks is a smooth and fluent transition to the walk by merely bracing his back and maintaining the contact with both legs. (Podhajsky, p. 114.)

There are several different things that these writers may be trying to describe when they talk about bracing the back to reduce the pace. I will take them up one at a time although they are very closely related. First there is the "rein as an extension of the back." Müseler says:

> The back is always the connexion . . . between legs and reins. The influences exerted by the legs and the reins can only be in harmony if a simultaneous action of the back effects an intimate connexion between them. (Müseler, pp. 51–52.)

The idea is that the rider's back unites his seat aids and rein aids. If he leans back one inch, for example, without changing the position of his arm, the seat bones press down more firmly and the reins are automatically shortened one inch. Read the above quotation from Wätjen again. This may be what writers mean who say you must never pull on the reins to stop the horse.

A second possible connection between bracing the back and slowing the horse is that when one braces "a bit more," one can also stiffen and cease to follow the movement of whatever gait the horse is performing. This tends to inhibit the movements of that gait. D'Endrödy describes this:

> The taking action of the seat [is] performed in the process of retardment. . . . In exercising this action, the rider should bend his upper body a bit further backwards from the ready position, which causes his seat-bone to press down deeper in the saddle.
>
> The pressing down of the seat-bone is carried out mainly by the muscles of the waist. However, the effect of the pressure becomes more pronounced due to the fact that the seat-bone cannot shift forward because the thighs, which cleave to the saddle and are fixed by the position of the knee, check any of its movements through the pelvis.
>
> With the aid of the taking action of the seat, the rider can exert a downward pressure on the horse's back, which tends to decrease the swinging movement of its spine and results in slowing down the motion of the horse. (d'Endrödy, p. 67.)

I have also heard this explained by Charles de Kunffy, and it can be found in his book, *Creative Horsemanship*. He clearly states that the back is stiffened and the seat ceases to follow the movement of the horse (pages 84–85, and 158–59).

A third version is that the seat used to stop the horse is identical with the action used to accelerate the horse. This is the point of the Seunig quote above. Müseler expresses the same idea:

> *If a rider, on a well-schooled horse, is bracing his back while having a good contact with his legs and if the reins simultaneously:*
>
> > *give—the horse will move on*
> > *do not give—the horse will stop. (Müseler, p. 52.)*

In my opinion, what works best in driving or slowing a particular horse, depends in a large degree on the horse's temperament. I am now working a horse so willing to stop (lazy?) that it is important to drive him forward when retarding and to use the rein very gently. I formerly had a horse which never wanted to reduce the pace and required a more energetic rein aid and a minimum of leg aid. The driving seat may also be more useful for warm-bloods, formerly the typical German-type of horse, than for Thoroughbreds. I have also heard that this aid is not as universally applied in Germany today as it used to be. If your horse is going forward satisfactorily, and reducing the pace satisfactorily, my suggestion would be to ignore the driving seat and continue as you are. But if you are having difficulties, there may be some useful suggestions here.

As I stated at the beginning of this section, there is much controversy about the use of the seat. A talented rider whom I know says that the driving seat did not make her horses go one bit better. Robert Hall used to warn his students that if the rider braced his back it would make a young horse hollow (or drop) its back and would somewhat flatten the back of a well-developed horse. He said that only the rider's leg could make the horse's hind legs more active. I have also heard the theory that the horse steps forward under the center of his body where the rider's weight is bearing down—and thus is induced to track up. And Wynmalen suggests that the weight might become an aid by association.

I recall one instructor saying that "shoulders behind hips" was driving, and "shoulders above hips" was restraining. I also recall that at an early show in my area I commented to a German-trained teacher who was present that all the horses lacked impulsion. "Yes," he said, "the riders have no strength in the back." You are apt to hear all sorts of things. I hope this makes it clear that there is much disagreement and confusion about the use of the back. Under these circumstances, the best thing to do is to follow your instructor's directions as long as your horse seems to be making progress. Usually an instructor has a method that works for him, and he should be able to judge what your horse requires. Since at this stage we are so far from perfection, we need not be unduly disturbed by this disagreement among the experts. It does seem, however, that more than one road leads to Rome.

Rein (and Leg) Aids

Aids are classified in a bewildering variety of ways. You are apt to be told to use rein or leg aids that are parallel, lateral, opposed, contrary, opening, or intermediary, to mention just some of the confusing terms. I will try to define them briefly and indicate where you can turn for more details if it is necessary.

First of all, aids may be distinguished according to whether or not they act on the same side of the horse's body. If the active aids are the right rein and right leg, for example, they both act on the right side of the horse's body and are called *lateral aids.* The opposite situation would be called *diagonal aids* when you use principally the right rein and left leg, for example, which do not act on the same side. American riders are customarily taught to go around corners using the inside rein and the outside leg. I hear this every day at my local stable where elementary English lessons are given. This is, or course, diagonal aiding. When these same beginners are taught to put their horses into the canter on the correct lead they use the outside rein and the outside leg, an example of lateral aids. (See Figure 85.)

Some writers stress that one starts with lateral aids and advances later to the use of diagonal aids. This seems to refer primarily to the change from leg-yielding to more advanced lateral work, such as two-track. Leg-yielding calls for lateral aids, that is, one rein turns the horse's head away from the direction he is going, while the leg on the same side pushes him sideways. Shoulder-in is similar. In a correctly flexed two-track, however, the predominant rein and leg act on opposite sides. The inside rein obtains a flexion to the inside, while the outside leg obtains the sideways movement. (See Figure 86.) The same is true of haunches-in and

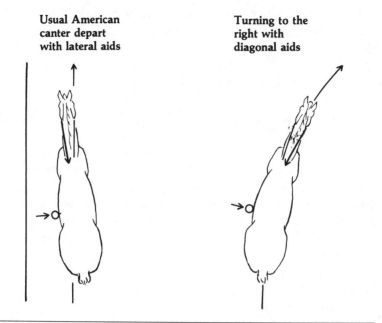

Usual American
canter depart
with lateral aids

Turning to the
right with
diagonal aids

Figure 85.   Lateral and diagonal aids.

Leg-yielding with lateral aids

Two-track with diagonal aids

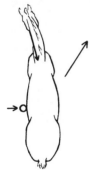 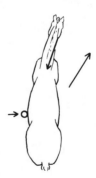

Figure 86.   Lateral and diagonal aids. In this diagram both horses
are bent. This happens in leg-yielding when it is done by a more
advanced supple horse.

haunches-out which also require diagonal aids. Now that you have done some of these exercises, you can easily understand the distinction between the terms "lateral" and "diagonal." Jackson goes the furthest into this type of classification, even using the terms "interior lateral" aids and "exterior lateral" aids, the general meaning of which you can guess. (See pages 65–67 in his book.)

A second classification of aids is the division into *bilateral* and *unilateral aids.* Bilateral means that the two reins act alike, and the two legs act alike. For instance, both legs drive and both reins yield—the horse accelerates. Or, the legs drive and the reins resist. This would increase collection; it could be called a half-halt. Unilateral, on the other hand, means that the two reins do different things, and the two legs do different things. An example would be a canter depart with the inside leg on the girth and the outside leg behind the girth while the inside rein maintains a flexion to the inside. Thus the two legs are acting differently, as are the two reins. (See Figure 87.)

About the only use of bilateral aids is when going straight forward and reducing or increasing the pace (but not canter departs). Most of the time we are, instead, using unilateral aids. Straightening and flexing, following curved tracks, and doing lateral work all require unilateral aids. Using alternating leg aids at the walk would

Half-halt with bilateral (or parallel) aids

Canter depart with unilateral (or diagonal) aids

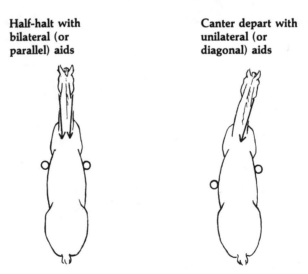

Figure 87.   Bilateral and unilateral aids (also called parallel and diagonal aids).

also be unilateral. The terms "unilateral" and "bilateral" are from Müseler. Charles de Kunffy uses this classification, but calls them *parallel aids* and *diagonal aids* instead of bilateral and unilateral. You can consult his book, *Creative Horsemanship*. Note that de Kunffy's "diagonal" aids are not the same thing as Jackson's "diagonal" aids.

A third type of classification defines the effects of the exact direction in which a rein acts, whether straight back, toward the side, or across the withers. These are all unilateral rein actions and usually have the effect of turning the horse. This seems to be a French type of analysis. Froissard goes into considerable detail, and Jackson has even more detail. In fact Jackson describes five main effects and two intermediate phases. I will quote from Froissard, and supplement his definitions with a diagram (Figure 88). As you read about the five rein effects, refer to the diagram, which shows the direction of action of the rein (the right one only is illustrated) and the resulting direction of movement of the horse.

THE FIVE REIN EFFECTS

The opening rein *(1st effect)* has a natural action upon the horse. It consists of drawing his nose in the direction one wants to take. . . .

The counter-rein *(2nd effect)* also called, the neck rein, acts upon the base of the neck which it nudges in the proposed direction. To turn right, make your left wrist act from left to right and from back to front. It is the only rein effect permitting you to manage your horse with a single hand. . . .

Both rein effects *[1st and 2nd]* act on the forehand which takes the new direction, while the hindquarters are content to follow the shoulders in this change. Since the action does not interfere with the forward movement, the horse does not tend to slow down.

By contrast the following three rein effects *[3rd, 4th, and 5th]* address the hindquarters. By a rational disposition of his reins, the rider opposes the shoulders to the haunches, whence their appellation of reins of opposition. This opposition impairs the forward movement which the rider's legs must painstakingly keep intact or restore whenever it tends to disappear. . . .

The direct rein of opposition *[3rd effect]* acts upon the haunches. The counter-rein of opposition in front of the withers *(4th effect)* acts upon the shoulders. The counter-rein of opposition passing behind the withers *(5th effect or intermediate rein)* acts upon the shoulders and the haunches. (Froissard, p. 155.)

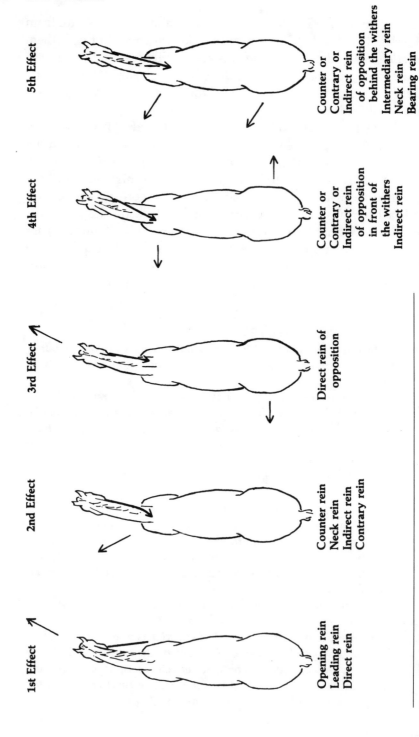

1st Effect

Opening rein
Leading rein
Direct rein

2nd Effect

Counter rein
Neck rein
Indirect rein
Contrary rein

3rd Effect

Direct rein of
opposition

4th Effect

Counter or
Contrary or
Indirect rein
of opposition
in front of
the withers
Indirect rein

5th Effect

Counter or
Contrary or
Indirect rein
of opposition
behind the withers
Intermediary rein
Neck rein
Bearing rein
Intermediate rein

Figure 88. The five rein effects.

The right direct rein of opposition *makes the horse turn right by pushing the haunches to the left. In performing this rein effect, the rider tightens the right rein in the direction of his right knee, after slightly relaxing the fingers of his left hand. . . .*

The right counter-rein of opposition in front of the withers *makes the horse turn left by throwing his shoulders to the left and his haunches to the right. . . . In performing this rein effect, the rider, increasing finger pressure on the right rein, shifts his right wrist to the left, passing in front of the withers.*

The right counter-rein of opposition behind the withers *displaces the whole horse toward the left. This rein effect is intermediate between the direct rein of opposition, which only acts upon the haunches, and the counter-rein of opposition in front of the withers, which only acts upon the shoulders. It thus falls to the rider, in shifting his right wrist toward the left, to determine how far behind the withers the right rein should pass in order to act with equal intensity upon shoulders and haunches. . . . (Froissard, p. 157.)*

Now let us consider the technique of the five rein aids, one by one, and note where and how they have been used in the exercises thus far described for First and Second Levels. I should point out that the diagrams in Chapters 9 and 10 do not attempt to distinguish between these various rein aids. This is chiefly because the writers whose descriptions they illustrate did not usually explain just which rein effect they were advocating. Most did not use the French terminology at all. Teachers are not usually very specific about rein aids when giving instructions to their pupils. For instance, I have found that the term "indirect rein" is often used collectively for the second, fourth, and fifth effects, and it is up to the pupil to figure out what to do. If you are confused, there is no substitute for asking your instructor to be more specific. But let me give you a hint. Ask your instructor to simply show you how to use your hand. It is usually better not to get into technical discussions as to the *name* of the rein effect that is wanted.

First Effect

The *opening rein* (leading rein, direct rein) is not supposed to act from front to rear, but rather to the side. This does not mean that there is no backward tension. Rather it means that there is no *increase* in backward tension. You simply maintain the contact (or tension) that you have, while moving your hand to the side. This is perhaps the most common way for dressage riders to ask the horse to perform turns and circles. Just what the *other* rein (the outside rein) does, will be dealt with presently.

Second Effect

The *indirect rein* (contrary rein, counter-rein, neck-rein) seems to require that the horse look to one side and turn to the other side. We all know that Western riders hold both reins in one hand and turn by means of the neck-rein. I am told that the Western horse *should* look the way he is going when neck-reined. However, the question pertinent to dressage riding is, do we ever use the neck-rein? I mean, in the narrow sense as defined above with the head turned away from the direction of motion and the hand acting toward the front. The answer seems to be "no" so far as the exercises used in modern dressage are concerned.* Only in leg-yielding and shoulder-in does the horse look to one side and move his shoulders to the other side, but the neck rein is not useful in these movements because it would put the horse back on one track.

The three *reins of opposition* are much used in dressage. You might almost say they are the hallmarks of dressage, partly because they require the horse to be in strong impulsion. Jackson says:

> They are so called because the effects are obtained by opposing the horse's shoulders to the forward impulsion of his hind quarters. It follows that they depend essentially on impulsion. Without impulsion there would be nothing to oppose. This presupposes a horse well "in front of the legs" and "on the bit". . . . (Jackson, p. 58.)

In other words, a horse performing the working trot!

Third Effect

The *rein of direct opposition* is probably the rein with which most nondressage riders turn their horses even without impulsion. If the horse is in impulsion, it requires use of the outside leg to *keep* the haunches from swinging out. We may use it for the turn on the forehand where it helps induce the haunches to swing sideways, a movement which, in this case, is *encouraged* with the inside leg.

---

*The neck-rein can be used for a turn on the haunches in which the horse looks away from the way he is turning. Jackson describes this. (Jackson, pp. 139–140.)

Fourth Effect

Indirect rein of opposition in front of the withers (contrary rein of opposition in front of the withers, or just indirect rein) turns the head to one side while moving the shoulders to the opposite side. It can straighten the horse by moving his shoulders over in front of his haunches. When doing two-track, it can bend the neck to the inside and *keep* the shoulders to the outside in front of the hind-quarters. In shoulder-in, the outside indirect rein can move the shoulders off the track combined with the inside rein of direct opposition which bends the neck a trifle to the inside.

Fifth Effect

Indirect rein of opposition behind the withers (contrary rein of opposition behind the withers, intermediary rein, intermediate rein, neck-rein, bearing rein).* This rein effect can produce leg-yielding (in two-track format) with a little help from a sideward-pushing leg. Leg-yielding can, of course, be done without it, especially when the horse is not yet doing a good working trot. In combination with the inside direct rein, which bends the neck to the inside, it can produce the two-track.

In using the indirect reins, it is usually stressed that the rider's hand must never cross the withers. This admonition need not be taken too literally. Look at Figure 89. It shows two points at which the rider might be holding the rein. If he is holding it at one point, his hand has not crossed the withers. If he is holding it at the other point, it has. The rein effect is exactly the same in both cases, but in the second case the rein is being held a little too long, and the rider must either shorten the rein or cross the withers. Certainly we do not always have our reins adjusted just right.

Now let us consider the use of the "other" rein. By this I mean the inactive rein. I have illustrated all the rein effects with the right rein, so in this context the left rein is the "other" rein. In describing

---

*Decarpentry makes some fine distinctions. The difference, as he describes it, between the indirect rein, the indirect rein of opposition, and the neck-rein is rather subtle. A foot-note in his book when read very carefully with the text makes these distinctions: Indirect Rein acts on *corner of mouth only* and flexes neck to same side (this must be rein effect 2); Indirect Rein of Opposition acts on *corner of mouth and side of neck* (this must be effect 4); Neck or Bearing Rein acts on *side of neck only* (not mouth) and moves the whole horse to the opposite side effecting the half-pass (this must be Effect 5) which can be done with slight flexion to opposite side brought about by using the other rein as a direct rein of opposition. (Decarpentry, p. 44 including footnote.)

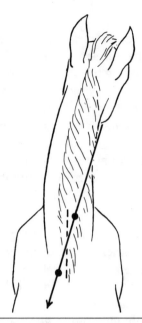

Figure 89. It is said that the hand must never cross the withers. However, when the rein is being held a little too long, the hand may cross with no change in the effect of the rein.

the three reins of opposition, Jackson says that in each case the nonactive rein first cedes (yields or gives) to allow the neck to bend and then "supports" the active rein, parallel to the horse's neck. (Jackson, pages 59–62.) In our examples this means that the left rein gives a trifle to allow the slight flexing of the neck, and then resists any further displacement of the neck. This is very important, because otherwise there is no "opposition" and the right rein will not work. It is because both reins are in firm contact that considerable impulsion is required to keep the horse from slowing down. Do not expect that you can easily use these reins and obtain the effects described. When you can do so, you and your horse will be well trained.

The uses of the five rein effects that I have cited are not very extensive, but you will also find yourself using combinations in dealing with special problems. For instance, in working with a horse that had a long-standing habit of cantering very crookedly on the right lead, it was necessary to use the right rein of opposition which helped push the haunches out onto the track, and the left indirect rein to keep the neck straight and move the shoulders inward. Needless to say, the horse had to be cantering with great vigor to continue forward against these rein effects. Some of the corrections in Chapter 9 for crookedness problems will be seen, on examination, to involve various combinations of these effects.

Besides the five effects described, there are also two intermediate reins, one between the third and fifth and one between the fourth and fifth. These are explained by Jackson (page 62) and I have illustrated them here. I shall not describe them further. The effects already described are probably as complex—or even more complex—than the reader can appreciate at this point. If in practice you have difficulty recognizing the exact effects of the five reins, this sentence from Decarpentry should be well appreciated:

> It is only on the well schooled horse, i.e. the submissive and educated horse, that the actions of the hands can be exactly defined. (Decarpentry, p. 42.)

However, with a horse trained in the French manner, the rein aids are ultimately of supreme importance:

> During dressage [he means during training] and with incompletely schooled horses the hand effects are insufficient to determine the positions the rider wishes to impose upon the horse. They can only do so with the co-operation of the legs used in a different manner from that which induces impulsion. The necessity of this co-operation diminishes as dressage progresses. As it approaches perfection the role of the legs is increasingly confined to the production of impulsion, and can progressively be restricted solely to this role as the horse becomes more eagerly submissive to the actions of the hands, which must eventually be able to determine by themselves all the positions required of the horse by academic equitation. (Decarpentry, p. 44.)

This discussion would be incomplete if we did not consider how the German school, which has very little to say about rein effects, manages on turns and circles. Müseler does not even describe the rein aids, which he says are overly emphasized by other writers. They should be "almost imperceptible." Ideally, he says, turns are executed by means of a unilateral back aid—pushing forward the inner seat bone only—and a slight shift of weight to the inside. See pages 51, 53, and 137–39 in his book.

Wätjen, who is usually so brief in his instructions, has a good deal to say about turning:

> All rein aids can act only from forwards to backwards and up-wards or vice versa, but must never act sideways. (Wätjen, p. 31.)

> The horse should be in the full sense of the word turned and not thrown around, so that it moves in a position properly adapted to the turn, bent in the ribs, which can be achieved by a correct guid-ance with the reins. In the actual turn the horse must be more bent with the inside rein, the outside rein supporting and regulating the position, the flexion and the turn. The outside rein is always pre-dominant, supported by the inside driving and the outside restrain-ing leg. The horse more or less receives the direction from the inside rein, according to the diameter of the turn. The restraining (outside) rein should act in the direction towards the rider's body, thereby enabling the horse to bend in the turn; should the outside rein be ap-plied sideways, then the horse would be thrown round. (Wätjen, pp. 39–41.)

> The horse is correctly bent if it responds to the inside rein and leg aids, but at the same time finds a support on the outside rein, its neck being well fixed at the withers. In this way it adopts a slight flexion of the whole vertebral column. The degree of the flexion is determined by that of the turn. (Wätjen, pp. 34–35.)

This is called going around the turn "on the outside rein." It sounds contradictory, but this is what happens. The inside rein ob-tains a bend while the outside rein maintains contact. Then the in-side rein is eased—it floats—and the horse continues, at least for a couple of strides, with his neck bent and a contact with the outside rein. When he begins to lose the bend, the inside rein reestablishes it and then eases again. The inside rein has an inhibiting effect on the inside hind leg. By easing it, the rider helps the horse maintain impulsion on turns and circles.

Wynmalen has an unorthodox approach to circling that is worthy of consideration. He notes that use of the inside rein to circle—in the manner of the rein of opposition—causes the horse's haunches to swing out. Since this is not desired, he explains that it is not necessary to use the inside rein to start a circle.

> Consequently, when riding to commence a circle, we have the horse collected, in front of the legs, straight, and on the bit with even con-

tact on both reins. Now, to commence the circle, there is no need whatever to take any action with the direct or opening rein. Instead, we lengthen the indirect rein. In circling to the right, we lengthen the left rein. Since we take no action with the right rein at all, the question of setting up a force of opposition to the haunches does not arise. But we have our horse well in front of our legs, maintaining undiminished impulsion; the effect of this impulsion causes him to re-establish equal contact with both sides of his mouth; he does that by bending his neck to the right. Which is exactly what we want! (Wynmalen, p. 145.)

Wynmalen advises this simple procedure only for large circles. It reduces collection rather than increases it because "the sum total [length] of our two reins is greater than it was before," so the horse must be doing a good working trot before commencing the circle. Wynmalen's instructions for smaller circles are more complex. You may want to read his whole discussion of the subject in *Dressage*, pages 143–47.

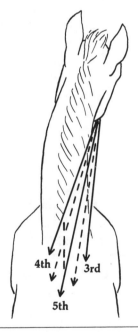

Figure 90.   There are two additional rein effects, between the 4th and 5th and between the 3rd and 5th. Consult Jackson's *Effective Horsemanship,* **page 62,** for explanation.

Another classification of rein directions is provided by the late Colonel Bengt Ljungquist, the former coach of the United States Dressage Team, in his book *Practical Dressage Manual.* According to Colonel Ljungquist, the rein acts either straight back (with a bending function) or toward the rider's hip on the same side (with a leading or supporting function). These would be, in French terminology, the direct rein of opposition (third effect) and the leading rein (first effect). It is interesting to see how this classification is used to explain a turn. The inner rein bends the horse and then, if the horse tends to cut the corner, as most horses do, the outside rein acts as a leading rein (outside hand moved a little to the side) to lead the horse further into the corner.

The second function of the rein acting toward the rider's hip, you will notice, is called "supporting." This is interesting because what it "supports" is the rider's leg on the same side. If you are doing a turn on the forehand, you are pushing the hindquarters around with your inside leg. You can "support" the effect of the leg by using the leading rein on the same side. In fact this is what you are no doubt already doing. Froissard would say to pull straight back to support the leg. Ljungquist says to use the leading rein. The "other" rein, he stresses, must always keep a contact. It does this in order to control the bend, that is, not to let the neck bend more than the body. Ljungquist discusses this subject on pages 41–44. Colonel Ljungquist's book is a very useful one. It was published privately in 1976, and was reprinted in 1977. Colonel Ljungquist died in 1979.

The Half-halt

At some time you will surely be asked to perform a half-halt by an instructor or clinic leader, and as there are several kinds some confusion may result. Actually the term "half-halt" covers quite a variety of actions with rather different purposes, so teacher and pupil sometimes have difficulty understanding one another. It seems to me that the subject can best be discussed if five meanings or uses of the word "half-halt" are recognized.

1. The French half-halt: an action to raise and extend the horse's neck and head.

2. Podhajsky's unilateral half-halt: a means to straighten the horse and correct the "soft side-stiff side" problem.

3. Any collected reduction of pace short of a full halt.

4. An action intended to collect the horse or to teach the horse collection.

5. A slight increase of collection that improves contact and attention.

When the term "half-halt" is used in my part of the country it refers to one of the last two meanings. I will dispose of the three uncommon meanings first.

What I call the French half-halt is a means to raise the horse's head if it is too low. This has already been mentioned on page 66 as a remedy for a horse that is overbent. It is very clearly described by Froissard, Decarpentry, and Chamberlin. I will quote from Chamberlin:

> The half-halt is used to lighten the forehand of horses which . . . lean heavily on the hand, or carry the head too low. . . .
>
> It is executed as follows: the fingers are firmly closed on the stretched reins, after which the hands are rotated inward and upward, with the little fingers moving toward the rider's chest. This is accomplished by vigorous rearward and upward twists of the wrists and forearms. The half-halt applies a quick, sharp reaction to the horse's mouth. Since contact with the mouth is not lost due to the taut reins, the reaction differs from a brutal jerk with a loose rein. The effect is to make the horse quickly lift his neck and head, throw more weight on to his hind-quarters, thus lighten his forehand and prevent his boring against the bit. The hands momentarily release all support after a half-halt and then establish the light, normal feel. The half-halt may be executed with one or both reins. . . .
>
> When a horse rounds his whole neck far over so that his face passes in rear of a vertical plane, the hand, or hands, must be carried far forward over the poll when administering the half-halt. This will lift and extend his head and neck. . . . Half-halts are used to lighten the forehand without decreasing the speed. *They are not concerned with halting.* (Chamberlin, p. 102.)

I have not had any personal experience with this technique.

The second meaning of the half-halt, Podhajsky's corrective for the "soft-stiff" problem, was thoroughly covered in Chapter 9, page 169.

The rest of the meanings all have something to do with collection. The third meaning seems as though it might be the "original" half-halt, being anything short of a full halt. We all perform this sort of half-halt frequently, but I never hear it referred to by that name. Müseler uses it to mean shortening the stride (as in the transition from extended trot to working trot) or coming to a walk. He calls these "half-parades." "Parade" is a German word for "halt." Similarly, Wätjen says:

> The half halt is executed in the transition from a more extended to a shorter movement. (Wätjen, p. 26.)

How should such a half-halt be done? Seunig begins with the aids for a full halt and then defines the aids for a half-halt. The aids are described as a sequence of events:

> Stimulating forward reach of the hindquarters, followed by halting them by leg pressure on both sides of the horse. Loading action of the seat by pushing the small of the back farther forward, keeping the upper body upright and sustaining action of the hands. More or less accepting pull on the reins, as necessary, with unchanged posture of the rider's upper body and passive legs. . . .
>
> If the controls do not co-operate in the sequence given—say, the accepting pull on the reins is made too early or the weight action becomes too much of a driving action because the upper body leans backwards excessively—the stop cannot be soft and fluid but is abrupt.
>
> The controls employed for the half halt are similar, the sole difference being that the hands allow motion to continue accordingly. Driving controls persist and outweigh the restraining ones. Stretching in one's seat and closing one's fingers will suffice for sensitive horses. (Seunig, pp. 133–34.)

Podhajsky describes it thus:

> The same aids are employed as for a full halt but to a lesser degree and are discontinued the moment the horse has responded. (Podhajsky, p. 40.)
>
> . . . the rule is that with any half- or full-halt—this rule may sound paradoxical—the rider first pushes forward and then reduces the

speed; only by the combination of the aids of the legs and the hands will the collection be preserved during the transition. (Podhajsky, p. 114.)

Here is Müseler's description of the half-halt:

. . . all these half-parades are executed in the same way: by driving the horse from rear to front into the passively resisting hand. (Müseler, p. 116.)

These actions to slow the horse, as from trot to walk or extended trot to working trot, are related to collection in that the horse is slowed down in a collected manner. He is "pushed together" as he is slowed down.

The fourth meaning, teaching the horse collection, or collecting him after he has learned to go in a collected manner, will probably not be done deliberately at this stage of training.

The fifth meaning, a slight increase of collection, is the most common version of the half-halt and includes a number of very frequently used applications. Since it involves only a *slight* increase in collection, it can be carried out at this stage of schooling. Several quotations will give a good idea of what is included.

The half-halt may be described as a "call to attention" to prepare the horse for the next command of his rider. It can be employed to shorten the stride, improve the contact and collection, and give notice to the horse that an exercise requiring greater proficiency is about to be demanded. (Podhajsky, p. 40)

Half-parades should, therefore, always be given before asking something new of the horse, i.e. before changing the direction or the pace or gait. A half-parade is the 'attention!' for the horse. . . . (Müseler, p. 116.)

The half-halt *is a signal given the horse to decrease its rate, or merely to improve its carriage, or to make the horse easier on the reins, when it bores on the bit and presses on the reins. In both of the latter cases the rate may be the same as before. (Seunig, p. 133.)*

The half-halt will help the horse to carry himself better and take a lighter contact with the bit. It may be used as a corrective, especially with a horse that is inclined to lie heavily on the reins. (Podhajsky, p. 40.)

Furthermore, by half-halts executed in smooth and quick rotation,

> *thè mental contact with the horse can be satisfactorily achieved. (d'Endrödy, p. 133.)*

So you would be likely to perform a half-halt to put the horse more on the bit (i.e., increase collection a trifle) before starting a turn or circle, before a canter depart, before shoulder-in, or at any time when the horse was coming off the bit, poking his nose, or becoming inattentive; also to correct too-strong a contact, although I am not familiar with this application.

Müseler is the greatest advocate of "giving the horse half-parades." In effect, he says the oftener the better. Not everyone, however, employs half-halts with great frequency. I recall Robert Hall saying that the horse should be attentive all the time and always ready to do something new; you should not have to warn him every time you were about to ask something of him.

Execution of the half-halt for these purposes involves some combination of leg, rein, and, for most riders, seat aids just as described above for the third meaning. "Double everything," I have been told. The rider drives "from rear to front into passively restraining hands" or "stretches in his seat (braces his back) and closes his fingers." It takes only a second or two. Sometimes the idea of reducing the pace seems to persist. I have heard the half-halt described as slowing the horse and then pushing on before an actual reduction takes place. d'Endrödy describes it in this way:

> *The characteristic feature of the half-halt is that the retardment involved is carried out only to the point where the horse mentally accepts the function by its momentary yielding (the sign of its willingness to retard), whether or not the physical movement of retardment has been completed.*
>
> *Bearing in mind this consideration, the half-halt is performed in the following manner:*
>
> *As a preliminary to the procedure, the rider drives on the animal. Then he carries out the retardment, following which he completes the half-halt by a newly applied drive-on.*
>
> *The extent of the retardment depends upon the sensitivity of the horse. . . . At the beginning of schooling the horse may even be brought to a standstill. . . . Finally, in more advanced stages of education it is sufficient for the rider to change his bearing to a passive tension of the hands and seat in order to bring about the horse's willingness to retard. (d'Endrödy, p. 133.)*

D'Endrödy often seems rather enigmatic to me, but there are those who understand him and regard him very highly. He seems to show a French influence, because the driving and retarding are not carried out simultaneously.

According to Müseler, the half-halt, like nearly everything else, can be brought about by bracing the back. In fact he says that the rider will reach a point when he automatically braces his back whenever he merely *thinks* of doing a half-halt, and in this way the half-halt will be effected without further action.

When your instructor asks you to perform a half-halt, it might be wise to ask him just what he wants you to do and how he expects your horse to respond, unless, of course, your first attempts seem satisfactory. There are so many reasons for the half-halt, and so many slight variations in its execution, that you and your instructor can quite easily have different things in mind. I might add that Robert Hall did not use the expression at all in his schools. As one of his instructors explained, "We just tell you what you are to do." This is not a bad approach to a complicated procedure.

Feel

A good deal was said about "feel" in the discussion of the working trot. You will also be developing "feel" as you work to develop a good turn on the haunches, and perhaps you will learn to feel whether your horse has squared up when he halts. There are a couple of other "feels" that it would be nice to acquire.

The first is *posting on a desired diagonal* without looking down to watch the action of the horse's shoulder. I have only found one way of feeling which foreleg is reaching forward at the trot, and this does not work, at least for me, on all horses. On some horses, however, I can feel my toes going *alternately* up and down when I am doing sitting trot. If you can feel this on your horse (I suggest you try with your eyes shut) it is quite easy to figure out how to rise on the desired diagonal. Pay attention to one toe and say "up, down, up, down" to yourself. Then start rising accordingly. Alas, the horse I am riding now does not give me this feeling, and I cannot feel his shoulders going forward and back or anything else that is helpful; so I must look down with my eyes when I want to post on a particular diagonal, being careful not to tilt my head.

Another thing that is nice to feel is *which lead the horse is on at the canter*. This can be felt by noticing the position your legs take naturally as the horse canters. It will be found that your leg on the leading side is a little in advance of the leg on the other side. I have no difficulty feeling this on various horses. Try it and see for yourself.

Müseler has a somewhat different version. He gives an example in which the rider has asked for the right lead, but the horse has taken the left lead. The rider tries to push the *right* seat bone forward, but when the horse takes the left lead, the *left* seat bone is moved forward by the horse. The rider feels this contradiction.

It is also to be hoped that you have developed a sensitive feel for *whether your mount is straight* or not. Not only should you know whether the hind feet are following the forefeet on curved tracks, but also whether the hind feet are following the forefeet on straight tracks! The latter is especially important at the canter, for horses have a natural tendency to canter with the haunches to the inside and judges always seem to be on the lookout for this fault. The straight horse has a lovely feel, like an engine running on a straight or curving track with the rear wheels of necessity faithfully rolling along behind the front ones. Then there is the feeling conveyed when impulsion is adequate at the canter with the hind legs coming well under rather than trailing out behind. All these feels are gradually learned if you pay attention to your teacher's comments and try to feel the difference when he says things are going well or badly.

Talent in developing feel varies tremendously from rider to rider. I think it is *the* prerequisite for progress, because if you cannot remember how something felt when, for a few moments, it was right, you are unlikely to be able to duplicate the proper execution of the movement, whatever it was, when you are practicing at home. But do not despair if it does not come rapidly. If you are persistent, and your teacher is patient, eventually you will feel and remember all the necessary things.

Weight Shifts

We have already discussed one kind of weight shift, or weight aid, for you will recall that bracing the back is often called using weight aids. But so far we have considered only the sort of weight shift that could be called "bilateral"—both seat bones acting in the same manner. They can both be weighted, or pressed down, or pushed forward. But it is also possible to shift the weight more onto *one* seat bone or to push *one* seat bone forward. So now let us consider the shifting of weight to one side.

You can think of this as weighting one side of your seat, or as lifting and "unweighting" the other side. What will happen? Try it sometime when your horse is walking across the arena in a relaxed way; he will probably start to turn or drift toward the side that you have weighted. Seunig explains it thus:

> As the horse's area of support from left to right—its transverse axis—is much shorter than its longitudinal axis, it is particularly sensitive and receptive to lateral shifts of the rider's weight. . . . It readily follows the mechanical persuasion of an increased load on the inner side. . . . (Seunig, p. 68.)

If your horse does not shift the first time you try, do it again with a loose rein and try it to both sides. I have had horses that shifted and also one horse that did not. If the horse follows the weight aid, it is helpful in keeping him on a straight course when doing the long diagonal at free walk. If the horse *begins* to deviate to the right, you can shift your weight a little to the left and thus *keep* him going straight. Of course the displacement of weight should not be visible to anyone other than a very observant instructor.

You may also unintentionally cause your horse to deviate by shifting your weight. For instance, I have had the experience of causing the horse's hindquarters to fall inward off the track when doing shoulder-in at the walk because my weight was excessively shifted to the inside. The horse followed the weight aid, and I could not keep his haunches on the track with my inside leg. An observant instructor who can see these things is indispensable. We cause many difficulties for ourselves by unwillingly giving all sorts of aids and being quite unaware that we are doing so. Then we are apt to blame the horse and think he is being disobedient.

Besides the simple weight shift to cause or prevent turning, there is the *unilateral back aid* in which one seat bone is pushed forward and kept in advance of the other. Müseler, as you might expect, finds this very important. I have mentioned his advice for turning and for canter departs which requires pushing the inside seat bone forward. See page 19 in his book. Seunig goes into more detail:

> The rider also uses a weight control [aid] to initiate turns and bends; this control consists in a flexing of the muscles of the small of the back on the side on which the turn is made, a resultant pushing

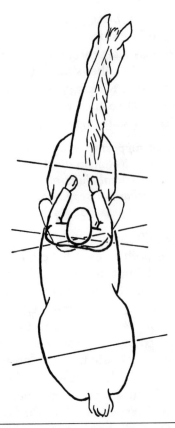

Figure 91. Riding a turn with hips parallel to the horse's hips and shoulders parallel to the horse's shoulders.

> *forward of the respective seat bone (which fixes the weight control), a lengthening of the inner leg, and a slight advance of the outside shoulder. (Seunig, p. 68.)*

Seunig's mention of the outside shoulder as well as the inside seat bone is related to the basic rule that the rider's hips should always be parallel to the horse's hips, while the rider's shoulders should always be parallel to the horse's shoulders. Figure 91 shows what happens when the horse is bent on a turn. I have never done this consciously, nor have I been corrected for not doing it. So my conclusion is that the rider is likely to line up his hips and shoulders automatically and need not be concerned about it. However, the German writers mention it a good deal, and I bring it up so that if your instructor corrects you, you will know what he is talking about.

Pushing the inside seat bone forward when you ask for the canter may be helpful in getting the correct lead. It is a technique which you may also find helpful if you are trying to overcome the common fault of former hunt-seat riders who tense their thighs and lift their seats out of the saddle on canter departs. But I have also heard disagreement about its merits as an aid. One side maintains that pushing the right seat bone forward is an aid for canter on the right lead. The other side holds that pushing the seat bone forward should not be an aid but should *accompany* the horse's strikeoff and harmonize the rider's seat with the horse's movement. There are even some riders who use weight on the *outside* seat bone as an aid in canter departs.

It is also sometimes possible to push the horse's haunches to one side by concentrating the weight on the *other* seat bone (but not pushing it forward). I have twice been instructed to do this. In one instance, I was directed to put weight on the inside seat bone to keep the horse's haunches on the track when doing shoulder-in at the trot; this was to correct a tendency of the haunches to fall in. The other instance was to put weight on the inside seat bone to straighten the horse and keep the haunches from falling in at the canter. These aids seem to be contrary to the effect of the weight aid in causing the horse to turn, but they proved to be the correct thing to do in these instances. I mention this because there are special instances when unusual measures will solve a particular problem for a particular horse.

Collapsing the Hip

This is a fault that a rider may have without being conscious of it. Judges comment on collapsing the hip whenever they see it, but the rider may not know what the judge means. The term is not self-explanatory and, in fact, it is not really the hip which is collapsed. Here is what happens: The rider is driving with the inside leg. In doing so, the leg works up, the seat slips to the outside, and in order to continue to sit upright the rider collapses the *rib cage* on the inner side. Figure 92 will make this clear. The inner hip is said to be collapsed.

The Aids Going Through

You may run across this expression, or your instructor may com-

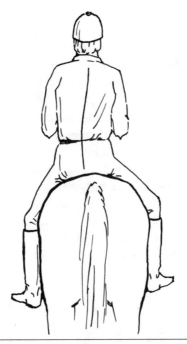

Figure 92.   The collapsed hip. Here it is the right hip that is collapsed.

plain that your aids are "stuck" or "escaping" and so not "getting through." Müseler relates the expression to the aids for a halt as follows:

> *The expression 'going through' means that the halt or parade affects the whole horse from head to tail. (Müseler, footnote p. 91.)*

If the horse does not halt but resists the bit by opening his mouth or fighting the bit, the aids are stuck. The aids "go through" if the horse responds to them rather than escaping or evading. Another example of evasion would be as follows: The rider attempts to turn, and the horse bends his neck but his body continues a little longer on a straight line before beginning to turn. The common expression is to say that the "shoulder falls out," or the horse "bulls." Müseler would say that the rein aid did not go through but escaped at the withers. For another example see the quote from Seunig on page 149 in Chapter 8.

13 Training in Preparation for Showing

If you are serious about showing you will have to keep this in mind in all of your work. As you make progress, you should become more systematic in your schooling; except when trail-riding, warming up, or consciously relaxing in some way, you should always be doing something definite.

When walking, the walk should always be either free walk on a loose rein, free walk on a long rein, or working walk. The trot should always be working trot or lengthened trot, and canter should always be working canter or lengthened canter. No crooked canters should be tolerated while working. No lazy gaits. Walk always energetic, trot on the bit, canter at a proper tempo. It is all right to warm up for a while at a natural trot before putting the horse on the bit, and it is all right to rest at a relaxed walk, but only if you are clear in your own mind when these rest periods begin and end and can also make it clear to your horse. Rest periods are necessary for both you and your horse. You cannot work *all* the time, but you *must* concentrate *all* the time you are working.

You should concentrate on and plan your transitions when working. It is so easy at the end of a period of trot or canter, when you are elated because something went well or are perhaps just tired, to simply let everything collapse into a lazy walk. Do not do this. No matter how your attention is flagging or how tired you are, do as good a transition as possible to walk, get the walk as good as possible, and only then, after a few strides of working walk, relax.

Always halt in a definite way. It is all too easy, especially when others are working in the same arena, to turn off the track at some ill-defined angle and, as soon as one is out of the path of the other riders, let the trot or walk die to a halt. Instead decide, for example, that you will make a 90 degree turn and halt in the center of the arena. Keep up the good trot or walk until it is time to halt, and then make the kind of halt you would make if you were about to salute the judge.

What do you concentrate on besides gaits and transitions? On every turn and circle you must bend your horse—unless he is supple and always bends himself. Every circle should be a definite size—not just any old size. Every shoulder-in should be done with your instructor's admonitions in mind, whatever they are: Do not bend the neck too much, try to keep the horse on the bit, keep up the impulsion, or watch your weight shift. The same goes for any other exercise you are practicing.

Try to carry on your training in fairly long, continuous segments. At the Fulmer School of Equitation, a lesson consisted of three segments of about 12 minutes each with three-minute rest periods in between. During the 12-minute working period the rider never halted but went on without interruption from one thing to another at the teacher's direction. During the three-minute rest the rider stopped in the center of the school and could ask questions and discuss problems. The Fulmer formula is a good one—when it fits the student. But on a hot day in summer, or a day when you are tired or your horse is uncooperative, six five-minute work periods with one-minute rest periods in between might be better. The important thing is to sustain impulsion and attention through the work period whatever its length.

A work period as long as you can sustain it also has the advantage that it is more like a dressage test and is better practice for competition. It is much better than trotting once around at working trot, then halting and deciding what to do next; then doing two turns on the haunches and stopping again to rest; then starting up again and trying several shoulder-ins, and so on. Instead combine all this into one work segment. For example, do working trot twice around the ring with maybe a small circle and a change on the diagonal. Then do a good transition to walk and two turns on the forehand, or more if the first two are not satisfactory. Follow these with a good transition to working trot, shoulder-in down one side and, if it is satisfactory, a change on the diagonal and a shoulder-in on the other hand. Finally a correct halt, and then a rest.

Another point to consider is how often to try a particular movement before going on to something else. You must not bore or overtire your horse by doing a movement too often, and yet you ought to repeat a successful performance often enough so that the horse learns something. Knowing when to continue and when to stop is a matter of judgement.

As a general rule, if a thing is done well you might do it about twice, then pat your horse and go on to something else. But if it is done badly repeat it until some improvement is noted, and then either do it once more or stop, depending on how long you have been trying and how the horse is reacting. If you realize that you are weak in this matter, try to do as your teacher has you do at lessons. Usually it is recommended to work on new movements at the end of the lesson and stop as soon as progress, however slight, is made. Horses are said to think about their new lessons in their stalls afterward, and do them better the next day.

Before a show you will review the tests you plan to ride, pick out the elements in them which you may not have been working on and give them extra attention. Perhaps you have not been doing "trot, halt, trot." Or maybe you have not been alternating periods of rising and sitting trot with attention paid to keeping the rhythm unchanged, or crossing the arena from "B" to "E," or doing lengthened trot sitting, or doing canter departs on large circles.

If you have been making transitions when you felt the horse was just right, you had better practice some at preselected points instead. Try to have the horse right when you reach the point you have decided on, but make the best transition you can anyway whether you and the horse are ready or not.

If you do not have a standard arena to practice in, you will have some special problems. It is well to check out the sizes of your circles. Measure a large circle and a 10-meter circle, and mark them in some way so you can be sure your circles and figure eights are the correct size. Figure 93 shows one way to draw a circle by

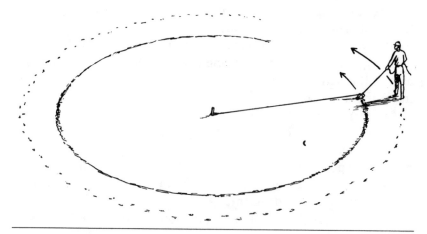

Figure 93. Drawing a circle. A stake, a thin rope, and a stone or chunk of concrete are needed. Keep the rope taut by pulling forward and outward. The rope can have several permanent loops for circles of various sizes.

dragging some heavy rough object that will leave a track. The hardest thing to practice without an arena of correct size is the three-loop serpentine. You will have to mark out some points for guidance in your practice area as best you can, and also study the diagram of the standard arena and fix in your mind the places where your loops should touch the sides of the arena. (Figure 40.)

If you have an arena to practice in, try to ride accurately around it, that is, straight down each side, as far into the corners as the size of circle you are currently performing will permit, and then just as straight along the end and at the same distance from the fence as when you were on the long side. If you do not have an arena, you ought at least to have some accurately drawn corners to your field and practice riding accurately through them.

Maintaining impulsion throughout a test may be a serious problem. Judges say, "Drive the horse more forward." But how? You cannot use your legs vigorously and continuously if it exhausts you; besides it looks bad. The horse is supposed to be "keen." I have two suggestions. The first is to warm up the horse thoroughly. When a lazy horse is really warmed up—which may take as much as 30 minutes of vigorous work—he may then "go by himself." Notice during training sessions whether a point comes each day when you stop using your whip and legs; then plan your warm-up so that you will not start the test before this stage is reached.

My other suggestion is to use your whip as much as necessary. Some say the whip should only be used to teach obedience to the leg, but most use it as an aid in its own right. It is certainly less tiring than endlessly driving with the leg, and your seat will be more relaxed and look better. Sometimes two or three good strokes with the whip are all that are needed to solve the problem.

If I have made it sound as though you must think of everything at all times and remember half a dozen things at once, I will admit that this is only an ideal. You cannot, of course, think of everything at once, but you can work on all aspects of the performance at one time or another. Gradually more of them will become automatic, you will be able to concentrate on other things, and your "rides" will get better and better. Dressage schooling is a matter of skill, persistence, intelligent planning, and concentration. The only one of these your teacher can give you is skill. The others must come from within yourself.

Another thing that I hope you realized some time ago as you were reading this book, is that when you are reading about dressage *every word counts*. Every word adds meaning, and no word must be lightly passed over. You must try to be aware of the meaning of every sentence and phrase. Careful reading is a must. Paragraphs must often be read again and again to extract every bit of meaning and usefulness.

After all this is said and done, remember that the whole process of riding and training is supposed to give you pleasure. If it does not, something is wrong. Perhaps you have missed your calling, maybe you have the wrong horse, or you are just being too deadly serious and trying to advance too fast. Or maybe you need to get out of the arena into the country once or twice a week. On the other hand, if you are enjoying your riding, if all your tensions and worries disappear while you are in the saddle, and if you and your horse are making progress, then, as the saying goes, you must be doing *something* right. In fact, probably a lot of things.

Glossary

Above the bit. *See* contact.

Accept the leg. *See* leg.

Aids. *See also* rein aids, weight aids. Aids are classified as follows
  Bi-lateral: same as parallel
  Diagonal: Rein acting mainly on one side, leg mainly on the other side.
  Lateral: Rein and leg aids acting predominantly on the same side.
  Parallel: Right and left aids doing the same thing, as, both reins resisting.
  Unilateral: also called diagonal. Right and left aids doing different things, as right leg on the girth and left leg behind the girth.
  Unilateral back aid: One seat bone weighted and pushed forward.

Aids going through Horse responds to the aids rather than evading or resisting them.

Aids stuck or escaping Horse resists or evades.

Asking down Giving quick, little tugs on one rein by closing and opening the fingers or bending and straightening the wrist; bit remains in contact throughout.

Back (horse's)
  Hollow: (also sagging, fallen, or down) The hollow between the withers and croup is larger, back is usually stiff, and trot is hard to sit. Stride is short.
  Rounded: (also arched, up) The hollow between the withers and croup is smaller, loin more horizontal, usually means back is relaxed and tail swinging.

Back Aids. *See* weight aids. Other expressions meaning essentially the same thing are action of the loins, seat aids, pushing buttocks forward, braced back, driving seat. *See* pages 233ff for discussion.

Balance Refers to the general agility or athletic ability of the horse, also more specifically to a desirable distribution of weight between the front and hind legs; ultimately the well-schooled horse is balanced when there is an equal distribution of weight between the front and hind legs which requires engagement of the haunches and raising of the neck which shifts some weight from front to hind legs.
  Central balance: Equal weight on fore and hind legs; collected gaits.
  Forward balance: More weight on fore than on hind legs; working gaits.
  On the forehand: More weight on the forelegs, or too much weight on the forelegs.

Balanced halt. *See* halt.

Bearing rein Neck rein.

Behind the bit. *See* contact.

Bending. *See* suppleness, lateral.

Bend, wrong Neck not flexed at poll, but farther back; poll not highest point of neck.

Bilateral aids. *See* aids.

Braced back. *See* back aids.

Cadence. *See* suspension.

Canter
> Counter: Rider intended that horse take outside lead, which horse did. Horse can take counter canter by remaining on original lead when changing the rein.
> Extended. *See* extended gaits.
> False: Rider intended one lead and horse took the other.
> Left: on the left lead.
> Lengthened. *See* lengthened gaits.
> Medium. *See* medium gaits.
> On the inside leg: Canter with inside foreleg leading.
> On the right leg: Canter with right foreleg leading.
> Working. *See* working gaits.

Canter depart Transition from halt, walk, or trot to canter.

Carries himself. *See* self-carriage.

Carriage Position of head and neck.
> Improved carriage: Neck raised, poll flexed and face nearer the vertical; occurs in collection.

Change the rein Reverse and go around the arena in the opposite direction; the most common way of doing this is to change the rein on the diagonal (*see* Figure 23).

Chewing A desirable action of the horse in which he carries out a swallowing action and produces foam; a wet mouth.

Circle
> Large: A circle 20 meters in diameter (about 65 feet); width of the arena.
> Small: A circle 10 meters in diameter (about 33 feet).
> Volte: The smallest circle of which the horse is capable, six meters in diameter (about 19 feet).

Collapsed hip A fault of the rider. *See* page 265 for discussion.

Collection (also collected gaits) The collected horse is in central balance with shortened frame, lowered croup, engaged haunches, and much impulsion.

Concave. *See* crookedness.

Contact
> Above the bit: Head too high, face may be approaching the horizontal; rein slopes downward from bit to rider's hand.
> Accept the bit: (also being on contact) Horse is not disturbed by and does not try to resist or avoid constant contact of bit; horse goes willingly forward on a stretched rein.

Flexing the jaw: (also yielding the jaw, chewing, *mise en main*) Jaw not clenched or stiff, some mobility of the jaw as in rhythmic swallowing or chewing, or opening the mouth slightly.

Floating rein: Not enough contact; rein wavers, sags at times.

On the bit: (moving into the bit, stretching onto the bit) Going freely forward with a steady contact, the neck stretched forward and flexed at the poll.

Stretched rein: Proper contact; continuous tension, rein remains straight.

Counter canter. *See* canter.

Crookedness This can refer to three distinct things: 1. Spine curved at canter, side of leading leg is hollow side. 2. Spine straight, but haunches or shoulders carried to one side so hind legs do not follow forelegs. 3. Spine or neck curved so one side is *always* hollow; asymmetry.

Concave side: (also hollow, soft, or difficult side) Concave side of horse with type 3 crookedness.

Convex side: (also stiff, hard, or constrained side) Convex side of horse with type 3 crookedness.

Crooked from right to left: (also asymmetrical to the right) Hollow on the right side.

Even loading: Right and left legs bearing equal weight; when this is true, horse is straight.

Decrease

of gait: (also decrease of pace or reduction of pace) Change from canter to trot, canter to walk, or trot to walk.

of rhythm or tempo: Fewer steps per minute (speed may or may not be affected).

of speed: Fewer yards per minute (rhythm may or may not be affected).

Diagonal aids. *See* aids.

Direct rein. *See* rein aids.

Downward transition. *See* transition.

Driving seat. *See* back aids.

Elasticity Springiness; horse barely seems to touch the ground.

Engagement (also engage the haunches) To bring each hind leg well forward under the body before placing it on the ground; at this stage of training, usually to track up; also to bend the three joints of the hind leg (also called lowering the croup).

Not engaged: (all strung out, losing the hind legs, hind legs trailing) Hind feet do not come far enough forward under body; hind feet remain on the ground too long and are too far out behind when they finally push off.

Even loading. *See* crookedness.

Extended gaits Most advanced stage of lengthening.

False canter. *See* canter.

Feel Ability of rider to detect what is going on under him by sensations reaching him through legs, seat, and hand.

Fixed hand. *See* hands.

Flexibility. *See* suppleness, lateral.

Flexion
> of the spine: See suppleness, lateral.
> of the jaw: See contact.
> of the poll: (also *ramener*) Flexing just behind the ears so the face is more vertical.

Floating rein. *See* contact.

Follow the movement. (also stick to the saddle, deep seat) *See also* seat. Hips and lower spine of rider are flexible so the rider's seat remains in contact with the seat of the saddle during trot and canter.

Forehand General term for the horse's shoulders and forelegs.

Free forward movement (also moving forward) Not just moving, but doing so at a good speed with willingness and eagerness to get somewhere.

Free walk. *See* walk.

Freedom of movement Taking long, relaxed strides without any sign of stiffness or constraint.

Gallop Canter, unless a racing gallop is specified.

Go large Come off the circle and proceed around the arena on the rail.

Half-halt (also half-parade) A more or less simultaneous checking and driving on that increases attention and collection; also the French half-halt, which is a method of correcting a horse that is overbent (*see* page 66).

Half-halt, unilateral Podhajsky's remedy for type 2 crookedness (*see* page 169).

Halt (also parade, which is a German term for halt)
> Balanced or square: The horse's four feet are at the corners of a rectangle, not a trapezoid or some other figure; weight is then equally distributed on all four feet if the horse is in central balance. (*See also* balance.)

Hands
> Educated: Hands, acting through the reins, do the correct thing at all times.
> Fixed: Hands stay in one place relative to the horse; if horse yields, the rein slackens.
> Good: Hands do not do anything unintentional; rider does not use reins to help him keep his balance; hands follow the horse's mouth.
> Inner or outer: *See* inner rein.
> Pulling: Hands exert constant traction to rear, coming closer to body when horse yields.

Haunches (also quarters) General term for croup and hind legs of horse.

Haunches-in, Haunches-out Lateral exercises. *See* Figure 60.

Head carriage. *See* carriage.

Hurry (also run, rush) Trot with too fast a rhythm.

Impulsion (also impulse forward) A desire or commitment to go briskly forward; performing with a certain pent up energy; maintaining a sufficient speed in all figures.

Indirect rein. *See* rein aids.

Inner or inside leg or rein Leg or rein toward center of arena, turn, or circle; or on side of leading leg at canter; or, if horse is bent, on the concave side of the horse.

Keeping the rein Maintaining contact.

Lateral aids. *See* aids.

Lateral movements (also work on two tracks, side steps, lateral work) Exercises in which the hind feet do not follow in the path of the forefeet. *See* Figure 60.

Leading rein. *See* rein aids.

Leg
> horse accepts the: Horse is not upset by rider keeping constant light contact with the calves of the legs.
> horse behind the: Horse does not respond to the driving leg.
> horse in front of the: Horse responds and advances freely when driven by the rider's leg.

Leg, inner. *See* inner leg.

Leg on the girth Top part of the calf on the girth, lower part of the calf behind the girth.

Leg-yielding A lateral movement. *See* Figure 69.

Lengthened frame Increased distance from nose to hocks (or points of buttocks); lowered neck, straightened poll, less engagement.

Lengthened gaits Steps longer and more suspension at trot and canter; increased speed with unchanged rhythm.

Lengthened stride (also lengthening, lengthening the trot, etc.) Covering more ground with the same number of strides per minute.

Lightness Horse does not hang on the bit or pull, responds to refined rein aids; also may be light to the leg, that is, respond to refined leg aids.

Longitudinal suppleness. *See* suppleness.

Loss of rhythm. *See* rhythm.

Lower the croup Bend hip, stifle, and hock joints causing croup to slope more downward to the rear; the spine also bends in a vertical plane; engagement.

Medium gaits Strides lengthened but not fully extended.

Mise en main. *See* contact, flexing the jaw. French expression meaning "put in hand."

Moving forward. *See* free forward movement.

On the aids Horse on the bit with impulsion, or horse attentive and responsive to all the aids; "putting the horse to the aids" is a German expression denoting the period of training during which this is accomplished.

On the bit. *See* contact.

On the forehand. *See* balance.

Opening rein. *See* rein aids.

Ordinary gaits Old term for working gaits.

Outer or outside leg or rein Opposite of inner.

Overbent (more properly, overflexed) The horse's face, when looked at from the side, is behind the vertical; the horse is not necessarily behind the bit.

Over flexion (also wrong bend) Flexing neck between second and third vertebrae or farther back so that the poll is not the highest point of the neck.

Overtrack Hind foot steps in front of corresponding forefoot print; said of walk and trot; most horses overtrack at working walk and lengthened trot.

Paces Called gaits in America: trot, walk, and canter.

Parallel aids. *See* aids.

Pirouette. Turn on the haunches, inner hind leg steps in place.

Posting trot Rising trot.

Putting the horse to the aids. *See* on the aids.

Quarters. *See* haunches.

Ramener. *See* flexion of the poll.

Reduction of pace. *See* decrease of gait.

Regularity
> of gait: Proper sequence and spacing of footfalls.
> of rhythm: Unchanging speed of footfalls.

Rein, inner or outer. *See* inner rein.

Rein, on the right Going around an arena or circle to the right.

Rein, stretched or floating. *See* contact.

Rein aids Direct, indirect, opening, opposed, leading, etc. *See* pages 244ff for complete description.

Rein back. Backing; a pace in two time, moving diagonal pairs.

Relaxation (also unconstraint) Any movement requiring muscular effort is being carried out with relaxation if no more muscular effort is expended than is required to perform it.

Renvers (also haunches-out) A lateral movement. *See*Figure 60.

Rhythm. *See also* regularity. The order and spacing of footfalls, as a two-beat rhythm, a three-beat rhythm, an irregular rhythm (an ambling walk, for example); the number of footfalls per minute, as a fast or slow rhythm.

Rhythm, loss of Irregularity of footfalls of the gait, or varying numbers of steps per minute, or an increase (or decrease) in the rhythm so that it becomes too fast (or slow).

Rising trot Posting trot.

Run (also rush or hurry) Trot with too fast a rhythm.

Seat
> Chair seat: stirrups too short and rider sitting too far back, hence thigh too horizontal.
> Deep seat: (also sitting down in the saddle, sitting deep in the saddle, sitting *in* the saddle, not *on* it.) Riding with long stirrups and seat bones pressing onto the saddle by the rider's weight; thigh as vertical as possible and weight resting firmly on seat, not thighs.
> Light seat: (also crotch seat) Posting the trot, weight on thighs rather than seat at the canter; used on green horses and when warming up schooled horses.
> Loose seat: Thighs and knees relaxed, not tense or gripping; staying on by balance rather than grip.
> Sitting forward in the saddle: This does not mean leaning forward; it means that the seat bones are in the center of the saddle rather than the back part of it.

Self-carriage Horse holds his head up, does not expect rider to hold it up with the reins; a rising of neck which comes with improved balance.

Shoulder-in Lateral exercise. *See* Figure 60.

Shortened frame (also pushing the horse together) Decreased distance from nose to hocks (or point of buttocks); raising neck, flexing poll and jaw, more engagement.

Side, hard, soft, concave, convex, etc. *See* Crookedness.

Side steps. *See* lateral work.

Sitting forward. *See* seat

Square halt. *See* halt.

Straight The horse is straight when the hind feet follow in the path of the forefeet; if on a circular path, the horse must be bent to be straight.

Stretched rein. *See* contact.

Suppleness
> Lateral: (also flexibility, bending, bent in the ribs, flexion) The uniform bending of the horse's entire body from poll to tail so as to coincide with the track the horse follows on curves and circles; bending of spine in horizontal plane.
> Longitudinal: Bending of the spine in a vertical plane; flexing the poll, raising the neck, rounding the back, lowering the croup; required in collecting and extending the gaits.

Suspension (also cadence) Refers to horse being in the air with all feet off the ground between beats of trot and bounds of canter; horses can trot and canter without suspension; a gait is said to be cadenced when the suspension is longer and the time the feet are on the ground is shorter.

Tempo Rhythm; increasing the tempo means taking more steps per minute.

Track-up Left hind foot steps into left forefoot print, and right hind steps into right forefoot print; said of trot and walk; for many horses, tracking up at the trot is a sign of adequate impulsion.

Transition
> Downward: Change to slower gait, as extended walk to working walk, or canter to trot.
> Upward: Change to faster pace, as working trot to lengthened trot, or walk to canter.

Travers (also haunches-in) A lateral movement. (*See* Figure 60.)

Trot
> Extended: *See* extended gaits.
> Lengthened: *See* lengthening.
> Medium: *See* medium gaits.
> Rising: Posting trot.
> Sitting: Rider does not post, but keeps seat in saddle following movement of the horse; this requires flexible back and hips of rider and is easier when the horse's back swings.
> Working. *See* working gaits.

Turn on the haunches (also pirouette) *See* Figure 82.

Two-track (also half-pass) A lateral movement. *See* Figure 60.

Two tracks A general term that includes three tracks, 3½ tracks, and four tracks. Work on two tracks: *See* lateral work.

Unilateral
>   Aids: *See* aids.
>   Back aid: Pushing one seat bone forward.

Upward transition. *See* transition.

Vibrations Working the bit back and forth through the horse's mouth, the idea being that it is hard to lean on something that is moving.

Volte. *See* circle.

Walk
>   Extended: *See* extended gaits.
>   Free, on a long rein: Long striding, energetic walk with neck stretched forward and down and very slight or floating contact.
>   Free on a loose rein: Same as on long rein, but no contact.
>   Lengthened: *See* lengthened gaits.
>   Medium: *See* medium gaits.
>   Working. *See* working gaits.

Weight aids Influencing the horse by shifting the weight: shifting weight to one seat bone; shifting weight to thighs or to seat; bearing down more heavily on the seat by bracing the back, or leaning back or both, or by following the movement of the horse more aggressively.

Working gaits Horse goes energetically forward with a good speed and rhythm with head and neck in the "on the bit" position; gaits at which most lower level work is done.

Wrong bend. *See* over flexion.

Arena Diagram

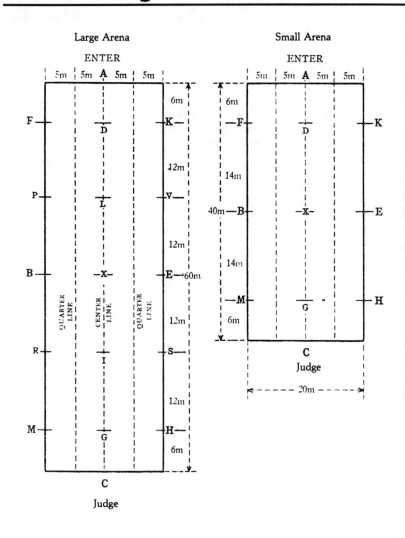

Large Arena

Small Arena

1987
TRAINING LEVEL TEST 1

			Points	Coefficient	Total
1	A	Enter working trot rising			
	X	Halt, salute, proceed working trot rising			
2	C	Track right			
	B	Circle right 20 m			
	B	Working trot sitting			
3	between F & A	Working canter right lead			
4	E	Circle right 20 m			
	between E & H	Working trot rising			
5	C–M–E–K	Working walk			
6	K	Working trot rising			
	B	Circle left 20 m			
	B	Working trot sitting			
7	between M & C	Working canter left lead			
8	E	Circle left 20 m			
	between E & K	Working trot rising			
9	A	Down center line			
	X	Halt, salute			

Leave arena at free walk on long rein at A

		Coefficient	
Collective marks:			
Gaits (freedom and regularity)		2	
Impulsion (desire to move forward, elasticity of the steps, relaxation of the back)		2	
Submission (attention and confidence; harmony, lightness and ease of movements; acceptance of the bit)		2	
Rider's position and seat; correctness and effect of the aids		2	
Maximum points possible: 170			

1987
TRAINING LEVEL TEST 2

			Points	Coefficient	Total
1	A	Enter working trot rising			
	X	Halt, salute, proceed working trot rising			
2	C	Track left			
	A	Circle left 20 m			
	B	Working trot sitting			
3	between M & C	Working canter left lead			
4	C	Circle left 20 m			
	E	Working trot sitting			
5	A	Working walk			
	F-E	Free walk on a long rein			
	E	Working walk			
6	H	Working Trot rising			
	C	Circle right 20 m			
	B	Working trot sitting			
7	between F & A	Working canter right lead			
8	A	Circle right 20 m			
	E	Working trot rising			
9	MXK	Change rein			
10	A	Down center line			
	X	Halt, salute			

Leave arena at free walk on long rein at A

Collective marks (same as Test 1):

Gaits	2	
Impulsion	2	
Submission	2	
Rider	2	
Maximum points possible: 180		

1987
TRAINING LEVEL TEST 3

			Points	Coefficient	Total
1	A	Enter working trot sitting			
	X	Halt, salute, proceed working trot sitting			
2	C	Track right			
	B	Circle right 20 m			
3	F	Working canter right lead			
4	E	Circle right 20 m			
	H	Working trot sitting			
5	C	Working walk			
	MXK	Free walk on a long rein			
	K	Working walk			
6	F	Working trot sitting			
	B	Circle left 20 m			
7	M	Working canter left lead			
8	E	Circle left 20 m			
	K	Working trot sitting			
9	FXH	Working trot rising			
	H	Working trot sitting			
10	MXK	Change rein			
11	A	Down center line			
	X	Halt, salute			

Leave arena at free walk on long rein at A

Collective marks (same):

Gaits	2	
Impulsion	2	
Submission	2	
Rider	2	
Maximum points possible: 190		

1987
TRAINING LEVEL TEST 4

			Points	Coefficient	Total
1	A	Enter working trot sitting			
	X	Halt, salute, proceed working trot sitting			
2	C	Track left			
	E	Turn left			
	X	Circle left 20 m			
3	X	Circle right 20 m			
	B	Turn left			
4	C	Halt 5 seconds, proceed working walk			
5	HXF	Free walk on long rein			
	F	Working walk			
6	A	Working trot sitting			
	E-B	Half circle right 20 m			
7	B	Working canter right lead and immediately			
8	B	Circle right 20 m			
	B	Straight ahead			
9	F	Working trot sitting			
	KXM	Change rein			
10	M	Working trot sitting			
	E-B	Half circle left 20 m			
11	B	Working canter left lead and immediately			
12	B	Circle left 20 m			
	B	Straight ahead			
13	M	Working trot sitting			
	HXF	Change rein			
14	A	Down center line			
	X	Halt, salute			

Leave arena at free walk on long rein at A

Collective marks (same as Test 1):		
Gaits	2	
Impulsion	2	
Submission	2	
Rider	2	
Maximum points possible: 220		

Reproduced with permission of the American Horse Shows Assn., Inc.

1987
FIRST LEVEL TEST 1

			Points	Coefficient	Total
1	A	Enter working trot sitting			
	X	Halt, salute, proceed working trot sitting			
2	C	Track right			
	B	Circle right 15 m			
3	KXM	Lengthen stride in trot rising			
	M	Working trot sitting		2	
4	E	Circle left 15 m			
5	A	Halt 5 seconds, proceed working walk			
6	FXH	Free walk on long rein			
	H	Working walk		2	
7	C	Working trot			
	M	Working canter right lead			
8	B	Circle right 15 m			
9	KXM	Change rein			
	X	Working trot sitting			
	M	Working canter left lead			
10	E	Circle left 15 m			
11	FXH	Change rein			
	X	Working trot sitting			
12	MXK	Lengthen stride in trot rising			
	K	Working trot sitting		2	
13	A	Down center line			
	X	Halt, salute			

Leave arena at free walk on long rein at A

Collective marks (same as Training Level):		
Gaits	2	
Impulsion	2	
Submission	2	
Rider	2	
Maximum points possible: 240		

1987
FIRST LEVEL TEST 2

			Points	Coefficient	Total
1	A	Enter working trot sitting			
	X	Halt, salute, proceed working trot sitting			
2	C	Track left			
	E	Half circle left 10 m returning to the track at H			
3	B	Half circle right 10 m returning to the track at M			
4	C-A	Serpentine of 3 loops, width of arena			
5	FXH	Lengthen stride in trot rising			
	H	Working trot sitting		2	
6	C	Halt 5 seconds, proceed working walk			
7	MXK	Free walk on long rein			
	K	Working walk		2	
8	A	Working trot sitting			
	F	Working canter left lead			
9	B	Circle left 15 m			
10	HXF	Change rein			
	X	Working trot sitting			
	F	Working canter right lead			
11	E	Circle right 15 m			
12	C	Working trot sitting			
	MXK	Lengthen stride in trot rising			
	K	Working trot sitting		2	
13	A	Down center line			
	X	Halt, salute			

Leave arena at free walk on long rein at A

	Collective marks (same):		
	Gaits	2	
	Impulsion	2	
	Submission	2	
	Rider	2	
	Maximum points possible: 240		

1987
FIRST LEVEL TEST 3

			Points	Coefficient	Total
1	A	Enter working trot sitting			
	X	Halt, salute, proceed working trot sitting			
2	C	Track right			
	MXK	Lengthen stride in trot rising			
	K	Working trot sitting			
3	A	Down center line			
	L	Circle left 10 m			
4	L-R	Leg yield right		2	
5	HXF	Lengthen stride in trot sitting			
	F	Working trot sitting			
6	A	Down center line			
	L	Circle right 10 m			
7	L-S	Leg yield left		2	
8	C	Halt 5 seconds, proceed working walk			
9	MXK	Free walk on a long rein			
	K	Working walk		2	
10	A	Working trot sitting			
	F	Working canter left lead			
11	B	Circle left 10 m			
12	H-K	Lengthen stride in canter			
	K	Working canter		2	
13	FXH	Change rein, at X change of lead through trot			
14	B	Circle right 10 m			
15	K-H	Lengthen stride in canter			
	H	Working canter		2	
16	MXK	Change rein, at X working trot sitting			
17	A	Down center line			
	X	Halt, salute			

Leave arena at free walk on long rein at A

	Collective marks (same):			
	Gaits		2	
	Impulsion		2	
	Submission		2	
	Rider		2	
	Maximum points possible: 300			

1987
FIRST LEVEL TEST 4

			Points	Coefficient	Total
1	A	Enter working trot sitting			
	X	Halt, salute, proceed working trot sitting			
2	C	Track left			
	S-L	Leg yield left		2	
3	L	Circle right 10 m			
	L	Straight ahead			
	A	Track right			
4	V-I	Leg yield right		2	
5	I	Circle left 10 m			
	I	Straight ahead			
	C	Track left			
6	HXF	Lengthen stride in trot rising			
	F	Working trot sitting			
7	A	Halt 5 seconds, proceed working walk			
8	KXH	Free walk on long rein			
	H	Working walk		2	
9	C	Working trot sitting			
	M	Working canter right lead			
10	B	Circle right 10 m			
11	K-H	Lengthen stride in canter			
	H	Working canter		2	
12	MXK	Change rein, at X change of lead through trot			
13	B	Circle left 10 m			
14	H-K	Lengthen stride in canter			
	K	Working canter		2	
15	A	Working trot sitting			
	FXH	Lengthen stride in trot sitting			
	H	Working trot sitting			
16	B	Turn right			
	X	Turn right			
	G	Halt, salute			

Leave arena at free walk on long rein at A

Collective marks (same):		
Gaits	2	
Impulsion	2	
Submission	2	
Rider	2	
Maximum points possible: 290		

1987
SECOND LEVEL TEST 1

			Points	Coefficient	Total
Note: All trot work is done sitting					
1	A	Enter collected trot			
	X	Halt, salute, proceed collected trot			
2	C	Track right			
	B	Circle right 10 m			
3	B-F	Shoulder-in right		2	
4	KXM	Medium trot			
	M	Collected trot		2	
5	E	Circle left 10 m			
6	E-K	Shoulder-in left		2	
7	A	Halt, rein back 3-4 steps, proceed working walk			
8	FXH	Medium walk			
	H	Working walk		2	
9	C	Working canter right lead			
10	B	Circle right 10 m			
11	K-H	Lengthen stride in canter			
	H	Working canter			
12	MXK	Change of rein, at X change of lead through the trot			
13	B	Circle left 10 m			
14	H-K	Lengthen stride in canter			
	K	Working canter			
15	FXH	Change rein, at X change of lead through trot			
16	C	Collected trot			
	MXK	Medium trot			
	K	Collected trot		2	
17	A	Down center line			
	X	Halt, salute			

Leave arena at free walk on long rein at A

	Collective marks:			
	Gaits (freedom and regularity)		2	
	Impulsion (desire to move forward, elasticity of the steps, suppleness of the back and engagement of the hind quarters)		2	
	Submission (attention and confidence; harmony, lightness and ease of movements; acceptance of the bridle and lightness of the forehand)		2	
	Rider's seat and position; correctness and effect of the aids		2	
	Maximum points possible: 300			

1987
SECOND LEVEL TEST 2

Note: All trot work is done sitting			Points	Coefficient	Total
1	A X	Enter collected trot Halt, salute, proceed collected trot			
2	C HXF F	Track left Medium trot Collected trot			
3	K-E	Shoulder-in right			
4	E	Circle right 10 m			
5	E-H	Travers right		2	
6	MXK K	Medium trot Collected trot			
7	F-B	Shoulder-in left			
8	B	Circle left 10 m			
9	B-M	Travers left		2	
10	C	Halt, rein back 3-4 steps, proceed working walk			
11	HXK K	Medium walk Working walk		2	
12	A	Collected canter left lead			
13	B	Circle left 10 m			
14	H-K K	Medium canter Collected canter		2	
15	FXH	Change rein, at X change of lead through the trot			
16	B	Circle right 10 m			
17	K-H H	Medium canter Collected canter		2	
18	MXK	Change rein, at X change of lead through the trot			
19	K A X	Collected trot Down center line Halt, salute			

Leave arena at free walk on long rein at A

Collective marks (same):		
Gaits	2	
Impulsion	2	
Submission	2	
Rider	2	
Maximum points possible: 320		

1987
SECOND LEVEL TEST 3

			Points	Coefficient	Total
Note: All trot work is done sitting					
1	A	Enter collected trot			
	X	Halt, salute, proceed collected trot			
2	C	Track right			
	M-B	Shoulder-in right			
3	B-K	Medium trot			
	K	Collected trot			
4	A	Down center line			
	X	Circle left 10 m			
5	X	Circle right 10 m			
	C	Track left			
6	H-E	Shoulder-in left			
7	E-F	Medium trot			
	F	Collected trot			
8	A	Halt, rein back 3 or 4 steps, proceed collected trot			
9	KXM	Medium trot			
	M	Collected trot			
10	C	Working walk			
	HXF	Medium walk			
	F	Working walk		2	
11	A	Collected canter right lead			
12	K-H	Medium canter			
	H	Collected canter		2	
13	C-I	Half circle right 18 m			
	I	Simple change of lead: proceed to S			
	S	Turn left		2	
14	F-M	Medium canter			
	M	Collected canter		2	
15	C-I	Half circle left 18 m			
	I	Simple change of lead: proceed to R			
	R	Turn right		2	
16	F	Collected trot			
	A	Down center line			
	X	Halt, salute			
Leave arena at free walk on long rein at A					
		Collective marks (same):			
		Gaits		2	
		Impulsion		2	
		Submission		2	
		Rider		2	
		Maximum points possible: 290			

Reproduced with permission of the American Horse Shows Assn., Inc.

1987
SECOND LEVEL TEST 4

			Points	Coefficient	Total
Note: All trot work is done sitting					
1	A X	Enter collected trot Halt, salute, proceed collected trot			
2	C HXF F	Track left Medium trot Collected trot			
3	K-E	Travers right			
4	E	Circle right 10 m			
5	E-H	Shoulder-in right			
6	MXK K	Medium trot Collected trot			
7	F-B	Travers left			
8	B	Circle left 10 m			
9	B-M	Shoulder-in left			
10	C	Halt, rein back 4 steps, proceed working walk			
11	HXF F	Medium walk Working walk		2	
12	between K & V	Half turn on haunches right		2	
13	between F & P	Half turn on haunches left		2	
14	A	Collected canter right lead			
15	E	Circle right 10 m			
16	E	Simple change of lead		2	
17	E-M MXK	Proceed in counter canter Change rein, no change of lead			
18	F-R R·	Medium canter Collected canter			
19	E	Circle left 10 m			
20	E	Simple change of lead		2	
21	E-F FXH	Proceed in counter canter Change rein, no change of lead			
22	M-P P	Medium canter Collected canter			
23	F A X	Collected trot Down center line Halt, salute			

Leave arena at free walk on long rein at A

Collective marks (same):			
Gaits		2	
Impulsion		2	
Submission		2	
Rider		2	
Maximum points possible: 360			

Bibliography

American Horse Shows Association. *American Horse Shows Association Rulebook.* New York, 1978.

Chamberlin, Harry D. *Training Hunters, Jumpers, and Hacks.* London: Hurst and Blackett, Ltd., 1938.

Decarpentry, General. *Academic Equitation.* London: Nicole Bartle and J. Allen, 1971.

De Kunffy, Charles. *Creative Horsemanship.* San Diego: A.S. Barnes and Co., 1975.

d'Endrödy, Lt.-Col. A. L. *Give Your Horse a Chance.* London: J. A. Allen, 1959.

Fillis, James. *Breaking and Riding.* London: Hurst and Blackett, n.d.

Froissard, Jean. *Equitation.* San Diego: A.S. Barnes and Co., 1967.

Jackson, Noël. *Effective Horsemanship.* Princeton, New Jersey: D. Van Nostrand Co., 1967.

Littauer, Vladimir. *Schooling Your Horse.* Princeton, New Jersey: D. Van Nostrand Co., 1956.

Ljungquist, Bengt. *Practical Dressage Manual.* Richmond, Virginia, 1976.

Müseler, Wilhelm. *Riding Logic.* London: Methuen, 1965.

Podhajsky, Alois. *The Complete Training of Horse and Rider.* New York: Doubleday, 1967.

Pony Club of Great Britain. *Training the Young Horse and Pony.* London, 1961.

Seunig, Waldemar. *Horsemanship.* London: Doubleday, 1956.

Wätjen, Richard. *Dressage Riding.* London: J. A. Allen, 1965.

Wynmalen, Henry. *Dressage.* London: Museum Press Ltd., 1953.

——— *Equitation.* 2nd ed., London: Country Life Ltd., 1952.